Unionization
and Deunionization

STUDIES IN INDUSTRIAL RELATIONS

Hoyt N. Wheeler and Roy J. Adams, *Editors*

Industrial Conflict: An Integrative Theory
   by Hoyt N. Wheeler

*Theories and Concepts in Comparative
Industrial Relations*
   Edited by Jack Barbash and Kate Barbash

*Unionization and Deunionization:
Strategy, Tactics, and Outcomes*
   by John J. Lawler

UNIONIZATION AND DEUNIONIZATION

STRATEGY, TACTICS, AND OUTCOMES

JOHN J. LAWLER

UNIVERSITY OF SOUTH CAROLINA PRESS

Copyright © University of South Carolina 1990

Published in Columbia, South Carolina, by the
University of South Carolina Press

Manufactured in the United States of America

Library of Congress Cataloging-in-Publication Data

Lawler, John J.
    Unionization and deunionization : strategy, tactics, and outcomes
/ John J. Lawler.
        p.   cm.—(Studies in industrial relations)
    Includes bibliographical references.
    ISBN 0-87249-662-7
    1. Trade-unions—United States—Organizing.   2. Trade-unions—
United States—Recognition.   I. Title.   II. Series.
HD6490.072U648   1990
331.89′12—dc20   89-21496
                                                                CIP

To my parents,
who have given substance to my life,
and Vinita and Elisa, who define its purpose.

CONTENTS

TABLES

DIAGRAMS

ACKNOWLEDGMENTS

A number of people were most helpful to me in the development and final preparation of this manuscript. First of all, I would like to thank Hoyt Wheeler and Roy Adams, the coeditors of this series, for their support and encouragement. Hoyt also provided detailed comments on the original manuscript, which greatly helped in focusing issues and identifying weak arguments. Two anonymous reviewers were most helpful in their detailed and insightful comments.

Colleagues both at the University of Illinois and the University of Minnesota helped me to shape and refine many of my ideas. Lauren Lerch, Lisa Reavlin, and Robin West Elliot provided research assistance. Support for some aspects of this study was provided by the Institute of Labor and Industrial Relations, University of Illinois, the School of Management, University of Minnesota, and the Institute of Business and Economic Research, University of California, Berkeley.

I wish to express my gratitude to Joe Garbarino, my dissertation chair at Berkeley, who first provided me with the resources and encouragement necessary to pursue the line of research which ultimately led to this book. Mal Walker, with whom I have collaborated on several studies concerned with union growth and decline processes, has provided a continuing flow of observations and insights over the years that have greatly informed the views expressed in this work.

Unionization
and Deunionization

CHAPTER 1

Introduction

Few would deny that the American labor movement now confronts its greatest challenge since emerging as a vital economic and political force a half century ago. A complex of internal and external forces has reduced dramatically the effectiveness of unions in representing employee interests. More important, these forces seem to threaten the very survival of organized labor in the United States. Yet American unions have long exhibited considerable resilience in the face of adversity. And there is now at least some evidence to suggest a recovery may be at hand.

Diminished union power is manifested in a variety of ways. Contract negotiations result in negligible wage increases or outright rollbacks of prior gains. Protracted strikes, ultimately lost by the unions involved, occur in companies in which labor-management relations were once said to be "mature" and stable. The political clout once wielded by organized labor is virtually nonexistent. But more than anything else, the erosion in union membership over the past fifteen to twenty years has gutted the labor movement of core constituents and called into question its institutional legitimacy.

This book is concerned with four major issues: (1) the efforts of unions to secure new members through organizing, (2) the counterorganizing techniques of employers, (3) the attempts of employers to dislodge established unions, and (4) the response of unions to such deunionization attempts. The focus is on the manner in which these activities relate to the contemporary problems of the labor movement. Although much has been written in this area over the past decade, this literature is diverse and would seem to lack a coherent and unifying framework. This book endeavors to integrate what we know about unionization and deunionization processes by developing and applying a model of union and employer strategic action.

1

STRATEGY AND THE STATE OF THE LABOR MOVEMENT

Although relatively stable throughout the 1950s, union density began to decline in the early 1960s, accelerating sharply in the 1970s. The proportion of the nonagricultural organized labor force decreased from just over 29 percent in 1970 to a current level of about 17 percent. Although relative union membership dropped during this period, absolute membership remained stable or increased slightly until the early eighties (i.e., membership grew, but at a rate less than the growth of the labor force). Yet even that figure has declined substantially in recent years. Total union membership, which peaked at just over twenty-two million in the mid-1970s, was down to about seventeen million in 1988.

A debate regarding the long-term viability of the labor movement has been in progress for several years. Initially, attention focused on changes in American economic, political, and social structure—factors largely outside of the control of any of the central "actors" of the industrial relations system. More recently, concern has turned to the role of the discretionary actions of unions and employers in responding to environmental conditions and in dealing with each other. Important elements in this analysis are the substantial increase in employer hostility toward unions over the past ten to twenty years and a corresponding decline in the capability of unions to design effective responses to this challenge by management.

In their recent book, Kochan, Katz, and McKersie (1986) largely define the dimensions of this argument by applying Child's (1972) "strategic choice" concept, widely used in the organizational theory literature, to the analysis of a variety of industrial relations issues. The essence of the strategic choice paradigm is that key organizational decision makers have significant discretion in selecting organizational actions and what they choose to do matters. Although the context within which choices are made may be seen as constraining, it is not viewed to be the sole determinant of action. Even though the strategy concept is not without its detractors, it seems likely that it will continue to attract considerable attention in the industrial relations field in the coming years.

Taken as a whole, the findings of a few of the more general contemporary studies of union growth and decline are indicative of the impact of union and management strategy on this process. In particular, these studies suggest:

1. *The decline in union membership is attributable to more than broad structural shifts in the economy (particularly with respect to industrial composition).*

Neumann and Rissman (1984) estimate that even though about 40 percent of the drop in union density that took place between 1956 and 1980 could be explained in terms of changes in industrial composition (e.g., the shift from heavy manufacturing to high-technology production and the service sector) fully 60 percent of the change resulted from declining unionization rates within industries. Thus, conditions specific to particular industries, even those traditionally hospitable to unions, must be considered sources of union decline.

2. *Much of the decline in unionization over the past three decades is the result of the decreased ability of unions to win certification and decertification elections.*

Dickens and Leonard (1985) decompose rates of change in union density for the period 1950–1980 into several sources of change: success rates for unions in certification and in decertification elections, the proportion of unorganized workers involved in certification elections, the proportion of organized workers involved in decertification elections, and "economic" sources. The last component is a residual category that measures all causes of change not related directly to the election process. Although economic change explains much of the shift in union membership over this period, a substantial proportion of the loss that occurred can be attributed to decreased organizing efforts by unions and the increased success of management in winning representation elections. For example, Dickens and Leonard estimate that had the rates of union organizing effort and success remained constant at the levels of the early 1950s union density would have declined only slightly between then and 1980.

3. *The drop in union success in organizing campaigns is largely the consequence of changes in union and management strategies and tactics.*

Declining union success in representation elections may be the result of structural change as well as shifting strategies. Freeman (1985), in a review of research on the impact of union and management campaign efforts, concludes that of the decline in union success in certification elections "perhaps 40% is due to increased management opposition; perhaps 20% is due to reduced union organizing effort; . . . [and] the remaining 40% is due in part to structural changes in the economy and . . . unknown forces."

The evidence, then, points strongly in the direction of the strategic choices of management and unions. Yet the processes of strategy formation and implementation in relation to organizing are not well understood; further research studies have been published since the

Freeman review, so that his assessment may no longer be supported. This book explores the topic of union organizing and employer resistance with the purpose of clarifying, if not always resolving, these issues.

OBJECTIVES

This book analyzes union and employer strategies specifically related to unionization and deunionization (henceforth *U/DU*) processes. *Unionization* as used here refers to active efforts by unions to expand representation by establishing new bargaining units (or perhaps by extending the coverage of existing units). Autonomous union growth, resulting from expansion of the economy or other passive mechanisms, is not directly considered here. Similarly, *deunionization* refers to active efforts to undermine established unions and reduce union representation and not to the effects of normal or structurally induced attrition.[1] *Unionization/deunionization strategies* refers to the action programs pursued by unions and employers in connection with unionization and deunionization efforts. Examples of U/DU strategic action include union target selection efforts, employer "positive labor relations" programs, the formal campaigns of both unions and employers prior to a representation election, "corporate campaigns" and "internal organizing" programs by unions, employer disinvestment in unionized facilities, and employer-initiated decertification campaigns.[2]

The central premise of the book is that what unions and employers do in U/DU efforts matters. Yet research on union growth has often implicitly or explicitly rejected this assumption, favoring the view that U/DU outcomes are fundamentally determined by exogenous contextual influences (e.g., Ashenfelter and Pencavel 1969; Bain and Elsheikh 1976). Union and management interventions are thus seen to be either irrelevant or simply manifestations of underlying contextual forces which do not independently affect outcomes. Even prior to the Kochan-Katz-McKersie book, this assumption of contextual determinism had been challenged as a result of the apparent association between union decline and the nature of contemporary employer and union strategies. A substantial literature has now developed on union and employer policies as these relate to U/DU outcomes. Although this research generally suggests that employer and union activities are important, our understanding of how U/DU strategies are formulated, implemented, and ultimately affect outcomes is woefully inadequate. Many studies are purely inductive exercises, and others, more theoretically sophisticated, often focus on a limited set of tactics without exploring interlinkages among various tactics and the overarching strategies from which these tactics derive. Moreover, different studies have reported conflicting results. We would therefore seem to have a loose collection of empirical findings in search of a unifying theoretical framework.

This book has five principal objectives:

1. Develop a strategic choice model of unionization and deunionization processes.
2. Describe the mechanisms involved in the formulation of both union and employer U/DU strategies.
3. Explore the role of outside parties, especially labor relations consultants, in generating strategies and influencing the outcomes of U/DU efforts.
4. Characterize U/DU strategies as implemented by employers and unions in relation to the strategic choice model.
5. Assess the impact of strategies and tactics on key U/DU outcomes.

PLAN OF THE BOOK

The remainder of the book is divided into nine chapters. Chapter 2 sets forth a *strategic choice model* of U/DU processes that is the foundation of the book. Recognizing that a limitation in the strategy literature is underconceptualization, this chapter sets forth a theory of strategy formulation and implementation, defining basic constructs that are built upon in subsequent chapters. Of particular significance is a presentation of the elements that define a strategy in the U/DU context, including a typology of elementary tactics.

Chapters 3 and 4 are concerned with the *formulation of U/DU strategies*. Theories of strategic decision making are reviewed as these relate specifically to U/DU strategic choices; empirical research on U/DU strategy formulation is reviewed, assessed, and integrated. Considerable attention is paid to both rational choice and behavioral decision theory. Chapter 3 deals with *union strategy formulation*. A choice model is proposed that explains the apparent strategic ridigity of unions; the initiatives promoted by the AFL-CIO in the organizing area are also examined in relation to strategy formulation. Chapter 4 addresses *management strategy formulation*.

An important force in contemporary U/DU processes is the labor relation consultant. Though consultants are involved to an increasing extent on the union side, especially in public relations work and "corporate campaigns," they are much more prevalent on the employer side. Chapter 5 is devoted to a consideration of *the role and impact of labor relations consultants.* A consultant typology is proposed, and data relating to their prevalence and activities are presented.

To simplify presentation of the material in this book, the U/DU process is broken down into three phases (chapter 2): the nonunion phase, the campaign phase, and the representation phase. Chapters 6, 7, and 8 consider *strategy implementation* in each of these phases. Types of strategies and associated tactics are identified; published studies as well as data collected by the author are used in characterizing strategic action. Strategy implementation is related back to the model proposed in chapter 2.

Chapter 9 reviews research and presents the results of empirical analysis by the author relating to *the impact of strategies and tactics on U/DU outcomes* for the various phases mentioned above. Chapter 10 summarizes the book, highlights its major conclusions, and develops policy implications.

Unionization, Deunionization, and Strategic Action:

A Theoretical Framework

This chapter develops the elements of a strategic choice model of U/DU (unionization and deunionization) processes. The model[1] is presented here in a fairly general form and is elaborated in subsequent chapters. Fundamental constructs are identified and causal linkages specified. The chapter begins with a consideration of the appropriate unit of analysis for the study of union growth and decline. A model of the U/DU process rooted in assumptions of contextual determinism is then presented. This serves as a foundation for the development of the strategic choice model, which occupies the remainder of the chapter.

LEVEL OF ANALYSIS

Although significant insights may be generated by studies conducted at different levels of analysis, the practice of granting a union exclusive representation for a defined group of workers (i.e., the bargaining unit) argues for analysis to be conducted principally at the bargaining unit level. The union status of a particular unit may be determined in a number of ways, most commonly through a polling of the preferences of bargaining unit employees. As a collectivity, workers may decide to establish a union when none exists, remove an incumbent union and return to nonunion status, or replace an incumbent union with a new union.

Aggregate-level studies, far removed from the locus of decision making regarding unionization, are apt to miss subtle group and organizational effects. Moreover, the familiar problem of aggregation bias is inherent in studies conducted at that level. In contrast, studies concerned solely with individual preferences and behavior related to unionism will necessarily understate the effects of U/DU activities that may be moderated by group processes. This is not to suggest that analysis at the individual level is irrelevant to an understanding of bargaining unit outcomes. Collective decisions derive from individual choices, and we need to have some fundamental understanding of these choice processes in the context of unionization in order to build an adequate bargaining unit–level model. This is especially important given that worker free choice with regard to union representation is a fundamental tenet of the National Labor Relations Act (NLRA). Serious policy questions have been raised regarding the extent to which certain tactics compromise free choice. Thus, individual choice processes will be considered as these relate to the proposed model.

Other factors argue for a primary focus on bargaining unit outcomes. Even though employees normally decide a unit's union status, other avenues abound. The National Labor Relations Board (NLRB) may order or withdraw certification, despite the outcome of an election, in response to actions brought before it by unions or employers. An employer may recognize a union without a certification election or withdraw recognition without a decertification election.[2] Employers may close unionized operations and relocate to nonunion regions; unions may abandon locals or formally withdraw from a bargaining relationship. New plants may be organized as the result of an accretion agreement. Employers may refuse to grant a contract to employees in a certified unit, thus effectively denying union representation. These alternative routes to unionization and deunionization affect a unit's union status in ways largely unrelated to employee preferences; all normally result from union and employer efforts. An adequate model of the U/DU process must also account for these bargaining unit–level outcomes. Again, purely individual-level models cannot accomplish this objective because of their narrow focus, and aggregate-level studies lack the richness of detail necessary to draw inferences regarding the impact of employer and union actions on those outcomes.

The model proposed here centers on U/DU strategies and outcomes as implemented at the bargaining unit (or potential bargaining unit) level.[3] Bargaining unit outcomes are linked most immediately to variations in union density. Contests between unions and employers over issues of representation are primarily waged within defined bargaining units. The regulation (or nonregulation) of union and employer conduct at the bargaining unit level is the focal point of public policy. Consequently, the evaluation of public policy and the identification of those areas where change may be warranted must ultimately concern actions that occur at the bargaining unit level. Yet bargaining unit strategies are not apt to be developed in isolation from the broader organizing programs of unions and the industrial relations policies of employers. Consequently, we shall also need to explore the nature of these more general strategies and the role they play in defining unit-specific strategies.

A given bargaining unit may pass through a series of U/DU phases. The types of outcomes and the techniques used in endeavoring to affect outcomes necessarily vary across phases. The three major U/DU phases that have received the greatest attention in the literature will be examined in depth in subsequent chapters. Each phase may be characterized in terms of current union status, which can change as a consequence of unionization (or deunionization) efforts:

Nonunion Phase

No strong union presence, although there may be some employee interest in unionization, or a union may be engaged in a preliminary organizing effort. The critical outcome in this phase is the establishment of a union presence in the unit of sufficient strength to demand recognition (thus initiating the campaign phase) versus continued nonunion status.

Campaign Phase

Follows a formal demand for recognition or filing of an election petition. The critical outcome is the establishment of union representation (through voluntary recognition, election victory, or the order of the NLRB or relevant regulatory agency) versus continued nonunion status.

Representation Phase

A union is established within a bargaining unit and has been certified by the NLRB (or relevant agency) or recognized by the employer without an election. There are several critical outcomes associated with this phase. The employer may engage in a deunionization effort, resulting in a return to nonunion status, the replacement of the incumbent union by an outside union,[4] or continued representation by the incumbent union. Alternatively, an outside union or an insurgent employee group might challenge an incumbent union, resulting in deunionization, the replacement of the incumbent union, or continued representation by the incumbent.

CONTEXTUAL FORCES AND
UNIONIZATION/DEUNIONIZATION OUTCOMES

Even though our objective is to develop a model of the U/DU process that incorporates union and management strategic choice mechanisms, we will begin by considering the elements of a model

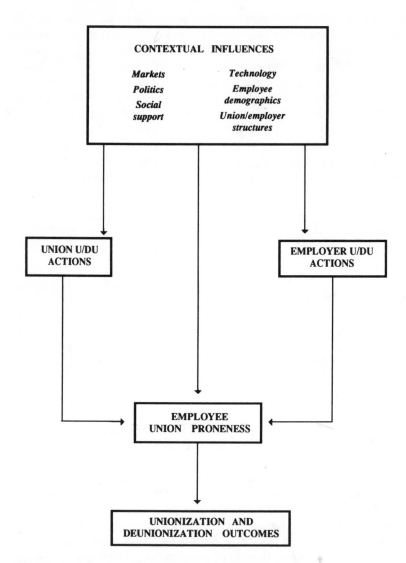

Diagram 2.1. Contextual influences and U/DU outcomes.

based on the assumption of contextual determinism (diagram 2.1). Most of the empirical union growth studies published in the late 1960s and throughout the 1970s (Fiorito and Greer 1982) are rooted in this assumption. Virtually none of these studies includes any direct measures of either employer or union actions, although some note the impact of employer and union actions and include certain contextual variables as proxies for these influences. Despite the limitation of the contextual union growth literature, important constructs and relationships are identified that are relevant in developing a strategic choice model. Moreover, studies continue to be published that assume union growth and decline are largely or exclusively determined by contextual forces. Thus, this basic model stands as an alternative against which the strategic choice model may be assessed.

One difficulty in developing a general model of the U/DU process is that the anticipated effects of variables included in the general model will differ across specific outcomes (e.g., certification versus decertification; see Lawler and Hundley (1983). To remain tractable, the general model of the U/DU processes proposed here is largely limited to identifying what seem to be important causal linkages without specifying strong hypotheses as to the expected signs of these effects.

ENDOGENOUS VARIABLES

Employees are seen as the central actors in determining the outcomes of U/DU efforts in contextual union growth models. Based on rationality assumptions, employee values and beliefs regarding unionism are presumed to determine *employee union proneness*. Union proneness derives from various contextual influences (either directly or indirectly, through actions taken by employers and unions). Dunlop's (1948) framework for analyzing union growth incorporates many of these features and has been the conceptual foundation for several union growth studies.[5] More recently, the union growth model proposed by Hirsch and Addison (1984, 9–42) is based on strong assumptions of rational decision making and contextual determinism.

Most empirical studies of union growth done by economists, whether macro or micro in focus, follow this line of reasoning. Employee decisions regarding unionization are assumed to be the product of a tradeoff between the expected costs and benefits of unionization versus those of nonunion status.[6] Studies written from an institutionalist perspective often at least implicitly assume similar processes.[7] Various behavioral studies complement this view by demonstrating relatively strong associations between worker motivational or attitudinal states and prounion behaviors and sentiments.[8]

The basic model assumes that *union and management actions* are mediating variables between exogenous contextual influences and U/DU outcomes. The proactive role of strategy in the process is either ignored or downplayed. It is not surprising, then, that even though the contextual union growth literature often alludes to employer and union policies there is minimal consideration of the form these policies assume in practice or the various ways in which specific actions might affect U/DU outcomes. Exogenous contextual influences serve as proxies for such actions. For the most part, union and employer actions are seen to act through union proneness in affecting outcomes. That is, actions are assumed either to have a direct effect on employee union proneness through influence efforts or a moderating effect on the relationship assumed to exist between union proneness and outcomes. The latter effect is seen to result from the facilitating or inhibiting impact that the infusion of resources into a U/DU effort is likely to have on the translation of employee motivations into action.

Following this perspective, the contextual growth model summarized in diagram 2.1 notes causal linkages running from both employer and union actions to employee union proneness. The mechanisms by which these effects are exerted are not specified, however, reflecting the limited discussion of this issue in the contextual union growth literature. The term *actions* is also purposefully ambiguous and is intended to connote both strategic programs and tactical initiatives. The strategic choice framework developed below decomposes this element into its constituent parts and considers the interrelationships among those parts.

EXOGENOUS VARIABLES

A wide range of contextual factors have been linked to U/DU outcomes. These factors are assumed to be predetermined and to affect outcomes by acting through intervening endogenous variables. For simplicity, the large number of variables that have been studied (Block and Premack 1983; Fiorito and Greer 1982; Heneman and Sandver 1983) are grouped into several basic categories. Some of these categories involve the specific characteristics of the workers, employers, and unions involved, but others relate to broader contextual characteristics. The following contextual influences are among those most frequently mentioned in the union growth literature.

Employee Demographics

The age, sex, race or ethnicity, and occupational characteristics of employees have all been linked to employee union proneness (Farber and Saks 1980; Moore and Newman 1975; Moore and Newman 1988; Stepina and Fiorito 1986; Lawler and Hundley 1983). Workers thirty to fifty years old generally have the most to gain from unionization and tend to be highly union-prone.[9] The concerns of female workers have not traditionally been high-priority items for most trade unions (which may also have discriminated against women in organizing efforts). This may well be changing as more unions focus specifically on women's issues (e.g., comparable worth, maternity leave, employer-provided day care), so that the relationship between an employee's sex and union proneness is no longer so clear. Despite past discriminatory practices by some unions, black employees have generally been found to be more favorably inclined to unionization than whites. How receptive the growing Asian and Hispanic components of the labor force will be toward unionism is less certain. And for the most part, employees in professional and white-collar occupations, at least outside of the public sector, have tended to be disinclined to unionize.

Employer Structure and Technology

The structural and technological characteristics of employer organizations are often discussed as important influences on employee union proneness. Authoritarian control systems and technologies that result in tedious work, physical danger, or discomfort may generate worker frustration and enhance employee union proneness (Hills 1985; Hundley 1988). In addition, structural arrangements and work processes may either encourage or limit the ability of workers to translate prounion feelings into action. For example, considerable noise in the workplace or limitations on the ability of employees to move around during work hours may reduce the likelihood of collective action. Despite the apparent importance of employer characteristics such as technology and structure, these variables have been investigated only to a limited extent. Most often, authors of empirical studies have included the size of the organization or bargaining unit as a proxy for a wide range of structural characteristics, including bureaucratization and employee differentiation. Other things being equal, studies tend to show that employees in larger units are less union-prone than those in smaller units. Dummy variables, used to control for employer industry or some other relevant employer characteristic, are also used. In general, these measures are rather weak and more work is necessary in developing cleaner indices of organizational technology and structure.[10]

Structure and technology would also be expected to be causally linked to employer policies. This issue shall be explored extensively when strategic choice processes are considered (below). Although the contextual union growth literature implies such a linkage, this notion is not well developed.

Union Organizational Characteristics

The structure and governance systems of unions are also suggested to be of importance in the contextual union growth literature. Brett (1980) notes the importance of group processes in expanding a base of support for unionization into a solid prounion majority. Even though both employee and employer characteristics will certainly impact on this consensus-building process, the political and structural characteristics of the union would intuitively seem to be perhaps most relevant. Maranto and Fiorito (1987) demonstrate internal union characteristics, such as democracy and centralization of decision making, to be related to election outcomes (i.e., more democratic, decentralized unions are more likely to win elections). Anderson, Busman, and O'Reilly (1982) demonstrate that leadership changes and the efforts of dissidents within unions are linked to decertification; other studies suggest that factors such as the level of dues and the union's ability to service units are also related to certification and decertification (Dickens, Wholey, and Robinson 1987; Dworkin and Extejt 1980; Chafetz and Fraser 1979). In addition, union characteristics should influence union policies. A theoretical treatment of this relationship by Berkowitz (1954), along with empirical studies by Voos (1987) and Block (1980), is taken up in chapter 3.

Economic Conditions

The relationships between U/DU outcomes and various economic influences are undoubtedly the most thoroughly analyzed by students of union growth and decline. Both the cyclical and structural properties of labor and product markets are assumed to determine attitudes toward collective bargaining. The impact of inflation, real wage adjustments, the union/nonunion wage differential, unemployment, market concentration, changes in employment, and product sales on employees are assumed to be related to the potential benefits and costs of unionization.[11] These factors condition current levels of job satisfaction, as well as employee expectations as to what unions will be able to accomplish and the extent to which employers are apt to retaliate for union activity.

Economic conditions can also directly influence union and employer policies. Unions and employers recognize that market conditions will impact on the results of contract negotiations; this in turn naturally affects their perceptions of the costs and benefits of establishing or disestablishing a bargaining relationship and their willingness to support or oppose the effort. The capacity of unions and employers to commit resources to U/DU efforts will also depend upon current economic conditions.

Legal and Political Environment

The argument whether laws and political conditions directly cause U/DU outcomes or simply moderate the impact of other influences has been around for some time and is not likely to be resolved. The distinction, for our purposes, is probably not all that significant. The extent to which workers feel protected or threatened by the legal system in pursuing union recognition can be assumed to affect their proneness to support unionization. Research on this issue has been more limited than is the case with many of the other classes of exogenous variables, often focusing on relationship between right-to-work laws and union membership or growth.

Social Environment

Dunlop (1948), along with many other institutionalist writers, stressed the importance of the social environment of the community within which organizing efforts occur in determining their success. Workers living in closely knit communities where unionism is highly legitimized are more apt to obtain tangible resources and moral support in organizing efforts than those who are more integrated into the broader community or those situated in antiunion areas. Measures of the social environment are often confounded by legal and political influences (and vice versa). In general, this issue has been underresearched, though there have been some recent efforts to distinguish social influences from other effects (e.g., Wessels 1981; Stepina and Fiorito 1986).

A STRATEGIC CHOICE FRAMEWORK

Fundamental limitations in the contextual union growth literature are apparent in light of recent research on U/DU strategies and tactics. In particular, the contextual approach treats employer and union policies as tightly bound to preexisting contextual conditions and downplays the significance of such efforts in determining U/DU outcomes relative to employee preferences. But the lack of an overarching theoretical framework that integrates the diverse research on U/DU strategies and tactics means that our understanding of what employers and unions do during unionization and deunionization efforts is piecemeal. If strategic actions are interlinked, and if the strategies of unions and employers are interdependent, then a model that accounts for these significant relationships is essential to a complete and undistorted view of union growth and decline processes. This is especially true if we wish to derive policy implications from this work.

THE STRATEGY CONCEPT

Much of the contextual union growth research has been influenced by Dunlop's (1958) industrial relations systems framework. In general, systems approaches emphasize contextual determinism and a consensus of values and beliefs among actors within a particular social system or subsystem. Systems are said to tend toward an equilibrium state; even though conflict may be overt and intense in periods of transition, it is assumed to be limited and contained once new equilibria obtain.

Systems theory has also played a dominant role in the development of organizational theory since at least the early 1960s. In particular, contingency theory perspectives (e.g., Thompson 1967) have stressed the existence of strong relationships between contextual conditions and organizational structures and processes. Yet contingency theory and related approaches are under increasing challenge by organizational theorists who emphasize the importance of managerial "strategic choice" in determining structure, processes, and context (Child 1972; Miles and Snow 1978). Moreover, organizations are said to be confronting increasingly turbulent—and often hostile—environments, making change and conflict ongoing processes; under such conditions, it may be that no clear-cut equilibrium state obtains (Pfeffer and Salancik 1978).

Although strategic choices may be constrained by contextual forces, they are also argued to reflect the decision maker's personal preferences and political interests. Consequently, strategic decisions may not lead to an optimal "fit" (from a contingency theory perspective) between context and management system. Managers may be willing to live with this, but they might also initiate actions to alter contextual conditions (e.g., change product lines or markets, relocate production facilities). Thus, organizational decision makers may be both *adaptive* and *proactive* in dealing with contextual constraints and contingencies. The strategic management literature of the last several years builds upon and expands the strategic choice concept.

A strategy can be viewed as a long-term plan by which key organizational players seek to achieve major objectives through a sequence of related steps. Strategies occur at different levels within organizations, with global strategies, formulated at high levels, giving rise to more specific strategies, which are formulated at lower levels (Freeman and Lorange 1985). Strategies may also be differentiated in terms of factors such as purpose (direct implementation versus context shaping) and focus (internal versus external). Organizational contexts are defined primarily in terms of various "stakeholders," who impose competing demands and create constraints for focal organizations. Strategic actions are adaptive or proactive responses to these contextual pressures. Strategies are implemented through various plans, policies, and tactics. The strategic management literature identifies many of these mechanisms. For example, the intraorganizational context may be controlled through structural arrangements that define authority and power. Influence techniques (e.g., persuasion, manipulation, coercion) may be advantageous in dealing with both internal and external constraints. External constraints may be avoided by shifting the organization into new environments; contextual control might also be accomplished by coopting, coalescing with, or absorbing stakeholders.

STRATEGIC CHOICES AND THE INDUSTRIAL RELATIONS SYSTEMS PERSPECTIVE

The concerns of researchers interested in the strategic management process mirror those of many industrial relations scholars. That is, approaching industrial relations from a perspective rooted in systems theory assumptions seems inappropriate in an era characterized by aggressive employer opposition to unions and ongoing conflict and disharmony. Rather than attributing U/DU outcomes largely to exogenous contextual forces, the strategic choice approach emphasizes the significance of the discretionary actions of employers and unions. Such actions are seen as only loosely coupled to contextual conditions; moreover, proactive strategic choices are often directed at altering contextual constraints.

The strategic choice perspective serves as the conceptual basis of the recent book by Kochan, Katz, and McKersie (1986). They identify fundamental elements and relationships in this framework, emphasizing the centrality of decision maker discretion and the interplay of contextual influences and strategic actions: "A key premise of our framework is that choice and discretion on the part of labor, management, and government affect the course and structure of industrial relations systems. Although contextual pressures are important and serve as the starting point for discussion of the determinants of an industrial relations system, the pressures do not strictly determine industrial relations outcomes" (Kochan, Katz, and McKersie 1986, 13-14).

A principal contention of the Kochan et al. book is that American employers have gained the upper hand in labor-management relations through a series of strategic initiatives. Thus, much of their analysis concerns the evolving nature of employee-relations strategies in firms and the increased importance firms are attaching to coordinating overall business strategies with human resource management strategies. The approach taken here is related to that of Kochan, Katz, and McKersie but differs in certain respects. First, discussion centers exclusively on unionization and deunionization processes. Second, Kochan et al. devote much of their book to an examination of strategic decisions made at the highest level in their three-tier system; these choices typically involve top-level executives and national union leaders and reflect global organizational concerns. The bargaining unit focus of this book means that greater attention is paid to the more specific strategies tied to particular U/DU efforts, choices that fall into the middle level of their hierarchy. Finally, Kochan et al. see management as the key player in shaping contemporary industrial relations outcomes and consequently concern themselves largely with managerial strategies. The nature and impact of union strategies, at least those related to U/DU activity, are treated

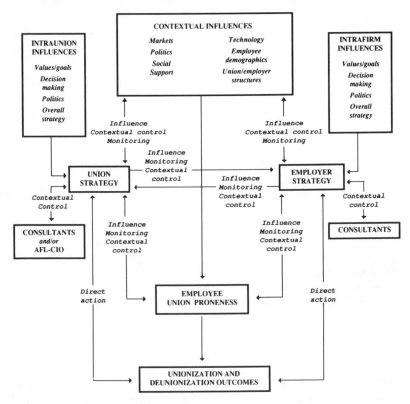

Diagram 2.2. Strategic choice framework.

more extensively here. The analysis presented here complements and extends the limited, but growing, literature focused on the nature of strategy formulation and implementation within unions (e.g., Dunlop 1990; Reed 1989c; Stratton and Brown 1988).

Having treated the components of organizational strategy in general, we turn now to strategic action within the context of U/DU efforts. The model proposed here (diagram 2.2) analyzes the formulation, implementation, and impacts of union and management strategic choices in relation to U/DU processes. As noted above, the purpose here is to delineate the basic constructs of the model, with subsequent chapters furnishing details.

STRATEGY FORMULATION

Both normative and descriptive models of strategy formulation and implementation have been proposed (Chaffee 1985). Analytical models (e.g., Grant and King 1979) posit that strategic planning proceeds through a series of steps, though the process may be recursive. As strategic choices involve important and nontrivial decisions, a wide range of influences, both internal and external to the organization, must be taken into account. A review of these conditions ought to suggest both problems and possibilities. Alternatives are then evaluated in terms of basic goals and objectives and a course of action is chosen. Analytical models stress the role of forecasting and rational optimization in strategic decision making, although it is recognized that professional judgment and qualitative decision techniques are often necessary in ambiguous settings.

Strategic decision making may, in practice, deviate from the ideal. Information processing can be distorted and choice rules altered because of uncertainty and complexity. In addition, organizational structure, authority relations, and political processes all impinge on the manner in which strategic decisions are made (Bower and Doz 1979; Mintzberg 1979; Mintzberg 1989, 25-42; Mintzberg, Raisinghani and Theoret 1976; Pfeffer and Salancik 1978, 62-91). Shrivastava (1983) has proposed a typology of strategic decision contexts and associated processes. He differentiates among rational bureaucratic systems, adaptive systems, and systems that are given over to political expediency.

As in the basic model, strategic choices are presumed to depend upon contextual conditions. In addition, employers and unions are expected to sense employee sentiments and adjust strategies accordingly. Since it is also posited that union proneness and context are influenced by strategic choices, there is obvious circularity in the process. To introduce determinancy, it is necessary to assume that some contextual influences are exogenous. Clearly some are. General economic conditions and basic public policy, for example, typically constrain U/DU strategies but are not usually targets of strategic initiatives. Moreover, the number of fixed contextual constraints will be greater the shorter the time horizon of the planning period.

There are other constraints that are apt to have an impact on strategy that are not a part of the basic model. The internal structures and political processes of employers and labor organizations are liable to affect the strategies of each. Unionization/deunionization strategies are also expected to be influenced by broader organizational strategies and goals. External consultants may shape the strategic choices of both management and unions, although consultants are much more prevalent on the employer side. The decision to use a consultant is also a strategic choice, however, and would be expected to be influenced by many of the same things that determine U/DU strategy. Finally, the values and preferences of key union and management decision makers are viewed as critical in the formulation of U/DU strategy. These organizational influences are indicated as causally related to union and employer strategies in diagram 2.2.

THE IMPLEMENTATION OF STRATEGY

As in the basic model of the U/DU process, the strategic choice approach posits the union proneness of employees to be a major factor in determining outcomes. Union proneness is shaped both by the organizational contexts within which employees function and by the environmental settings. Unlike in the basic model, union and management policies are more central in the process and are treated as more complex in character.

One definition of strategy that is especially useful in understanding the interaction of employers and unions in U/DU efforts is provided by Mason and Mitroff (1983, 33): "Strategies are plans for acquiring power. Power in this context refers to the human control of the energies necessary to achieve human purposes.... The kind of organizational power includes power over other human beings, exercised with or without their consent, with or against their 'will,' and with or without their knowledge or understanding." Both sides typically couch discussion of organizing and counterorganizing in win-loss terms, with the primary object of control efforts being bargaining unit employees. The balance of power between union and employer, which largely establishes the "winners" and "losers" in U/DU campaigns, is influenced by the manner in which each addresses contextual constraints and possibilities. Responses may be adaptive in character, in which case the parties work within the parameters established by various contexts. Alternatively, proactive responses involve the use of methods that transform contexts. Even though changed contexts present new constraints, these are anticipated to be more favorable to the organization or the interests of the decision maker.

The strategy concept is often criticized for being amorphous (e.g., Lewin 1987). It is difficult, if not impossible, to observe a strategy per se, and usually only the expressions of strategic action are seen. Yet in trying to understand the diverse activities that unions and employers engage in during unionization and deunionization efforts, strategy provides a helpful unifying framework. Moreover, managers and union officials discuss what they do in such situations in terms of strategic plans and objectives. As has already been noted, strategies are not always rational and well articulated. They can be the consequence of poor planning, distorted thinking, and emotional reactions. Thus, U/DU strategy is defined as the underlying process that generates discretionary organizational actions in unionization and deunionization efforts; no strong assumptions are made regarding what is proper strategy in a normative sense. This definition still assumes a latent construct not directly observable. Although this may still be troubling to some readers, strategy is no more elusive as a construct than utility, beliefs, attitudes, needs, and a host of other equally amorphous concepts used by social scientists. An implemented U/DU strategy is revealed through its interrelated elements that can be directly observed, including the *strategic mission*, the *targets* of strategic efforts, the *integration* of strategy within and across bargaining units, and the *tactics* used to accomplish strategic objectives.

STRATEGIC MISSION

The mission encompasses both key objectives and a guiding philosophy. It provides a sense of identity for those involved in strategic action and thus conditions responses to unforeseen circumstances. In normative models of strategy the articulation of an explicit mission statement is a key step in developing a strategy. The mission statement does not enumerate specific organizational actions to be used but does set the tone. This clearly constrains action and will result in the greater likelihood of particular tactics being used. Although the strategic mission may be well defined, as normative theory suggests, the notion of strategy used here does not presume that this will be so in all cases. The strategic mission may be implicit, ambiguous, and subject to change.

STRATEGIC TARGETS

Since the bargaining unit is the focal point of our analysis, we can meaningfully differentiate between *intraunit* and *external* aspects of U/DU strategy. The former embrace activities that revolve immediately around the bargaining unit and the employees within that unit. The latter involve responses to environmental elements distinct from the unit and its members. For example, a company's decision to locate a plant in a right-to-work state and a union's reliance on a "corporate campaign" or a consumer boycott are clear examples of externally directed strategic actions. Each involves an attempt to alter contextual conditions in order to increase the likelihood of desired outcomes. In contrast, "captive audience" speeches by employer representatives, as well as the use by union organizers of mass meetings and visits to the homes of bargaining unit employees, are classified as internally directed strategic actions.

A special and very significant form of external strategic action occurs when unions and employers target one another. Such *strategic interaction* includes efforts to influence an opponent and to foresee its actions. As in negotiations, statements made during campaigns send signals to the other side regarding a party's intentions and staying power. Unions and employers also engage in efforts to alter an opponent's capacity to act. An employer may initiate what amounts to a nuisance suit against a union by alleging financial loss as a result of union misconduct during a strike. Such litigation would consume union resources and could divert attention from actions more central to its objectives. If the union should lose the suit, a large award could seriously deplete its treasury.

A prime example of aggressive strategic interaction is the continuing interchange between Texas Air Corporation's president, Frank Lorenzo, and the various unions representing workers at Eastern and Continental airlines (both owned by Texas Air). Texas Air became the subject of extensive safety inspections by the Federal Aviation Authority and Department of Transportation as a consequence of union publicity campaigns questioning airline safety practices.[12] In response, Texas Air and Eastern initiated a $1.5 billion suit in 1988 against both the Airline Pilots and Machinists under provisions of the Racketeer Influenced and Corrupt Organizations Act

(RICO).[13] RICO has been criticized in many quarters as it has often been used—or misused—in business cases in which there is no hint of criminal conduct.

Unions also pursue means of curbing employer behavior in U/DU campaigns, with strikes and picketing being classic examples of such activity. Alternatively, a union may negotiate a neutrality agreement with an employer, effectively removing the employer from an active role in the campaign. In cases of interunion competition, patterns of strategic interaction can be very complex. A union may cooperate with a rival union in some areas while forming at least a tacit coalition with the employer in other areas. Alternatively, unions with overlapping jurisdictions may enter into noncompetition agreements.

A further distinction must be drawn between *primary* and *secondary* targets of strategic action (MacMillan 1979). If a change sought is a desired end in and of itself, then the contextual entity toward which the strategic action is aimed is the primary target. But many strategic initiatives are undertaken with the purpose of indirectly affecting a primary target. External strategic actions often fall into this category. A secondary boycott is a clear example of this type of approach. Another is a "corporate campaign" by a union, which may entail a public relations effort to discredit an employer. The impact upon the primary target (e.g., the firm's clients, stockholders, business partners) is not the principal objective; rather, the intent is to alter the stance of the employer, which is the secondary target.

In some instances an action may have the principal objective of affecting both the primary and secondary targets. A union dissident involved in a decertification effort may be harassed or disciplined by the union (e.g., fined or expelled from the union). This serves both to quiet the dissident and to dissuade would-be dissidents. Employer discrimination against union activists has a similar double-barreled impact.

STRATEGIC INTEGRATION

Although unions and employers may design strategies that are specific to particular bargaining units and U/DU phases, strategies may be integrated across U/DU phases and bargaining units. Employer strategies during the campaign phase are often little more than stop-gap measures undertaken in response to unanticipated union drives to obtain recognition. Employers may concentrate on defeating the union in an election without developing plans for dealing with those conditions that gave rise to the organizing effort.

Consequently, the employer may be highly vulnerable to unionization in the future, even if the union is defeated in the short term. In contrast, many employers with strong commitments to operating on a nonunion basis take considerable care to integrate union-avoidance activities. Executive-level managers have the responsibility of coordinating strategy at the corporate level. Thus, U/DU strategy is integrated within and across bargaining units; it is also well reconciled with broader business strategies. Multinational firms often coordinate union-avoidance programs on a worldwide basis.

Much of the current thinking on organizing in the AFL-CIO (American Federation of Labor and Congress of Industrial Organizations) stresses strategic integration. Realizing that a union is likely to be rebuffed in an initial campaign, organizers may link a series of campaigns in a particular unit. Employer promises made during one campaign are monitored; if unfulfilled, they may come back to haunt the employer in a subsequent campaign. The "associate membership" program now being promoted by the AFL-CIO is one means of maintaining contact with unit employees, monitoring conditions, and integrating activities over time until the union is successfully organized. The federation is also involved in efforts to increase interunion strategic integration, as exemplified by joint organizing programs, the encouragement of union mergers, and an agreement to limit organizing competition among affiliates.

TACTICS

Tactics are the specific actions through which strategies are expressed. In its simplest form a strategy can be defined operationally as a complex of interrelated tactics. Although strategies are complexes of tactics, it is important to recognize that there are multiple levels that build toward a fully implemented strategy. Three distinct levels of strategic action can be identified.

General Strategies

Free-standing and complete programs of action by which the union or employer seeks to achieve a desired long-term U/DU outcome.

Substrategies

Identifiable complexes of elementary tactics focused on particular and limited objectives. They are not fully self-contained and only make sense when combined with other substrategies and elementary tactics.

Elementary Tactics

Specific and immediate actions that can be used to achieve U/DU outcomes but only in combination with other elementary tactics. Unlike substrategies, which are limited as to what they can accomplish and as to how they can be intermingled, elementary tactics are more versatile: they may be combined and recombined in a variety of ways, and they are the fundamental building blocks of all strategies and substrategies.

As an example, a union may implement a general strategy in its effort to organize a particular bargaining unit. As part of its general strategic program, an organizer may establish an in-plant committee and pay home visits to bargaining unit employees, which are expressions of elementary tactics. In addition, a "corporate campaign" may also be undertaken to pressure the employer into voluntarily recognizing the union. A corporate campaign is a substrategy composed of several elementary tactics (influence, contextual control, monitoring). However, a corporate campaign is pursued here in association with other substrategies and elementary tactics.

The strategic management and organizational theory literatures have identified a wide range of tactics that organizations use in responding to external and internal contextual constraints (e.g., Thompson 1967; Pfeffer and Salancik 1978; Mason and Mitroff 1983). These writings are helpful in generating a typology of elementary tactics used by employers and unions in U/DU efforts. The categories of this typology are defined here along with illustrative examples of associated tactics in practice. Subsequent chapters will provide a more extensive treatment of the nature of the elementary tactics and the ways in which these are linked to the major substrategies and general strategies commonly utilized in each of the three principal U/DU phases.

Elementary tactics (influence, contextual control, monitoring, and direct action) are represented in diagram 2.2 as intervening between strategy and other elements of the model. Lines with arrows pointing in two directions indicate that strategy both causes and is affected by the element in question (e.g., contextual influences); the indicated elementary tactics mediate these relationships in ways discussed below.

Influence

Influence tactics entail the use of various forms of interpersonal communication and social interaction to encourage a strategic target to *interpret* or *reinterpret existing* contextual conditions in ways favorable to the strategist. Influence techniques include rational persuasion, manipulation, and the use of symbols and symbolic action. Their focus may be intraunit (e.g., individual, small group, and mass meetings; distribution of letters, posters, handbills, and other forms of written communication) or external (e.g., public relations campaigns).

Influence tactics may be divided into two subcategories. *Conversion* tactics involve attempting to convince strategic targets that they will be better off, or at least no worse off, if they act in a certain way. Company orientation programs for new employees usually involve conversion objectives. The keen interest many firms have in establishing "corporate cultures" is often linked to union-avoidance efforts. "Captive audience" meetings and small group meetings during organizing campaigns are often used by employers as the means of converting employees to an antiunion position. *Intimidation* differs from conversion in that the content of the message is coercive in character; targets are threatened with negative consequences if they do not behave in a desired manner. Threats may be viable or illusory, and symbolism is frequently used to increase the credibility or salience of a threat (e.g., bulky sergeants at arms in union meetings or a highly visible plant security force).

Influence tactics are widely used in U/DU efforts, though there is considerable controversy as to their effectiveness. The theoretical importance of such tactics is highlighted in the organizational behavior literature, which stresses the role of meaning construction in the management process (Weick 1979), in organizational politics (Pfeffer 1981), and in interorganizational relations (Pfeffer and Salancik 1978). Targets of influence efforts (e.g., bargaining unit members) often lack complete information on issues of importance (the impact of collective bargaining, the character of potential union leaders, costs of striking, etc.). Those who would effectively influence others are able to supply, or give the impression of supplying, relevant information. This imbues those individuals with power through their ability to filter and focus information in ways supportive of personal objectives. Of course, manipulation and outright deceit might also be used. The structuring of patterns of social interaction are also important in exercising influence. Isolating dissidents and malcontents in the workplace, as well as planting supporters or provocateurs, will likely affect the inclination of groups of employees to support unionization or deunionization.

Influence tactics are extensively used in large part because they are relatively inexpensive to implement. Yet as the success of influence tactics frequently relies on illusion, they are liable to work only in the short run unless continually reinforced. Ultimately, people may come to realize that union or employer claims are of little substance and react accordingly. For example, there is evidence that suggests that a "backfire" effect occurs when employers engage in overly aggressive union-avoidance efforts. That is, the net impact of the employer's strategy may be actually to *increase* the likelihood of unionization. In addition, intimidation tactics have a significant disadvantage that is not likely to result from conversion tactics. Targets of intimidation tend to harbor resentment and hostility toward their tormentors that may translate into retaliation should the opportunity arise.

Contextual Control

In contrast to influence tactics, contextual control tactics affect preferences and perceptions by *altering* contextual conditions.[14] In addition, modifying contextual conditions may inhibit or enhance the ability of strategic targets to act in certain ways, thus shaping outcomes independently of preferences or perceptions.

Intraunit contextual control tactics relate to the generation of structures, policies, and practices within the bargaining unit. Bargaining unit employees are likely to be imbedded in multiple structures and subject to different sets of policies, depending on the U/DU phase. Absent any union involvement, structure and policy are determined exclusively by the employer. When a union first appears, a structure emerges that links employees to that organization (e.g., an organizing committee is formed, with representatives in different departments), and union rules and bylaws regulate the conduct of at least those who are active in the organizing attempt. Should the union gain recognition, union structures and policies become more pervasive. Although unions and management may establish internal contextual conditions unilaterally, certain conditions may be the product of negotiations or established by some outside entity (e.g., the NLRB or other government agencies). Consequently, internal contextual control tactics may require external action as well.[15]

Specific policies regarding pay, promotion, working conditions, access to management, and other aspects of the employment relationship are important features of internal contextual control efforts. This is particularly true in the nonunion phase, in which management may implement changes in personnel policies as part of a "positive labor relations" program. Structural features, such as the lines of authority and communication within the unit and between the unit and employer or labor organizations, may be altered through contextual control tactics in order to affect the success of intraunion conversion, intimidation, and monitoring tactics.

Intraunit contextual control tactics play a central role in the control and coordination of the behavior of bargaining unit employees that is immediately related to U/DU efforts. On the union side, the establishment of a network of supporters and of a well-functioning organizing committee is normally imperative to the success of an organizing drive. During the representation phase, structure and union policies serve to maintain discipline and member solidarity in the face of any challenges by the management or an outside union. Disloyal members may be subject to disciplinary action or informal sanctions that are encouraged by the union leadership. Employer contextual control tactics undertaken within the bargaining unit are often designed to restrict prounion activities by employees through company rules (e.g., prohibitions against wearing union insignia or soliciting support for the union during work time). Union activists may be reassigned to jobs in which they do not have much contact with other employers; they may be fired or subject to other discriminatory (and illegal) treatment. A common technique in union-avoidance campaigns is selective hiring in which employers screen out job candidates with characteristics believed to be associated with union proneness (e.g., having prior work experience in a unionized company).

External contextual control tactics may be divided into two subcategories. Unions and employers are often in the position of having some choice over the contexts within which they will act. Unions do not pursue all organizing opportunities, usually choosing those with the greatest potential payoff. Employers may locate (or relocate) plants in areas where social and political conditions are not conducive to unionization. Both employers and unions use NLRB procedures to affect bargaining unit composition. All of these approaches are examples of *contextual selection,* a process of opting into contextual settings or niches that already possess favorable characteristics.

Contextual selection opportunities are not unlimited and sometimes may simply be unavailable. In any event, unions and employers may be precluded from readily moving once established in a particular setting. Yet they may be able to modify conditions through *contextual transformation* efforts. The rules and procedures of the NLRB (or relevant regulatory agency) may be used to impose constraints on the other side during certification and decertification elections. Both sides may secure the aid of community institutions. Religious leaders are sometimes enlisted to support or to oppose unionization; the support of the local media, merchants, banks, courts, and police agencies might be obtained. Unions and employers may attempt to coopt one another. Employers can provide assistance to the least disfavored of competing unions. Although overt aid would be illegal, tacit support of a particular union is not uncommon. Union organizers are also able to build alliances with sympathetic managers. External contextual control tactics appear to be increasingly important components of the organizing strategies of some unions and have been touted by the AFL-CIO (1985) in an era in which pursuing recognition through NLRB certification elections is seen to be a losing proposition. Boycotts, community outreach programs, coordinated organizing campaigns, and corporate campaigns are all examples of external contextual control tactics of unions.

Monitoring

An important objective in almost all U/DU efforts is the acquisition of reliable information. Unions and employers monitor each other's actions, those of employees in the election unit, and relevant external influences. The use of surveys and polls (which can also be used as influence tools) is widespread on both sides.[16] Unions are apparently increasingly likely to spend considerable time prior to initiating an organizing drive assessing the possibility of victory and estimating organizing costs. Although available published data on the target firm may be examined, organizers will also try to contact employees (usually away from the work location) to develop an understanding of the social dynamics of the firm and employee sentiments. Employers are frequently advised by consultants to train first-line supervisors in proper—and effective—means of discerning union activities at the shop floor level. Employers also engage in illegal monitoring tactics, such as the interrogation and surveillance of employees with respect to union matters.

Direct Action

Finally, a union, but more often an employer, may be in a position to determine the outcome of unionization or deunionization effort unilaterally through direct action. An employer may close a unionized facility, outsource materials produced by union workers, or automate the functions of union workers. Direct recognition of a union by an employer as well as an employer's withdrawal of recognition are other examples of enactment activities. Unions are rather more limited in their ability to achieve outcomes by direct action. One traditional approach, now illegal except for a limited form allowed in the construction industry, is the establishment of a closed shop. Ironically, the most prevalent union direct action tactic may, in fact, be withdrawal from a U/DU effort that it recognizes to be a losing proposition.[17]

CHAPTER SUMMARY

A general model of the unionization/deunionization process is proposed in this chapter. Although the initial representation election campaign is often the most important phase in the process, the other phases are of increasing significance. The personnel policies of non-union employers are often designed with union-avoidance objectives in mind, even in the absence of overt union organizing activity. Moreover, employers are now much more prone to attempt to dislodge established unions or prevent newly certified unions from winning an initial contract. Hence, the model is designed to be useful in analyzing outcomes in all three of the principal phases of the U/DU process. The model focuses on outcomes at the bargaining unit level, as these are most relevant to union representation under the American system.

Although building upon research on union growth that presumes outcomes to be effectively determined by contextual conditions, the formulation and implementation of employer and union strategies are the core features of the model. The strategic choice perspective, which is the theoretical basis of the model, leads to several important observations regarding the nature of the U/DU process that are at odds with the conventional growth literature:

1. U/DU outcomes are shaped by the strategies of employers and unions, as well as contextual influences.
2. Strategies are not exclusively dependent upon contextual influences, as they also reflect the preferences, perceptions, thinking practices, and political interests of key union and management decision makers.
3. The cognitive processes and motives of decision makers may lead to distorted views of reality and the development of strategies ill-suited to actual conditions.
4. In contrast to systems theory assumptions, overt conflict and disequilibrium may be the norm in the union-management arena, leading to abrupt and discontinuous change.

CHAPTER 3

Rigidity and Renewal:
Strategic Choice Processes in Unions

To understand the nature of U/DU strategies, it is necessary to appreciate the underlying decision-making processes of management and unions. Strategic choices are shaped by the manner in which information is assimilated and interpreted and by the decision rules that are applied. These factors are affected by the quality of the information available, the values and perceptual systems of key decision makers, and the distribution of power and control within the organization. Changes in the structural characteristics and institutional relationships of labor and employer organizations can therefore impact the strategic choice process and, ultimately, the strategies pursued. A number of important public and organizational policy implications follow from an understanding of how U/DU strategies are formulated.[1]

The general treatment of decision making in the strategic management literature has been covered in chapter 2. This chapter examines the specifics of union strategy formulation as these relate to the more general framework; the management strategy formulation process is taken up in the following chapter. The nature of U/DU strategy formulation in unions is explored here from two distinct perspectives. We begin by considering strategy formulation as a rational planning process. Since the literature does not lend strong support to the notion that unions develop U/DU strategies in this manner, we turn to an examination of strategy formulation in terms of behavioral decision theory and the institutional characteristics of unions. An alternative model is proposed that incorporates notions of political action and nonrational behavior. The chapter concludes with a look at contemporary developments in U/DU strategic decision making within unions, particularly as influenced by the report issues in 1985 by the AFL-CIO Committee on the Evolution of Work.

RATIONAL PLANNING: THEORY AND EVIDENCE

Rational choice models of organizational decision making are predicated upon four basic assumptions: clearly defined goals, utility optimization within resource constraints, tractable and programmable problems, and the availability of information. This approach has the advantage of generating determinant predictions of how organizations will act in particular circumstances. Even though rationality assumptions seem tenuous at best when applied to decision making in unions, a few authors have tackled the issue of optimal union strategic planning in the organizing area. These approaches are similar, though different, to efforts to develop rational choice models of union decision making in relation to bargaining activity (e.g., Bellinger 1989; Atherton 1973; Farber 1984).

ECONOMIC THEORY AND UNION ORGANIZING

Berkowitz (1954) proposed a rudimentary framework for analyzing the economics of union decision making with regard to organizing new bargaining units. A union's choice to establish a new bargaining unit is posited to depend upon the marginal contribution of the unit to the net revenues of the national union. Primary investment costs in the organizing campaign are assumed to be the salaries of organizers and support personnel, the costs of materials, and the administrative costs associated with representation election procedures. The probability of obtaining recognition is seen to be an increasing function of the level of union investment in the campaign, given the attributes of the unit. Experienced union leaders and organizers should be able to estimate the investment necessary to secure the support of a majority of those in the bargaining unit. Subsequent costs of administration, should the unit be successfully organized, are also presumed to be taken into account. Berkowitz assumes that the marginal increment in direct dues payments is the principal benefit accruing to the national union resulting from organizing new workers (though he also notes important secondary benefits).

The Berkowitz framework posits a mechanism by which rational union leaders use cost-benefit analysis to answer key questions relating to organizing activity: Should an organizing effort be undertaken? If so, how much should be committed to the effort? What level of services should be provided to the unit if the union is recognized? Berkowitz proceeds to critique his own model, however, arguing that certain aspects of the union organizing process render the rational choice perspective of limited usefulness as either a descriptive or normative model. His concerns revolve around violations of some of the strong rationality assumptions set forth above. First, he maintains that the risk and uncertainty associated with organizing render optimal decision making difficult at best. The greater the informational deficit associated with a decision problem, the less confidence one can have that a given choice will be appropriate to the conditions that ultimately obtain; indeed, to the extent risk can be measured, it is possible to calculate the expected opportunity loss associated with a given decision.[2] Berkowitz proposes a deterministic model of decision making and therefore has not directly incorporated risk and uncertainty into his analysis. Yet optimization, with certain modifications, is clearly a viable decision method under conditions of risk and uncertainty.

In most situations union organizers are likely to have some prior expectations as to the nature of critical relationships in the decision framework used to determine the degree of investment in the organizing effort. Seasoned union organizers are apt to have knowledge of factors such as the probability of union victory in the campaign given various resource expenditures during the campaign, the likelihood of successfully negotiating an initial contract (given certification), and the chances of decertification given different levels of service provided to the unit after negotiating a contract. Even in the absence of sufficient historical data to establish numeric probabilities, subjective probabilities, based on professional judgment and experience, may be used to establish the expected stream of benefits to the union as a function of investment both in organizing activity and postcertification service to the unit. Rational union leaders would then choose the levels of organizing effort and service that would maximize expected benefit to the union.

As risk increases and begins to border on uncertainty, the quality of choices made by means of mathematical optimization, whether implicitly or explicitly used in the strategy formulation process, begins to deteriorate. Various game theory approaches have nevertheless been developed to aid decision makers in providing some analytical structure to very ambiguous problems. Among the best known of these techniques are the so-called "minimax" and "maximin" solutions.[3] Various behavioral techniques may also be used in ill-structured settings to assist in clarifying options and relationships; examples include "brainstorming," the Delphi technique, and dialectic policy analysis (Grant and King 1979).

A second major concern raised by Berkowitz is his recognition that not only the level but also the form of organizing activity and postcertification service matters in determining organizing outcomes. As he notes: "The qualitative differences in both organizer and worker may overwhelm the quantitative differences" (Berkowitz 1954, 588). That the mix of organizing techniques is situation specific does not, however, preclude the use of optimization methods in devising union U/DU strategies. We could envision union organizers and leaders, rather than simply choosing the optimal level of resource investment in a particular organizing effort, as simultaneously selecting optimal levels for a mix of organizing activities.

A final question raised by Berkowitz is whether "it is politically possible in a union to operate according to an economic calculus" (Berkowitz 1954, 589). Political considerations can be accommodated within a quantitative choice framework. Economic choice models recognize that a decision maker's utility is subjectively experienced. Individuals may act as rational optimizers even if outcomes are only evaluated in intangible terms. Furthermore, to the extent that it is possible to scale decision-maker utility, as well as subjective expectations, numeric methods can be used to select optimal strategies.

EMPIRICAL STUDIES

Although Berkowitz provides no test of his model, other authors have also studied the level of union organizing activity within a rational choice framework and report empirical findings. These studies are more recent than Berkowitz's paper, which was written at the apex of union power. They consequently focus on linkages between the strategic choices of unions with respect to U/DU activity and the labor movement's membership decline over the past three decades. Research approaches differ; in one instance election activity is used as an indicator of union investment in organizing, but estimates of actual monetary expenditures are used by another author.

Election Activity

Block (1980) builds on themes developed both by Berkowitz and institutionalist analysts of union administrative practices. He proposes a model of the allocation of union resources to organizing activity predicated on the assumption that both leaders and rank-and-file members act as rational utility maximizers. To simplify matters, unions are presumed to have only two basic functions: organizing new members and providing services to current members. Block argues that the marginal utility of union growth declines at higher levels of unionization for both leaders and the rank and file. Rank-and-file utility is posited to level off with union density at relatively high levels of unionization, since increments in union power are likely to decrease as a function of union density. The increasing marginal costs of extending union representation, coupled with political pressure from the rank and file, are argued to lead to a decline in the marginal utility of union growth for union leaders. Hence, investment in organizing activity is hypothesized to decline after some threshold of unionization is reached.

Block tested this model by analyzing union organizing activity in a cross section of sixty-five national unions for the period 1972–1978. Since no direct measure of union investment in organizing activity was readily available, he used the number of representation elections per one thousand current union members as a proxy dependent variable. There are obvious difficulties here. To be a valid indicator of the intensity of union resources committed to organizing activity, it must be assumed that the average level of resources consumed per election are roughly equivalent across all unions in the sample. But this assumption is suspect, if for no other reason than the existence of considerable variation in the average size of election units. To say that two unions are each involved in roughly five elections per one thousand members in a given time period does not seem to suggest equivalent resource expenditures on organizing per member if the average unit size for the first union is two or three times that for the second. At minimum, the empirical analysis should have controlled in some manner for the *number* of employees involved in these elections. Moreover, considerable resources may have been invested by unions in organizing activity that did not result in an election (e.g., unsuccessful card drives, campaigns resulting in direct recognition). Unless non-election organizing activity is strongly correlated with election activity, Block's measure is apt to be unreliable and possibly biased.[4]

The principal independent variables in Block's analysis are the unionization rate for the national union's primary jurisdiction and the proportion of the union's membership that is in its primary jurisdiction; both are hypothesized to be negatively related to organizing efforts. Although in theory the relationship between both of these independent variables and organizing activity first rises and then declines, Block uses a sample of unions with relatively high penetration rates in the primary jurisdiction and expects the maximum of the function to be generally exceeded, hence the hypothesized negative relationships.

Membership concentration in the primary jurisdiction is intended to measure the extent to which union leaders experience pressure from the rank and file; that is, if the membership is concentrated rather than dispersed in the primary jurisdiction, then rank-and-file preferences are going to be more immediately felt by leaders in democratic unions. Block further addresses the issue of intraunion politics by including certain union structural properties in the analysis that are presumed to measure the democratic character of the union. The argument is that leaders in more democratic unions will be more responsive to member preferences; hence the negative relationships hypothesized for the principal independent variables will be stronger. These relationships are tested by examining various interaction effects.[5]

The results of his analysis generally support the principal hypotheses. Union density in the primary jurisdiction, membership concentration in the primary jurisdiction, and the interaction of these two variables all negatively impacted organizing activity. However, the interaction terms involving union structural characteristics were all found to be insignificant. The overall explanatory power of the model was also quite low, with adjusted R^2's in the range of .05 to .13. Although these weak results may be attributable to the data problems suggested above, the relatively small sample size, and poor model specification,[6] they clearly suggest that the rational choice framework proposed by Block does not reflect, in the main, the U/DU strategic decision processes of unions.

Expenditures on Organizing Activity

Three related studies by Paula Voos also tackle the issues of how unions allocate scarce resources to organizing activity. Unlike Block, Voos constructed a data series on union organizing expenditures from the financial records of several national unions over the period 1953-1977. Although, as she notes, there are clear limitations to the reliability of some of these data, her approach provides the first good approximation of the allocation of union resources to the organizing process. Voos (1984) found that over the period studied the proportion of union budgets allocated to organizing declined slightly (from a high of about 23 percent in the mid-1950s to around 19 percent in the early 1970s). Contrary to what many might have expected, however, real organizing expenditures per union member actually increased, by nearly 40 percent over the period studied. More important, real expenditures per *organizable worker* exhibited something of an upward trend over the period studied.[7] She thus rejects the argument that declining union commitment to organizing has substantially contributed to the difficulties that private sector unions are experiencing in organizing new members.

Voos examines the decision-making process of unions with respect to expenditures on organizing activity by first considering the costs versus benefits of a union organizing new members. She estimates that the cost (in 1967 dollars) of organizing an additional union member was between approximately $200 and $600 (Voos 1983). Unlike Berkowitz (1954), however, who suggests a broad range of financial benefits associated with expanding union representation, Voos concentrates exclusively on increased wages to currently represented workers resulting from greater union coverage. She estimates that by extending union coverage by one employee there was between a $100 and $800 annual increase in earnings (in 1967 dollars) for employees already covered by a contract (the amount of increase depending upon characteristics of the industry). Since the discounted incremental earnings stream would obviously be several times the annual figure, it is clear that on average the costs of organizing new members are far exceeded by the benefits, at least as expressed in very tangible terms. Consequently, a rational assessment of the organizing environment would suggest that unions should substantially expand organizing activity. That they do not suggests to Voos that other decision mechanisms may be at work that do not conform rigidly to the assumptions of economic theory.

Voos (1987) has also analyzed determinants of the proportion of total national union budgets allocated to organizing activity. She largely adopts Block's (1980) model. Besides using a different (and preferable) dependent variable, Voos excludes the union structural measures used by Block and employs some different control variables. Various specifications of the model are estimated, and different measures of union density in the primary jurisdiction are also considered. As with the Block study, however, their results are rather disappointing, with Voos being able to explain at most only 15 percent of the variance in relative expenditures on organizing. Moreover, the only statistically significant independent variable in the analysis was union density in the primary jurisdiction, which was negative in sign (as in the Block study).

RATIONAL PLANNING: AN ASSESSMENT

That unions approach the problem of formulating U/DU strategies in a rational manner is an appealing proposition. It lays open the possibility that we may readily model the process and fairly reliably anticipate how union leaders and organizers will respond in various circumstances. Those directly involved in U/DU efforts tend to portray themselves as carefully reviewing options and selecting the best course of action for both the membership and the union as an institution. Yet given the literature that we have considered here, a rational planning model does not seem especially appropriate for understanding union U/DU strategy formulation.

Berkowitz (1954) pointed out some of the conceptual difficulties associated with viewing decisions regarding the allocation of union resources to organizing within a rational choice framework. Although factors such as risk and uncertainty, problem complexity, and organizational politics do not preclude rational decision making, all contribute to creating an environment in which the strong assumptions of rational choice theory are violated. The behavioral decision literature that has developed over the past twenty-five to thirty years suggests that such conditions do promote nonrational action within organizations. The interaction of these influences further limits the viability of conventional rational choice mechanisms. Moreover, the empirical research reviewed above would seem to suggest that the allocation of union resources to organizing activity is only very weakly explained by a rational choice model.

Research on union U/DU strategy formulation is quite limited, and it would be imprudent to reject the rational choice framework absent additional studies. Even though existing studies provide a strong foundation for future work, there are deficiencies in this literature that should be addressed. Research to date focuses on the level of resources allocated to organizing rather than on the manner in which unions might choose among alternative strategies. Thus, significant qualitative decisions regarding organizing *techniques*, as opposed to organizing *intensity*, are largely ignored. Closely related to this issue is the need for micro-level studies of the strategic decision-making process. Existing research analyzes highly aggregate outcomes in terms of variables far removed from the locus of decision making; a better understanding of decision-making practices would derive from direct studies of union leaders and organizers in field settings. Finally, research on this topic is now rather dated. Berkowitz wrote over thirty years ago, and the data used by both Block and Voos are ten to twenty years old. The difficulties of the labor movement, especially in recent years, seem to have jolted union leaders and may have transformed decision-making processes, inducing greater reflection and more careful planning. It is quite possible that contemporary research would suggest rationality in U/DU strategy formulation to be more prevalent.

POLITICS, COGNITIVE PROCESSES, AND STRATEGIC CHOICES

If U/DU strategies are not devised within unions through rational planning techniques, then by what means are they? Difficulties abound in addressing this question. Unions vary considerably in terms of the locus of authority for embarking on organizing efforts; the international may take the lead in some unions, while intermediate bodies or local unions are principally responsible in others. Choice processes may reasonably be expected to differ across hierarchical levels within unions. Democratic practices found in unions are crucial, as the authors reviewed above all noted. Finally, critical strategic choices in many U/DU efforts may be made by those outside of the union. Organizing efforts are often initiated by employees who subsequently contact a union for assistance. By the time the union intervenes, the tone of the campaign may already have been established.

Recognizing these limitations, we shall proceed to construct a model of strategy formulation that derives from organizational theory perspectives centering on the nature of power, politics, and decision-making processes. The diversity of strategy formulation processes within the labor movement means that this model is very broad and efforts to apply it to particular circumstances will require appropriate augmentations. Although our purpose here is to gain insights into U/DU strategy formulation, it is difficult to differentiate this process from other forms of strategy formulation. Consequently, we proceed by first sketching a general model of union decision making that is then applied to the issue at hand.

THE UNION EFFECTIVENESS PROBLEM

A fundamental assumption of the rational choice perspective is that organizational goals are unambiguous and widely shared (at least by those in a position to affect outcomes). In simple organizations with relatively homogeneous participants, this notion seems quite tenable. It becomes more questionable in large, complex, and diverse organizations, as reflected in the considerable interest scholars have shown in the nature of organizational power and politics over the past several years. Conditions are particularly unfavorable to the formation of consensual goals in labor organizations. Unions lack tangible and readily quantifiable goals. Students of the labor movement have long debated what union objectives should be in principle, especially with regard to collective bargaining and wage negotiations. Yet uncertainty continues as to the ends unions pursue even with respect to what most would regard as a central function. Ambiguity is even greater concerning more peripheral matters.

The lack of clarity as to fundamental union goals is compounded by the diversity of interests within labor organizations. Unlike corporate shareholders, who have a common interest in a firm's profitability, diverse groups within the union's rank and file will often hold incompatible notions of union effectiveness. Even heroic efforts by union leaders to reconcile conflicting member interests are likely to be unsuccessful; hence, the interests of certain members will inevitably be subordinated to those of others. Conflicts also exist between the interests of members and a union's leadership. In a business firm, the values and preferences of managers—taken to reflect those of shareholders—are presumed to shape organizational policies. The interests of lower-level participants are expected to give way to hierarchically defined goals.[8] But in a labor union the rank-and-file members are, in principle, simultaneously in both superordinate and subordinate positions. The union is established to serve their interests, yet to do so necessitates the coordination and control of member behavior. Hence, union leaders may need to emphasize the union's institutional concerns at the expense of what the members perceive as their immediate interests.

Efforts to understand the nature of these fundamental conflicts within unions are long standing in the industrial relations field (Strauss 1977). Kochan (1980, 174–176) considers the processes by which union objectives might form, noting conflicts between the concerns of leaders and the rank and file. Other authors (e.g., Lipset, Trow, and Coleman 1956; Lester 1958; Sayles and Strauss 1967; Barbash 1967; Edelstein and Warner 1976) have explored the union democracy issue. Although there are important differences in structure and process across unions (Fiorito and Hendricks 1987), the governance systems of American unions tend to be oligarchical and, many would argue, relatively nondemocratic. Intraunion political action and the exercise of power are the dominant forces shaping the destinies of labor organizations (Dunlop 1990).

What is known about the political dynamics of unions would seem to lead to the rejection of models of union decision making based on *predefined* and *objective* criteria of union effectiveness. We might suppose definitions of effectiveness to be subjective, reflecting the interests of those currently in power. Even though politically based choices may be accommodated within a rational choice framework, it is necessary to have knowledge of the values and preferences of those within the dominant coalition. This is not always a simple chore. Even entrenched union leaders may have difficulty articulating long-term goals, though short-term operational objectives may be readily identified. Moreover, political relationships and patterns of influence may be complex and shifting, so that dominant interests cannot be readily discerned.

Organizational theorists have developed several alternatives to conventional rational choice models. One approach that seems especially applicable to trade unions has been proposed by Pfeffer and Salancik (1978) and is rooted in the *resource dependence* perspective on organizational effectiveness and action.[9] Their work emphasizes linkages between the external environment from which an organization must draw resources critical to its survival and the internal balance of political power. The Pfeffer and Salancik framework will be adapted here to the trade union context.

The resource dependence perspective argues that organizations confront a multiplicity of demands imposed by environmental entities that supply critical resources. The basic problem confronting organizational authorities is *not* the optimal attainment of long-term goals. Rather, concern focuses on building a viable coalition of resource suppliers. This is made problematic by the wide array of potentially conflicting, externally imposed demands. Organizational effectiveness is defined primarily in terms of the strength of an organization's bargaining position *vis-à-vis* its environment. Within such a context organizational authorities are necessarily preoccupied with resolving immediate crises, so that the pattern of organizational action over time is not apt to be consistent with the optimal attainment of remote and abstract long-term goals. The only meaningful index of organizational effectiveness is seen to be the preservation of a coalition of resource suppliers. Indeed, long-term goal statements may often be fashioned *after* the fact to justify organizational actions.

The resource dependence perspective suggests the following formal definition of union effectiveness:

Proposition 1
   Labor unions are effective to the extent that exchanges are structured with the environment to ensure a predictable and steady flow of resources critical to the union's survival.

Critical resources include a wide range of tangible and intangible factors, including the recruitment of new and retention of existing members, employer cooperation, financial support, governmental support, and legitimacy in the broader community. The suppliers of these resources must be induced to enter into a coalitional arrangement, in which the union is the focal point. Thus, coalition management is central to understanding union strategy formulation. This process suggests that the dynamics of organizational decision making are far different from those of rational planning. The focus is short run, rather akin to Lindblom's (1959) notion of organizational decision making as a process of "muddling through."

RESOURCE DEPENDENCIES AND UNION DECISION MAKING

Building on their resource dependence concept of organizational effectiveness, Pfeffer and Salancik (1978, 39–91) delineate aspects of an organizational choice model incorporating political action and behavioral decision processes. A number of propositions relating to union decision making and strategy formulation are derived from their work and considered here. Before developing these propositions, certain concepts must be defined.

Dependence is the most fundamental concept in the Pfeffer and Salancik framework, though it is also an integral aspect of much of the contemporary organizational literature. Dependence and power are social forces that are closely linked and largely mirror images of each other. *A* is said to be dependent upon *B* to the extent *B* is capable of supplying a critical resource to *A*, *A* has few or no alternatives to obtaining the resource from *B*, and *A* cannot force *B* to supply the resource through the use of sanctions. Conversely, the *power* of *B* over *A* is said to vary inversely with *A*'s dependence on *B*.[10]

As coalitions, organizations must be seen as complexes of participants (both individuals and social groupings, including other organizations). Organizational boundaries are fuzzy. At the nucleus of the organization is a core of tightly controlled participants and activities; radiating from the nucleus are other participants across a gradient of control. At the periphery of this complex are those entities clearly outside of the organizational coalition. Organizational participants can thus be categorized in terms of their level of inclusion in the organization. *Partial inclusion* is an important concept, since elements of the organizational coalition not fully under the control of the incumbent authorities of an organization are sources of dependence and possibly problematic. In the case of trade unions we might think of potentially organizable workers, as well as those already represented by a union, as only partially included union participants. Similarly, workers may be viewed as only partially included participants in employer organizations. Hence, bargaining unit members may be simultaneously considered to be external sources of dependence for both employers and unions (as is reflected in diagram 2.2).[11]

Unionization/deunionization efforts can be interpreted, then, as contests for control between employers and unions over mutual sources of dependence.

Having developed a definition of union effectiveness and established basic concepts, we turn to those propositions derived from Pfeffer and Salancik that define union decision-making practices.

Proposition 2
Union governance is an essentially political process.
Both the lateral and hierarchical conflicts of interest inherent in unions suggest that internal union decision making is power based. Dominant groups and individuals emerge through political action. The assumption that politics drives union choices is, of course, consistent with much of what has been written in the industrial relations literature.

Proposition 3
Dependence relationships affect the stability of a union.
To the extent that a union is dependent on an external (or partially included) entity, there is the risk that the agent will be unwilling or unable to provide critical resources. This poses a threat to the viability of the union.

Proposition 4
Internal political power in unions derives from the ability to cope with critical resource dependencies.
The resource dependence perspective is largely concerned with the linkages that exist between the management of external dependencies and internal political equilibria. Those who best contain the dependencies confronting unions are in positions to translate their competencies into political influence. In a sense the dependency is transferred from the external entity to those union leaders or members. The notion that those who deal well in reducing organizational risks are able to exercise political power within the organization is widely accepted in the organizational literature.

Unions may encounter dependency problems in the many arenas in which they must operate. Organizing new members and retaining the existing ones are but two classes of activities critical to union viability. Negotiating contracts, providing services to organized workers, lobbying and other forms of political action, and establishing working relationships with other unions and social movement organizations are also major concerns for most unions. The interplay among these various sources of dependence leads to the balance of power within the inner circle of a union's leadership. Not all dependencies will be equally demanding, either over time or across unions. Those who cope with the most immediate dependency problems will exercise the greatest influence within the union. Changing dependency patterns might be expected, then, to lead to a realignment of political relationships. Yet power can be self-perpetuating since power holders have at their disposal the means to shape future dependence relationships through strategic action.

Proposition 5

Those with power seek to institutionalize control by creating and preserving dependencies favorable to their positions and by eliminating unfavorable dependencies.

The essence of the resource dependence perspective is that organizations such as unions are apt to confront a *multiplicity of conflicting dependencies.* Although organizations cannot be expected to satisfy all demands that are placed upon them, strategic action may alter dependency patterns. Some dependencies may be eliminated through proactive policies, but others may remain as continuing sources of uncertainty and risk. By making strategic choices consistent with their competencies and personal preferences, power holders create conditions that support the maintenance of their power bases. Thus, the relationship between dependence and intraorganizational power is reciprocal. This observation parallels the argument of the strategic choice literature (discussed in chapter 2) that strategies are not completely determined by contextual constraints but also reflect the personal interests and perceptions of strategic decision makers.

Proposition 6

Critical resource dependencies and contextual conditions are often complex and uncertain. Since perceptions of reality may be socially constructed, power holders may seek to create and preserve self-serving definitions of reality within unions, so that true dependencies may be obscured.

The preponderance of research on human information processing and decision making clearly suggests that uncertainty and complexity alter the thinking practices of individuals in such a way as to preclude purely rational decision making.[12] To varying degrees, individuals find ambiguity aversive. When ambiguity is great and rational information-processing methods either fail or are difficult to implement, individuals may pursue ways of reducing ambiguity through a variety of cognitive devices. In particular, ambiguity makes people more open to social influence attempts and more likely to rationalize past actions.

In organizational settings, attribution, rationalization, dissonance reduction, cognitive distortion, and related processes lead to the development of an *organizational paradigm* that serves as a model of the world in which the organization operates and as a means of interpreting reality (Pfeffer 1982, 226-253). The essence of this "socially constructed reality" is to reduce equivocality and to create at least the perception of certainty (Weick 1979); the greater the initial level of ambiguity, the more likely it is that these processes will dominate the thinking within organizations. Of course, the paradigm will tend to depict the conditions confronting a union in a biased or outdated manner. It is in the interest of power holders to reinforce the extant union paradigm, which can be expected to support the view that they are able to cope with critical union dependencies. Indeed, goal statements may often be fashioned *after* the fact to justify union choices and actions. Power, therefore, can be institutionalized through the manipulation of *perceived* dependencies, as well as by shifts in the actual pattern of dependencies. Murray and Reshef (1988) explore paradigm construction processes as these relate specifically to American unions, noting various contextual forces that historically shaped union paradigm construction. They also discuss how the extant paradigm under which American unions typically function is inappropriate to contemporary conditions but quite resistant to change.

The resource dependence model offers an alternative to a rational choice framework for understanding union strategy formulation. It addresses what are seen as fundamental weaknesses in rational choice models and depicts activities within unions—as well as other types of organizations—that seem more consistent with the realities of organizational life. The resource dependence approach is also consistent with other theories of individual and organizational decision making that emphasize political or behavioral processes (e.g., Weick 1979; Hogarth 1987; Kahneman, Slovic, and Tversky 1982; Cyert and March 1963). Although empirical studies lend support to many of the hypotheses that derive from the resource dependence perspective (Pfeffer and Salancik 1978), none of this research specifically involves unions. The model of union action that has been proposed here must be subject to rigorous testing before it is accepted as valid, but that is beyond the scope of this work. It is a general framework applicable to the overall functioning of a union. With appropriate modifications it could be used to understand broad strategic action at the national or international union level as well as the more limited concerns of locals and other subunits.

STRATEGIC RIGIDITY

The resource dependence model offers an interpretation of union strategy formulation clearly at odds with a rational choice approach. With some notable exceptions mainstream American unions have often shown great rigidity in the face of dramatically changing conditions. Unfortunately, empirical studies of strategic decision making in unions are quite limited in comparison to work that has been done on decision making in business organizations.

Bok and Dunlop (1970, 138–188) provide a comprehensive and generally critical assessment of the nature of trade union administration as they found it on the eve of labor's present crisis. The organizational structures, personnel management practices, and planning and control systems typical of unions over the past few decades are all viewed as seriously deficient. In general, they observe that the "principles of administration are little more than common sense, and labor leaders are instinctively aware of most of them. With few exceptions, however, union officials have not devoted much conscious effort to implement these precepts" (139). In a similar vein Lester (1958) traced significant changes in the administrative practices of unions in the postwar years, observing that mature unions tend to become highly bureaucratic and "sleepy monopolies."

As it has become increasingly evident over the past decade that management has seized the initiative in the industrial relations arena, unions have been castigated, often by friends of organized labor, for being stodgy and inflexible. Raskin (1986, 3–4), speculating on the potential for strategic change in the American labor movement, observed that unions still seem generally unresponsive to shifting economic, political, and social conditions: "The inability of most unions to comprehend or cope with these transformations, coupled with a sluggishness of spirit making many of them prisoners of intertia, has caused a downhill slide in membership, muscle, and public regard that assumed dismaying dimensions at the start of this decade."

Others share Raskin's assessment. In an analysis that focuses specifically on the issue of paradigm construction within unions in the manufacturing sector, Murray and Reshef observe that inertial forces render many unions ill-equipped to react strategically to contemporary pressures. Their overall conclusion is that "altered environments mean unions must change, whereas paradigm maturity suggests they may not be able to" (Murray and Rashef 1988, 615). In addition, Kochan, Katz, and McKersie (1986, 3–20) proceed from the assumption that unions are now largely reactive organizations, with management defining the boundaries within which unions must operate (both in the U/DU area and other aspects of labor-management relations). Kochan et al. (as well as Raskin) feel that events currently unfolding within the labor movement, for example, as epitomized by the statement on priorities issued by the AFL-CIO in 1985, suggest the possibility of fundamental change. Yet considerable resistance to such change would appear to remain within labor organizations.

Since unions tend toward strategic rigidity, we need some understanding of the forces that generate that condition. This is particularly important in discerning the inherent potential for change within the labor movement. Some argue that the innovative approaches that have been undertaken in some unions are revolutionary, but these may be only transitory; pressures favoring conventional approaches to organizing and bargaining could well dominate in the long run. In addition, a knowledge of strategy formulation practices should be useful to union leaders in fostering creative policies and overcoming resistance to change.

The resource dependence model is used here to explore aspects of union strategic decision making that give rise to rigidity. Pfeffer and Salancik (1978, 225–256) argue that organizational change is closely related to the manner in which the organizational contexts are perceived, the assessment of organizational performance, and the nature of leadership succession. These processes are considered here as they would typically seem to occur within unions.

Distortion of Information

Ambiguity gives rise to paradigm construction resulting in distorted and biased views of union constraints (proposition 6). Union leaders are likely to ignore information that tends to disconfirm the established paradigm (which, after all, is supportive of the existing distribution of power) and to attach disproportionate weight to information that reinforces the paradigm. Organizational paradigms are built and reinforced in many ways. Power holders are often in the best position to interpret events to those with less direct knowledge of a situation, construing information in at least a partially self-serving manner. This often occurs within unions. Walton and McKersie (1965, 281–309) point to the significance in labor-management negotiations of intraorganizational bargaining, which frequently involves manipulation, deception, and other elements of the meaning construction process.[13] In addition, Walker (1981) discusses the general nature of meaning construction in union governance, concentrating in particular on the role of myth making and ritualism within labor organizations.

The distortion of information resulting from paradigm construction efforts can lead to organizational rigidities that preclude appropriate responses to new dependencies, perhaps even after the union's position has seriously deteriorated. Miles and Snow (1978, 28–30) characterize organizations that exhibit such rigidities as "reactors," reflecting their failure to anticipate environmental problems and their reliance on outmoded strategies to respond to crises. Leaders in reactor organizations can be expected to attribute failure to external events perceived to be totally beyond their control, thus obviating the need for paradigmatic change. This is not simply a matter of lengthy informational lags—which might well be expected in complex and uncertain settings—but rather of the systematic filtering and reinterpretation of information in ways supportive of the established paradigm.

These processes are quite evident in the initial reaction of labor to the decline in organizing success that became so apparent in the 1970s. The "saturation" effect, coupled with profound changes in the values and preferences of American workers, did not occur spontaneously. Observers of the labor movement had been predicting these problems for more than twenty-five years. Most labor leaders chose to avoid confronting what had not been immediate, though potentially very threatening, problems. Organizing was deemphasized. Although Voos' (1984) data indicate a slight increase in real expenditures per unorganized worker in the period 1953–1977, we have already noted questions that have been raised as to the method used to deflate the expenditure data. In any event, there is no question that there was no growth—and very probably a decrease—in the proportion of union budgets devoted to organizing.

As the consequences of inattention to organizing could no longer be denied, unions portrayed these events as largely the product of sinister forces beyond their control. "Union busters" and militantly antiunion employers, later joined by conservative politicians, were all depicted as participants in a monolithic conspiracy to undermine the labor movement. The solution sought revolved around efforts to change the NLRA to make life more difficult for those who would challenge unions. The intention was to recreate an environment, through the long-established instrument of legal action, in which traditional union approaches to organizing and collective bargaining could continue unimpeded.

Union leaders seemed genuinely perplexed, indeed betrayed, when appeals for relief were often greeted with indifference and even animosity by traditional allies. There is little doubt, as later sections of this book will demonstrate, that employer aggressiveness has played a major role in declining union representation. The mistake made within the labor movement, however, was to see this as virtually the only important factor and not part of a broader and interrelated complex of hostile forces. Thus, unions acted to preserve ingrained perspectives and methods, rendering union leaders the "prisoners of inertia" that Raskin maintains they have become.

Assessment and "Sense Making"

Cognitive distortion and the failure to discern changing dependencies are not exclusively the products of political ambition. Organizational leaders must justify their actions to those to whom they are accountable. Behavioral decision theory suggests that humans strive to *appear* rational even if their actions have been unintentional. Thus, people tend to engage in retrospective "sense making," which involves dissonance reduction, ex post facto attributions of motives, and other forms of rationalization.[14] Many of the institutional practices of unions contribute to the distortion of perceptions through sense-making activities.

Unions, as are other organizations, are subject to assessment and evaluation. That is, they must establish their worth, especially to critical coalition participants, in order to ensure a continued flow of resources. Thompson (1967) considers different approaches to organizational assessment, noting that quantitative and efficiency-based means of assessment, which are quite consistent with rational choice models of organizational action, are most likely to be encountered in settings characterized by goal clarity, goal consensus, and considerable certainty regarding cause-effect relationships. When these conditions are not met, organizations place considerable emphasis on standards of *comparability* in legitimizing their actions. That is, the organization tends to mimic the policies of similar other organizations, and these actions are then justified by noting that they are consistent with conventional practices. In addition, leaders in organizations operating under conditions of ambiguity may seek to justify the organizations' current actions in terms of its own past practices. Both standards of assessment involve sense making and rationalization. Goals are inferred from actions, unlike the rational choice assumption that goals precede and determine actions. When inferred goals serve as a basis for future actions, current practices become in effect self-perpetuating. The consequence of all of this is an organization that is rigid and noninnovative.

The assessment of unions through internal and external comparisons is most readily apparent in wage setting and contract negotiations. Union leaders have historically justified contracts in terms of established patterns and the extent of improvement on prior contracts. Although the political pressures to which industrial relations scholars have long attributed this phenomenon are undoubtedly partially responsible for wage spillover, there is strong evidence to suggest that it is also rooted in *uncertainty* regarding market conditions (Lawler 1982); union negotiators appear to cope with uncertainty and ambiguity through sense-making activities that revolve around comparisons. Even though we do not have direct evidence to suggest comparison processes at work in the choice and assessment of U/DU strategies, it is theoretically reasonable, and certainly practical, for unions to assess performance and identify policies by comparing current organizing activity to past practices and the actions of other unions. This would generate a bias toward retaining established techniques, avoiding experimentation, and expanding expenditures on U/DU efforts only very slowly.

Strategic rigidity and the persistence of established policies can also result from sense-making and assessment processes in the external environment. The interaction among trade unionists from different labor organizations, as well as between unionists and representatives of other sectors of society (e.g., government, business), leads to the perceptions in the broader community as to what actions are appropriate to unions. As definitions of acceptable union strategies are established in the institutional environment, the tendency of individual unions to conform to these expectations would be reinforced. For example, Meyer and Rowan (1978) note that institutionally determined expectations serve as important determinants of organizational structures and policies. And Stinchcombe (1965) argues that a population of organizations imposes standards of structure and action on those organizations falling within the population, reflecting conditions prevalent at the time of the population's emergence; deviations from population norms place organizations at risk of failure (termed the "liability of newness").

Trade unions that deviate from conventional strategies are clearly at risk of being sanctioned by other unions. In extreme cases the AFL-CIO may take formal action against deviant unions and their leaders. Such measures do not always work well. The expulsion of a strong union, for example, may have little impact on either its viability or behavior, as witnessed in the actions taken against the Teamsters in the 1950s. Yet leaders of smaller and weaker unions, which depend on broad-based support within the labor movement, may be restrained in the pursuit of innovative policies. The opposition of mainstream unions mobilized by George Meany against what were seen as the disruptive views of Walter Reuther is a clear example of this mechanism at work. The current leadership of the federation, which advocates significant change, confronts similar resistance.

Leadership Succession

Pfeffer and Salancik further maintain that an organization's ability to respond to critical dependencies is linked to patterns of leadership succession. If leaders emerge in response to current and real dependency problems, then organizational effectiveness is promoted. But this changing of the guard displaces established leaders and reorders power relationships within the organization. As we have seen, one important way of institutionalizing power is by building and maintaining a supportive organizational paradigm. Incumbent leaders may preserve established paradigms by engineering the succession process so as to reduce the possibility of paradigmatic change.

The nature of leadership development and succession in unions has been highlighted by various authors (Sayles and Strauss 1967, 76–88; Quaglieri 1988; Bok and Dunlop 1970, 172–186; Strauss 1977; Friedman 1970; Dunlop 1990, 17–18). A reading of this literature suggests unions are traditionally vulnerable to leadership succession practices that preserve entrenched power elites. Potential union leaders are groomed in elective office or staff positions for several years, which serves to indoctrinate and socialize them. Although there is some circulation of staff and officers among unions, most positions of any power are virtually closed to outsiders. An almost xenophobic fear serves to insulate established paradigms from disruptive influences.

NEW DIRECTIONS IN STRATEGIC THINKING

The resource dependence model proposed above depicts the process of union strategy formulation in admittedly bleak and discouraging terms. Not withstanding these sources of rigidity, significant effort within the labor movement is now being directed toward bringing organizational structures and decision-making processes into alignment with contemporary conditions. This is not to say that these new approaches have as of yet fully succeeded, nor is it to predict that they will. The changes under way within a number of unions affect many aspects of union functioning in addition to U/DU activity, including collective bargaining, union governance, and interunion relations. This section, however, will deal principally with strategic innovations that are related to organizing or deunionization efforts.

PRESSURES FOR CHANGE

The resource dependence perspective does not hold that misperceptions and strategic rigidity invariably result as organizational leaders endeavor to cope with critical dependencies. Ambiguity and conflict promote these phenomena, but such pressures may be overcome. Organizational paradigms and patterns of leadership succession can evolve that reflect true dependencies. One way in which an organization might be induced to change is through exposure to extreme environmental shocks that profoundly and undeniably threaten its viability. Self-deception is only possible in the absence of sharply defined images.

There is much to suggest that the American labor movement may be undergoing this type of transformation (Dunlop 1990, 6–7). The willingness of major unions to engage in "concession bargaining" and experiments in labor-management cooperation in the early part of the 1980s provided the first solid evidence of an openness to change. Despite strong counterarguments, some authors have proclaimed a new era of objectivity and realism on the part of unions (Freedman 1982). Although this apparent shift in strategic thinking first revolved around the bargaining positions of unions, there have been other changes in the manner in which unions conduct their affairs. Many of these innovations relate either directly or indirectly to the development of U/DU strategies.

Whether the promise of change is to be fully realized remains an open question. The American labor movement has, on occasion, demonstrated a capacity to transform itself rapidly, most notably during the Depression. But there have also been a great many false starts. Innovative perspectives have often been allowed to languish or have been the objects of determined repression. We shall now examine and evaluate the potential as some of the shifts in union practices that reflect new approaches in strategic thinking about U/DU efforts.

THE AFL-CIO REPORT

Although the AFL-CIO provides assistance in organizing campaigns, basic strategic decisions have traditionally been the responsibility of affiliated national and international unions. Yet the federation acts as an ideological gatekeeper; the statements of its leaders define mainstream unionism and influence the policies of affiliates. Consequently, pronouncements by the AFL-CIO relating to appropriate organizing techniques or responses to employer deunionization initiatives can be of critical importance in establishing strategic themes.

Few actions taken by labor organizations in recent years have generated as much attention as a report issued by the AFL-CIO Executive Council at its annual meeting in February 1985. Saddled with a rather cumbersome title, *The Changing Situation of Workers and Their Unions,* the report (as it is hereafter referred to) constitutes a wide-ranging assessment of the problems confronting American unions. That the report at least implicitly criticizes past practices and suggests a number of decidedly nontraditional stratagems marks it as a kind of *What Is To Be Done?* for the contemporary labor movement.

A Strategic Agenda

Relatively short, the report is part polemic, part recipe book. Although it lashes out at both the Reagan administration and perceived deficiencies in the law, it also recognizes the changing characteristics of American workers and their often ambivalent or negative views of unions. Policy recommendations revolve around organizing techniques, approaches to representation and collective bargaining, and union structure and governance. Suggestions specifically related to U/DU strategy include:[15]

1. The establishment of *associate membership* programs, in which workers not currently in established bargaining units could be affiliated with unions in order for unions to build and maintain contact with those individuals.
2. The use of *corporate campaigns* to reduce or eliminate employer opposition during organizing efforts and after union recognition.
3. The establishment of experimental organizing committees by the AFL-CIO, similar in some ways to the organizing committees of the 1930s.
4. Better training of organizers and expanded use of technology in organizing efforts.
5. Greater involvement of rank-and-file members in the organizing process.
6. The exercise of greater care in selecting organizing targets.
7. Experimentation with novel organizing techniques.
8. The establishment of procedures to resolve organizing disputes among unions.

Although the report stressed a number of themes, the need to expand organizing was clearly given high priority. Articles appearing in various union publications subsequent to the release of the report often emphasized the importance of renewed commitment to organizing, apparently in an effort to sell the program to rank-and-file union members. The issues raised by the report, in particular organizing, were featured in the Executive Council's report to the 1985 AFL-CIO convention.[16] Various AFL-CIO and union-sponsored conferences have been held to discuss the new agenda proposed in the report and to promote adoption of the recommendations by affiliates. Recent actions taken by the AFL-CIO and its affiliates have served to implement many of the recommendations regarding organizing (McDonald 1987), including development of associate membership programs, the issuance of union-sponsored credit cards at favorable interest rates, and the establishment of multiunion organizing projects.

Implications for Strategy Formulation

The AFL-CIO report is significant in three aspects. First, it makes substantive suggestions regarding trade union policy that both are innovative and often run contrary to the tenets of mainstream unionism (this is even more apparent in the recommendations relating to the nature of union representation). Second, the report not only promotes substantive policies but also encourages fundamental change in the decision-making processes of unions. It argues for greater involvement by the rank and file in union governance, more professionalism and sophistication on the part of staff members, and increased care by union officials in evaluating options. In short, it is a formula for partially opening an insular labor movement and dislodging outmoded and counterproductive perspectives generated through the paradigm construction mechanisms identified above.

A third, and perhaps most significant, aspect of the AFL-CIO document is not so much what it said but the manner in which it was drafted. The Committee on the Evolution of Work, composed of the presidents of several of the nation's largest unions (e.g., Albert Shanker [American Federation of Teachers (AFT)], Lynn Williams [Steelworkers], William Winpisinger [Machinists], Gerald McEntee [American Federation of State, County, and Municipal Employees (AFSCME)]), along with other high-ranking union and AFL-CIO officials, developed both this report and an earlier, companion report, *The Future of Work* (AFL-CIO 1983). But there was also extensive input from outside experts. The Lou Harris organization gathered and analyzed survey data of worker perceptions of and feelings toward unions. Several of the country's leading authorities on unions and labor management relations, including Tom Kochan, Richard Freeman, James Medoff, and Paul Weiler, provided significant input to the deliberations of the committee. Although the AFL-CIO may have traditionally served to insulate the labor movement from disruptive influences and to preserve orthodoxy, the manner in which these two reports were generated presents unions with an alternative approach to strategic decision making, one which makes extensive use of outside expertise and perspectives.

There are some who see in these new programs a redefinition of the traditional relationship between the AFL-CIO and its affiliates.[17] Certain changes will generate new decision-making structures requiring greater interunion coordination, with the federation often assuming a central role. Multiunion organizing programs coordinated by AFL-CIO staff, a program to limit interunion competition during organizing drives, and the creation of the Office of Comprehensive Organizing Strategies and Tactics (to assist affiliates in mounting corporate campaigns) all represent a greater involvement by the federation in the internal affairs of the affiliates. Aspects of the report not directly related to organizing also stress greater centralization within the labor movement (e.g., the encouragement of union mergers). Emphasizing that affiliates will continue to be autonomous in most matters, AFL-CIO president Lane Kirkland also suggested the extent to which the role of the federation might be expanded in the formulation of organizing and bargaining strategies: "I firmly and strongly believe we must be part of the general staff [of affiliated unions] at the inception rather than serve as ambulance drivers at the bitter end [of a labor dispute]; that we ought to be part of the decision-making as to whether or not this is the [labor management] battle to take on; whether or not an accurate appraisal of the circumstances has been made."[18]

STRATEGIC CHANGE: PROSPECTS AND PROBLEMS

Despite an auspicious beginning, signs are mixed as to whether the AFL-CIO report will promote widespread and sustained change. The labor press, especially AFL-CIO publications, continues to tout the report's agenda as the basis of a new beginning and stresses the need for such a transformation. This suggests, among other things, that not all within the labor movement are favorably inclined toward the report's recommendations and a selling job is still needed. There was something less than full consensus on the part of the committee members. For example, Machinists president William Winpisinger, a member of the committee, objected in particular to proposals such as the associate membership program, characterizing them as "tinkering."[19] The associate membership program has caused a stir among union officials in general, as they see it diverting scarce organizing resources to create a nebulous membership category. Indeed, virtually all of the construction craft unions rejected the approach when the AFL-CIO report was first issued.[20]

A more fundamental objection to the report, which seems to be expressed primarily by lower-level officials, relates to the manner in which it was developed.[21] This process is characterized above as a model for strategic decision making in unions. Maybe so. Yet many organizers, district officials, and local officers seem to view the report as a "top-down document," drafted by an elite with little understanding of the wants and needs of working people. The central role of academics and other outside experts, rather than field organizers, in drafting the report reinforced this perception. In appears, then, that implementation of the report proposals could be thwarted by crucial union functionaries who believe that their role in the policy-making process has been usurped.

There are other difficulties in eliciting the cooperation of union officials. They are being asked to undertake programs that are unfamiliar, often experimental, and quite risky. Moreover, these moves are politically threatening because they necessarily restructure power relationships. The possibility of increased intervention by the federation in organizing and related activities, coupled with the likelihood of greater centralization within affiliated unions, poses additional threats to the political positions of lower-echelon officers and staff members. Craft and Extejt (1983) studied nontraditional approaches to organizing in the period preceding the release of the AFL-CIO report. Their work also suggests that political barriers within unions strongly inhibit the willing acceptance and active cooperation of many key union officials in the implementation of new programs. Heckscher (1988, 234–237) is likewise pessimistic about the potential for change within the contemporary labor movement. He notes several recent strategic moves that have failed largely because of internal resistance or an inability by unions to carry through, noting that: "While major unions are engaged in the slow and painful process of transforming their own structures, it seems likely that much of the driving force for new forms of representation will come in the end from outside the formal boundaries of the labor movement—from 'new unions' with relatively little historical baggage and from associations and pressure groups" (Heckscher 1988, 237).

The problems of strategic rigidity that arise through the organizational processes described in the resource dependence model thus continue to plague unions. New approaches to strategic thinking at the apex of the labor movement, although a necessary condition for revitalizing unions, could well fail without complementary shifts at lower levels.

It may be unwarranted, however, to be excessively pessimistic about the prospects for both lasting change in the strategic decision-making practices of unions and the ability of unions to implement new approaches. That the report was issued at all is testimony to the determination of the top leadership of the AFL-CIO and many of the affiliated unions to create a climate of renewal. Despite resistance and limited initial success, the report's proposals have continued to be given high priority by the federation (McDonald 1987). New directions in strategic thinking are also evident within unions, as reflected both in the characteristics of certain organizing departments and the planning processes adopted by some unions. Although Bok and Dunlop (1970) were pessimistic about union administrative practices twenty years ago, Dunlop is now more sanguine regarding the prospects for the enhancement of strategic processes, noting that "the difficult environment that has confronted American unions during the past decade has stimulated considerable study, review, and experimentation in new methods of management and administration" (Dunlop 1990, 6–7). Yet he also notes that "a judgment on the effectiveness and outcomes of these newer methods must necessarily be deferred for a while" (7).

At least a few national and international unions have moved on the report's recommendations with apparent success, perhaps setting the stage for broader acceptance.[22] There seems to be a clear distinction between what Reed terms "progressive" and "traditional" organizing departments with respect to the characteristics of staff (Reed 1989c) and organizing techniques utilized (Reed 1989e).[23] Progressive departments are generally found in unions that organize primarily in emerging sectors, and traditional departments are more typical of unions operating in basic manufacturing, mining, and construction. In comparison to traditional departments Reed found that organizers in progressive departments are more likely to be women, to be younger, to be more educated, and to be more socially mobile. Organizers in progressive departments also are less apt to be drawn from the rank and file or to have followed the conventional career path for union officials. Thus, it would appear as if a cadre of a new style of organizers is emerging, one which is perhaps less attached to outmoded perspectives and faulty paradigms.

Although the elaborate and sophisticated strategic planning procedures used in most large-scale businesses are not common in the labor movement, national and international unions now seem more prone to engage in multiyear planning than apparently was the case at the time Bok and Dunlop (1970, 138–188) were writing. Certain unions have undertaken wide-ranging strategic planning efforts that, at least in principle, call for major internal restructuring and even shifts in institutional identity (Dunlop 1990, 25–52). Some examples include the report prepared by the United Steelworkers' Committee of Future Directions of the Union[24] and the activities of the Project 2000 Committee in the Bricklayers' Union (Bensman 1988).

Stratton and Brown (1988) surveyed more than one hundred national and international unions on the nature of strategic planning processes within those organizations. Although very few of the unions studied engaged in what they characterize as "complete planning" (i.e., general plans and goal statements supplemented by specific action plans), about 35 percent were classified as "incomplete planners" (general plans and goal statements but no specific action plans). Unions that engage in active planning were also found to be more aggressive on the organizing front and more prone to utilize certain innovative tactics; moreover, planners experienced a greater membership growth rate than nonplanners. Even though only a minority of national organizations pursue multiyear planning, the indications are that interest is increasing and that these activities may become more widespread. This tendency should be promoted by changes in the nature of the leadership succession process also occurring in some unions (Schwartz and Hoyman 1984).

CHAPTER SUMMARY

There has been fairly limited research dealing specifically with the nature of union U/DU strategy formulation. Empirical studies present little evidence to suggest that such strategies are devised by the processes assumed under conventional rational choice models. This should not come as much of a surprise, since much of what we know about the role of power in unions would lead us to anticipate that these decisions are political in character.

The resource dependence perspective is used to construct a model of internal union decision making that explains the strategic rigidity of unions over the past couple of decades in the face of clear environmental change. The model posits strategic rigidity results from the interaction of contextual ambiguity, the conflicting demands placed upon unions, and the politicized nature of unions as organizations.

This has been especially true in regard to the U/DU process. Most unions have been reluctant to commit necessary resources to organizing and to experiment with new strategies and tactics.

Yet not all is bleak for the labor movement. Pressures for change have begun to breach the formidable defenses of the trade union establishment. The 1985 AFL-CIO report provided an outline of the possibilities for change. Many unions have experimented with methods touted in the document, although acceptance has not been all that widespread as of yet. Relatively recent studies of union organizing processes and strategic decision making suggest fundamental changes have taken place, or are under way, in a number of American unions (though these are still in the minority).

CHAPTER 4

Seizing the Initiative:
Employer Strategy Formulation

In contrast to what has been written concerning unions, the analysis of U/DU strategic decision making by management is much more thoroughly developed. The literature relevant to the strategic choice model proposed in chapter 2 is reviewed and evaluated here. Theoretical approaches that speak to the fundamental nature of management U/DU strategy formulation are examined first. As managerial attitudes toward unions are highly relevant within a strategic choice framework, research relating to trends in and influences on such attitudes will also be reviewed. Finally, empirical research bearing on U/DU strategy formulation by management is considered, and suggestions are made concerning future research on this topic, especially in regard to methodology.

STRATEGY FORMULATION PROCESSES

In the preceding chapter strategic choice practices in unions were characterized as tending toward rigidity and stodginess (though something of a spiritual revival is under way). In contrast, the thrust of contemporary analyses of management strategic thinking on U/DU and other employee relations issues is that management policies typically involve reasoned choices rooted in well-articulated values and beliefs. A recognition among union leaders of this difference has clearly been a factor in generating many of the changes in strategic thinking and action now under way in the labor movement. Some authors disagree with this assessement of management strategy formulation, however, arguing that strident antiunionism is often an emotion-laden and nonrational response.

60

HUMAN RESOURCE MANAGEMENT

The increased attention of employers to strategic planning in human resource matters is not merely an outgrowth of their concern to limit the strength and influence of unions. Two broad trends in economic and social development would seem to be principally responsible for management's evolving posture. First, the use of financial and other extrinsic incentives is of diminishing effectiveness in obtaining the compliance of increasingly skilled and affluent workers with organizational objectives. The demands that employees place on management for more meaningful work and greater participation in organizational decision making are well documented and have been widely discussed in the organizational behavior literature since at least the 1950s.

A second and somewhat more recent phenomenon has been the intensifying complexity, turbulence, and hostility that now seem to characterize business environments. An important implication of this is that management is less able to coordinate and control employee activities in a hierarchical and bureaucratic manner.[1] As decision making becomes more decentralized and fluid, individual employees, including those in nonmanagerial positions, are expected to exercise greater discretion and act in a more autonomous manner. A fundamental problem for top management under these conditions is ensuring that independent employees will behave in ways consistent with organizational objectives. The development of nontraditional coordination and control systems to accomplish this end has necessitated increased attention to the design of supporting human resource management systems (Kravetz 1988, 1–35).

The evolving sophistication of employee management systems as a consequence of these pressures has been chronicled by many authors. In a now classic piece Miles (1975, 8–19) proposes a three-category typology of management systems. The "human resource" approach, the most advanced system in his framework, focuses on the motivation of worker behavior through the creation of intrinsically fulfilling work and some level of worker participation in organizational decision making. Mile's work derives largely from a recognition of evolving worker values. More recently, Lawrence (1985) identifies five distinct stages in the evolution of American employee management systems. The highest level of development is characterized as a "commitment system," an approach that addresses both evolving worker values and increasingly problematic organizational environments. Heckscher (1988, 85–113) also explores these themes, though often in a critical vein, in his examination of "managerialism," a central feature of which being what he terms "coordinated independence."

The enhanced professionalism and influence of human resource management (HRM) specialists in organizations reflect upper-level management's concern with the quality of employee relations. This new sophistication has important implications for decision making in the personnel area. Human resource management specialists are able to design more effective personnel management systems. Staffing, compensation, performance evaluation, training, and other personnel functions are more likely to be grounded in research findings than structured on an ad hoc basis. But more significant for our purposes here, the HRM field has become increasingly concerned with strategic planning processes. This concern largely emanates from upper management's correspondingly higher concern with the development of organizationwide strategies.

We have examined the basic elements of strategic thinking in chapter 2, noting that these involve considerable management discretion in endeavoring to link organizational capabilities to environmental possibilities. Strategic management implies a much more dynamic and global process than contingency theory and related perspectives, since managers are envisioned as actively reshaping constraints usually taken as given. It is argued that managers must be more attentive to strategic planning than in bygone days since contextual change and uncertainty are now so much more pervasive. Managers of organizations situated in relatively placid settings would have little need to be concerned with orchestrating strategic change.

Models of organizationwide strategic planning and change have thus naturally led to models of HRM strategic planning. The literature in this area has been extensive in recent years, and at least one journal, *Human Resource Management*, devotes itself primarily to HRM strategy. Works by Fombrun (1983), Dyer (1984), Dyer and Holder (1987), and Devanna, Fombrun, and Tichy (1984) provide general overviews of the field. Human resource management strategy involves the integration of the various personnel management functions into an overall system that in turn complements broader strategic concerns. For example, a company that pursues a strategy of aggressive growth and diversification is likely to be favored by an HRM strategy stressing skill acquisition and innovative thinking by employees. Human resource management strategies range from very broad, corporatewide plans to those specific to organizational subunits.

What we appear to be seeing as a consequence of the HRM revolution, then, is an increasingly systematic and objectively rational approach to personnel management. Human resource management strategies almost always have important U/DU implications, though these may or may not be intended. The point is that this trend, conditioned by forces that extend beyond management's interest in containing unions, has very likely contributed to greater rationality in the formulation of management U/DU strategies. Unfortunately, the models of HRM strategy formulation developed to date, although rich in conceptual insight, are clearly wanting in terms of theoretical rigor. Causal relationships tend to be vaguely specified, and analytical consistency across studies is lacking. The strategy studies also tend to be quite weak methodologically, with authors frequently relying on limited case studies and qualitative analysis. This is, of course, true of the strategy field in general. As the field is new and developing, we might hope to see these problems remedied with time.

LINKING BUSINESS AND INDUSTRIAL RELATIONS STRATEGIES

Though grounded in many of the same perspectives as the HRM strategy literature, Kochan, Katz, and McKersie (1986) largely developed their notions parallel to and independently of that work. Their book represents the culmination of a multiyear project, involving a number of collaborators and centered at MIT. The essence of their argument is that as a consequence of both environmental pressures and opportunities management has now taken an aggressive lead in defining the nature of the industrial relations system. As noted in chapter 2, this competitive and proactive stance by management is at odds with earlier industrial relations perspectives based on assumptions of mutual legitimization and trust by unions and employers (Dunlop 1958). Yet some question whether the paradigm proposed by Kochan el al. really deviates all that much from systems theory[2] and suggest that the strategy concept is underdeveloped.[3] Lewin (1987) also reviews the industrial relations strategy literature and raises a number of conceptual and methodological concerns.

Data from a Conference Board survey suggested to Kochan (1980, 191–208) that there has been a considerable and increasing centralization of industrial relations decision making at relatively high corporate levels. In addition, old-line labor relations specialists, who tend to be viewed as relatively sympathetic to trade unions, are being supplanted by a new wave of HRM specialists (Kochan and McKersie 1983). Although the growth of the HRM field was originally promoted by the forces described in the previous section, HRM specialists bring union-avoidance skills to businesses that are now particularly valued by a great many top executives. Hence, they have gained substantial power in organizational decision making.

Kochan and others proceeded to develop a general framework for the analysis of corporate industrial relations policy. First proposed in an article by Kochan, McKersie, and Cappelli (1984), this became the conceptual core of *The Transformation of American Industrial Relations* (Kochan, Katz, and McKersie 1986). They start from the position that industrial relations policies must be understood at three levels: workplace relations, collective bargaining and personnel administration, and long-term strategic decision making. This approach parallels the tendency of management writers to differentiate among the operational, administrative, and strategic levels within organizations.

The key argument made by Kochan, McKersie, and Cappelli is that the highest level in this system, where overarching corporate strategies are formulated, has largely been ignored by industrial relations scholars. This is understandable, since industrial relations issues have only infrequently been of major concern to corporate strategists in the postwar period. But this has clearly changed over the past decade or so. As executive views of unions have become more hostile and environmental pressures have grown, corporate strategies are now more apt to deal directly with the issues of avoiding, containing, and dislodging unions. A clear linkage is thus established between the formulation of business strategies and industrial relations strategies, much as more general HRM strategies are argued to be linked to business strategies.

AN ALTERNATIVE PERSPECTIVE

Neither the HRM nor the business/IR strategy literature fully addresses the important issue of nonrational decision making in business organizations. As discussed in our treatment of union strategy formulation, behavioral decision theorists have long argued that ambiguity and complexity in organizational contexts create conditions that promote choice processes that deviate from the rational ideal and generate decisions that are suboptimal in relation to initial goals (e.g., Cyert and March 1963; Lindblom 1959; Weick 1979). Decision making under these conditions is likely to be characterized by such practices as a limited and sequential consideration of alternatives, the distortion of information, nonoptimizing choice rules (e.g., "satisficing"), rationalization, and commitment to past choices (Hogarth 1987). Yet environmental ambiguity and complexity are the very conditions that the strategy literature suggests promote increased rationality in corporate management, industrial relations, and human resource management.

What, then, does this imply for managerial strategy formulation? The increasing uncertainty, complexity, and resource dependencies of the contemporary environment may induce management to seek greater stability and clarity in environmental relations. But we know choices made under these conditions are likely to be influenced by anomalous decision processes. To make sense of economic adversity, managers could point to unionism as a visible symbol of inefficiency and external threat (along with other factors such as excessive government regulation, alleged Japanese unfair trade practices, and the like).

That unions undercut the economic performance of firms is a view quite consistent with, and thus reinforced by, the contemporary popular image of unionism. The empirical evidence supports this view to some extent in the sense that unionized firms tend to be less profitable than equivalent nonunion firms (Freeman and Medoff 1984, 181–190). Yet we also know that unionization seems to contribute to greater employee productivity, and the evidence on reduced profitability is mixed. Moreover, empirical results would suggest that the impact of unionism on firm performance is apt to be minimal in the competitive environments typical of the emerging industries in which management union-avoidance activity is most pronounced.

By treating unionism and other external forces as scapegoats, management exempts itself from accepting a fair share of responsibility for its current problems. Such a process of sense making follows from behavioral theories of the attribution of causation (Heider 1958), which suggest that individuals are most likely to infer, though corroborating evidence may be lacking, that a highly salient external force is responsible for a particular event.[4] The response of the Reagan administration to the air traffic controllers strike in 1981 fits quite neatly into this framework. Now seen as a watershed in American labor relations, the strong action taken against the Professional Air Traffic Controllers' Organization (PATCO) could have validated and legitimized the managerial view of unionism as antithetical to American competitiveness.

With unions identified through such cognitive mechanisms as threatening, managers, unsure of how to proceed, may rely on imitation, another common decision-making heuristic, to select union-avoidance strategies. Once in place, these policies are apt to become self-justifying and self-perpetuating. These arguments could explain the spread of both positive labor relations programs in nonunion settings and aggressive union-avoidance efforts during and after representation campaigns. Additional factors enter the picture if we focus specifically on election campaigns. Union organizing drives, once fully manifested, often come as a shock to management. Such highly charged and threatening situations are especially likely to engender aberrant decision-making practices (Janis and Mann 1977) and produce emotional, possibly irrational, responses.[5] It may well be that under such circumstances, management may overreact, creating a "backfire" effect in which excessive resistance actually aids the organizing effort.[6]

The issue of nonrationality and emotionalism in management union-avoidance activity has also been examined from power and social dominance perspectives. Barbash (1984, 75–84) argues the pluralist Wisconsin-school view that much of management opposition to unionism is related not to the economic consequences of collective bargaining so much as to management's desire to retain control. As he observes: "Over the above efficiency there undoubtedly is a "taste for power" in management's resistance to the union. . . . For many employers it may be that the real hurt in the relationship with the union is in the sharing of . . . power more than in sharing [wealth]. . . . When the luster of economic advancement diminishes, it is the joy of power (or self-actualization, if you like) which really makes managers' jobs interesting" (Barbash 1984, 78). This interpretation is not, strictly speaking, inconsistent with the strategic choice perspective, which is based on the assumption that managerial choices are strongly influenced by personal preferences and power considerations. The difference, however, is that Barbash asserts managerial antiunionism to be more often a visceral rather than a calculated response to potential power loss. Thus, the threat posed by collective bargaining to the "joy of power" supersedes most other considerations. In contrast, a strategic choice approach would treat power loss as one of a number of criteria factored into a reasoned decision.

Wheeler (1986) builds on Barbash's basic framework but adds social dominance arguments derived in large part from sociobiology to form what he terms an "institutional/biological perspective." His arguments draw from material in his earlier book on industrial conflict (Wheeler 1985). The essence of dominance theory is that the "thirst for obedience" and the reaction to a threatened loss in dominance are largely instinctive rather than calculated. Thus, he states:

"As we would expect in social dominance hierarchies, we find that managers are attached to their position and its dignity and respond vigorously, sometimes even brutally, to threats to their status. ... This, of course, creates inherent difficulties when one attempts to devise egalitarian forms of organization ..." (Wheeler 1986, 11).

The Barbash and Wheeler view that management opposition to unionism may be more impulsive than reasoned are bolstered by some streams of theory and research in the organizational behavior field. For example, a number of authors have explored affect-based behavioral processes, maintaining that behavior is often highly emotional, habitual, and scripted.[7] Analyses using longitudinal data (Staw and Ross 1985; Staw, Bell, and Clausen 1986) support the presence of a strong dispositional component in certain employee work attitudes; similar processes could be responsible for determining managerial attitudes regarding unions and collective bargaining.

IMPLICATIONS

The HRM and business/industrial relations strategy perspectives posit that management is quite actively concerned with building well-integrated and rationally structured employee relations systems. The industrial relations and personnel functions, once largely self-contained and peripheral, have become central concerns in many companies, especially those operating in the emerging and high-growth sectors of the economy. With HRM and industrial relations policies hypothesized to be linked to broader business objectives, overall strategic decision making in this area is seen to be assuming an increasingly rational flavor. Indeed, much of the contemporary practitioner-oriented literature centers on strategic planning and decision-making techniques.

Although this literature primarily concerns the development of broadly defined industrial relations and HRM strategies, there are obvious implications for the manner in which employers formulate strategies in specific U/DU efforts. As these programs derive from the broader strategies, we should expect considerable care to be taken in deriving specific strategies and in integrating these across units. This is especially so in companies with strong union-avoidance policies. It is not uncommon for such firms to establish units at the corporate level charged with the responsibility of coordinating union-avoidance efforts on a companywide basis. In addition, individuals in these units frequently act as troubleshooters who are dispatched to facilities in danger of organization. Acting as internal consultants,

able to put in place programs known to be effective in crisis
ns. Outside consultants often serve the same function in firms
wiц. .mited or no internal union-avoidance capabilities. In either
case the assistance of union-avoidance specialists may reduce the
possibility of panicky managers—fearful of the implications of "losing" to a union—reacting in an ill-considered and counterproductive
manner.

Yet we also know that employer reactions to unions may be
nonrational or emotional in character. Labor relations consultants
have prospered to no small extent because companies wishing to
operate on a union-free basis were caught off guard by union organizing campaigns, often as a consequence of poor strategic planning. And
as we shall see later, the advice of union-avoidance specialists is not
always grounded in accepted theory and may offer clients comfort
without substance. Profit-oriented organizations, in contrast to
unions, however, possess a goal of major significance that can be
readily measured on a regular basis. Environmental signals are less
prone to be misread or distorted. Thus, the pressures associated with
the economic and social changes so often posited as the source of the
labor movement's weakened condition were experienced much sooner
and more immediately by employers. It is really only in the last few
years that union leaders have come to appreciate and respond to
conditions that had been evident to management years earlier. In net,
then, it would seem that the strategic choice approach has something
of an edge, absent empirical evidence, as an explanatory framework.

MANAGERIAL ATTITUDES TOWARD UNIONS

A central argument in the strategic choice literature is that key
decision makers exercise considerable discretion, with their judgments reflecting personal values and preferences. Hence, knowledge
of managerial values is crucial in explaining management strategy
formulation.

TRENDS

Management sentiments regarding unions have clearly varied
over time. The period from the late 1940s through well into the 1960s is
seen by most observers to have been one of relative accommodation
and placidity. It is conventionally viewed as an era of "mature" labor-
management relations (Lester 1958) in which most employers that
dealt much with unions refrained from ungentlemanly conduct. In-

dustrial relations scholars of the time sought to characterize managerial labor relations philosophies, identifying as progressive those
ideologies that appropriately balanced the economic interests of firms
against the institutional requirements of unions. Even though relationships may have been "adversarial," conflict was seen to be contained by mutual legitimization, as in Dunlop's (1958) systems notion.

That management truly accepted the concept of unionism during
labor's golden age is a highly suspect notion. Many suggest that
management's apparent acquiescence to union interests represented
more of a strategic retreat than a spiritual conversion (e.g., Kochan,
Katz, and McKersie 1986, 14). The power of the unions in the postwar
era necessitated management assuming a more moderate position.
Yet even as employers appeared to be relatively cooperative, so the
argument goes, they sought to undercut the labor movement by
securing institutional changes, such as the enactment of the Taft-
Hartley and Landrum-Griffin acts. As economic and social conditions
shifted, management acted opportunistically to exploit fully its new
advantage. A less sardonic view of events, which seems to be the
dominant perspective in the industrial relations field, holds that
increasingly hostile attitudes toward unions by management resulted
in large part from the failure of unions to react reasonably to new
economic realities (e.g., Raskin 1979; Pestillo 1979).

Inferring motives from actions is a dangerous business, and we
simply have little hard evidence of how management truly felt about
unions in the 1950s and 1960s. Fortunately, some quantitative data are
available concerning management sentiments in more recent times.
Studies conducted by the Conference Board (Freedman 1978, 1985)
report the results of two surveys (in 1978 and 1983) of corporate
executives in several hundred of the nation's largest firms. The targeted firms were largely unionized, though companies varied considerably in terms of degree of unionization. As these studies were
primarily concerned with the management of labor relations, the
analysis of management attitudes toward unions per se was not a
principal concern. However, the surveys did ask respondents to indicate whether their firms attached greater priority to forestalling
unionization or to achieving the best bargaining results in contract
negotiations. This is not, of course, a direct measure of managerial
attitudes with respect to unions and still suffers to some degree from
the problem of inferring motives from actions. Also, the question has
meaning only for companies that already have some degree of unionization, so it does not tell us anything about the relative intensity of

union-avoidance sentiments in union-free firms. Yet these data still provide a good proxy for attitudes and attitude change in unionized firms.

In the earlier survey only about one-third of the unionized firms reported "keeping the company as nonunion as possible" (versus "achieving the most favorable bargain possible") to be the principal labor relations objective (Freedman 1978, 5). Since a panel study design was used, changes in management sentiments within firms can be tracked over time. Using both waves of the Conference Board survey, Cappelli and Chalykoff (1986) compared the answers from unionized firms that responded to both the first and second surveys. They found a substantial movement by the "best bargain" firms into the union-avoidance camp, with nearly 50 percent of the firms studied listing union avoidance as a primary labor relations objective in 1983. A very substantial reorientation in management values plainly occurred in this period, and there is little reason to believe that this trend has reversed itself.

INFLUENCES

Although we have data suggestive of the growing intensity of management hostility toward unionism, research centering on the determinants of managerial attitudes is still quite limited. Kochan (1980, 188–191) reports simple correlations between various characteristics of a firm and the importance its managers attach to avoiding new union organizing (using data from the first Conference Board survey). By far the strongest correlate was the firm's current level of unionization, which was found to be negatively associated with the union-avoidance goal. The current wage level of the firm and industry union density were observed to be moderately and negatively correlated with the union-avoidance goal, but none of the other factors considered (including profit rates, relative labor cost, and product market concentration) were found to be significantly correlated with this variable. Personal interviews with corporate executives further suggested that the firm's current degree of organization is the best predictor of commitment to union-avoidance objectives. Cappelli and Chalykoff (1986) also examined some of the correlates of union avoidance, using both 1978 and 1983 Conference Board surveys. As with Kochan's analysis, they report that the firm's level of organization is the strongest correlate of such sentiments. Unfortunately, these findings provide a less than satisfying explanation of employer attitudes toward unionization since we have no way of knowing causal order.

A study conducted by Walker and Lawler (1982) provides a more detailed analysis of managerial attitude formation, though it is limited in that it focuses on administrator attitudes toward faculty collective bargaining in a single university system. Although the results are therefore not fully generalizable, contemporary universities and colleges often confront complex and turbulent environments and thus operate under conditions not dissimilar to those confronting modern corporations. Administration in higher education is increasingly a function of professional managers rather than of academics. These conditions are especially applicable to the California State University (CSU) system, which was used in the Walker and Lawler study. In addition, higher education has been in recent years one of the few growth areas for unions (Garbarino 1986).

The survey, which sampled the opinions of about 250 campus-level administrators throughout the CSU system, was conducted prior to the certification of a bargaining agent and in the midst of protracted organizing drives undertaken by two faculty organizations, the United Professors of California (UPC) and the California Faculty Association (CFA).[8] Around 55 percent of the administrators surveyed opposed bargaining in any form. Since it was generally recognized that a strong majority of faculty supported unionization, however, it is not surprising that a substantial proportion of administrators indicated that they supported certification under one or the other of the competing unions. That is, since bargaining was assured in any event, it would not be unreasonable for those in managerial positions to favor a particular union for strategic reasons, especially given the different ideological positions of the two unions involved. Administrators drew sharp distinctions between the UPC and CFA; those supportive of collective bargaining were three times as likely to favor the more conservative and "protective" CFA than the militant and "aggressive" UPC.[9] These differences were also apparent in the beliefs administrators expressed regarding the likely consequences of bargaining under each of the faculty unions; the CFA was consistently evaluated in a more favorable light than the UPC.

The authors considered the effects of a wide range of perceptual and affective factors on administrator support for bargaining in the CSU system. Administrators who labeled themselves politically conservative were much more likely to oppose bargaining than moderate or liberal administrators. Although not a surprising finding, it does suggest a strong linkage between general values not immediately related to collective bargaining and managerial views of unionism, a key element in the strategic choice perspective. Their views were also found to be conditioned by considerations related directly to faculty bargaining. Administrators who saw bargaining as working well in higher education generally were less likely to oppose it. Moreover, various expectations regarding the impact of bargaining under each of the competing unions were found to be quite strongly related to support for bargaining. In sum, administrator attitudes appear to have been well grounded in personal values and the rational assessment of relevant organizational conditions, findings that support strategic choice formulations. However, since the study did not specifically consider alternative processes, such as those suggested by Barbash or Wheeler, the notion that management U/DU strategies are at least in part impulsive and emotionally driven cannot be ruled out completely.

THE EMPIRICAL ANALYSIS
OF UNIONIZATION/DEUNIONIZATION FORMULATION

Although most of the empirical research on employer U/DU activity has been concerned with the impact of strategies and specific tactics on outcomes, some authors have directly studied the determinants of strategic decision-making processes. This section reviews the conceptual approaches and findings of several such studies.

UNION AVOIDANCE AS AN INVESTMENT DECISION

Focusing on strategic decision making specific to a single representation election campaign, Greer and Martin (1978) assume that management must choose from among four mutually exclusive alternatives: (a) do nothing in opposition to the union; (b) oppose the union by means of a legal campaign; (c) oppose the union by committing an unfair labor practice (discharge of union activists); or (d) oppose the union by both means. This represents an obviously simple view of the choices typically confronted by management during a campaign, but it is sufficient to gain some general insight into the manner in which campaign strategies are developed. The methodology used by Greer and Martin would have rendered a more complex model analytically intractable.

Greer and Martin treat the choice of campaign strategy as an investment decision, in which costs and benefits are measured exclusively in monetary terms. Since each of the four options available to management has the same benefit stream, management's problem is reduced to selecting the alternative that minimizes the expected present value of the cost stream. Option a, for example, is associated with higher union wages weighted by the probability of union victory, given that the employer refrains from opposing the union. Alternatively, option c is associated with the expected costs of committing a single unfair labor practice (expected back-pay award from the NLRB for an illegally discharged employee) *plus* higher union wages weighted by the probability of union victory, given that the employer engages in an illegal discharge. It is also assumed that the more aggressive the actions of an employer, the greater will be the reduction in the probability that the union will win the election (thus, the union's victory chances will decrease steadily from option a to option d). The authors derive cost expressions for each of the four alternatives.

Greer and Martin apply simulation techniques to model employer choices in hypothetical situations using published data, along with certain reasonable assumptions, to estimate the costs of alternative options. The principal conclusion of their study is that management is justified, at least in *economic* terms, in pursuing aggressive union-avoidance campaigns, often involving illegal activities, under almost all reasonable scenarios. Indeed, option c, which involved the use of illegal discharge, was found to be warranted by economic criteria even if the action only reduced the chances of union victory by 4 percent. However, Greer and Martin have not incorporated a way of appreciating *intangible* and *indirect* costs and benefits into their analysis. For example, a company engaged in an aggressive union-avoidance campaign may be the object of a consumer boycott or may have its image as a responsible corporate citizen tarnished if it discharges employees for union activities.

The importance of the Greer and Martin study for our purposes is that it demonstrates that the drift toward more aggressive union-avoidance strategies in recent years may be understood to a significant extent in terms of the apparent cost effectiveness of such conduct. That is, it may not be necessary to posit shifting managerial values in order to explain these new strategic choices. Of course, the Greer-Martin study is concerned with only a very limited set of strategic options and is consequently quite simplistic. In addition, the information used in the simulations is dated; changes in union victory rates, new studies that cast light on the impact of employer union-avoidance activities, and shifting NLRB policies would undoubtedly alter the numeric results of the Greer-Martin simulations. The basic model proposed by the authors could be greatly enriched by the extensive research that has been done on employer U/DU activities in recent years. Moreover, it should be possible to construct a fairly elaborate model of the U/DU process incorporating both union and employer strategic decision-making processes, so that the dynamics of strategic interaction might be simulated.

STRATEGY AND INNOVATIVE PERSONNEL PRACTICES

Building on the conceptual themes developed in *The Transformation of American Industrial Relations* (Kochan, Katz, and McKersie 1986), Kochan, McKersie, and Chalykoff (1986) did further analysis using the Conference Board data. Their study was principally concerned with the impact of various innovations in personnel practices on union growth and decline at the corporate level. Those results will be considered later. Of special concern here are their findings with respect to the determinants of workplace innovation as part of a union-avoidance strategy.

An index of innovative personnel practices, especially those strongly linked to union-avoidance activities, is analyzed in terms of contextual influences, corporate structure, and managerial attitudes. The principal contextual variable included was product market competition, which was expected to increase the use of innovative practices, since firms operating in highly competitive settings would have the greatest incentives to limit union influence. Corporate structure was measured by the relative power of line versus industrial relations managers in industrial relations policy making, the reasoning being that the former have been more interested in developing programs to weaken union influence. As argued above, structure should be important in affecting strategy formulation since it establishes or influences authority relationships, communications patterns, and political relationships within organizations. Finally, Kochan, McKersie, and Chalykoff considered the impact of managerial values and attitudes on personnel policy innovation. This is a key variable in the strategic choice framework, as the opportunity for decision makers to exercise personal discretion in strategy formulation is really what distinguishes this approach from those that stress contextual determinism. Commitment to union avoidance as a policy objective and the firm's current level of unionization were used as alternative indicators of management's union-avoidance sentiments.[10]

Kochan et al. estimated separate equations for union and nonunion facilities, the reasoning being that antiunion sentiments were expected to *increase* innovation in nonunion facilities but *decrease* innovation in union facilities (which such employers would probably be interested in phasing out anyway). The findings provide general support for the model. Parameter estimates are of the expected signs, and the overall equations are statistically significant. Yet the findings are weaker than what might have been anticipated. The model explains only about 12 percent to 16 percent of the variance in level of innovation, and certain critical relationships, although correct in sign, are not statistically significant (despite a sample size of nearly three hundred). In particular, market competitiveness was not found to be significant in any of the estimations, and commitment to union avoidance as a corporate policy was insignificant in the nonunion facilities equation (where we might expect the effect to be especially strong). The unionization variable was found to be negative and significant in the nonunion equation (as anticipated), but this could be attributable to many factors other than employer sentiments.

Thus, although the Kochan, McKersie, and Chalykoff study provides some support for the argument that management U/DU strategies are formulated through a rational selection process that reflects managerial values, it is equally clear that other forces are very much at work. The study was, of course, limited to large firms that already had some degree of unionization. One wonders to what extent these results generalize to the substantial proportion of businesses that have no union presence, as well as to smaller organizations.

USE OF LABOR RELATIONS CONSULTANTS

While consultants may influence employer U/DU strategy, the decision to use a labor relations consultant is itself a strategic choice. One study of the impact of consultants on election outcomes also considers the issue of consultant selection to some extent. Lawler (1984) proposes and tests a model in which both consultant use and election outcomes (union win/loss) are treated as endogenous variables. A rational choice framework is used to model the propensity of employers to use consultants. Consultant propensity is hypothesized to be an increasing function of the likelihood of union victory; other variables in the analysis include product market measures, with consultant propensity expected to decrease with improving market conditions. The study is, however, limited to a sample of certification elections in grocery stores and supermarkets, so that the range of influences on consultant choice is restricted. In addition, the study focuses only on the decision to use or not use a consultant that engaged in activities reportable under Landrum-Griffin.

The results of the empirical analysis largely conformed to theoretical expectations, with a reasonably strong fit of the model to the data. The importance of this result for our purposes is that it suggests employers evaluate their options with respect to consultant use in cost-benefit terms; the decision is thus not merely a panicky reaction to the threat of unionization. But we should not necessarily conclude that clients are properly evaluating consultant efficacy since perceptions of the impact of consultants on organizing outcomes could still be distorted by consultant marketing techniques. Moreover, the fit of the model is less than perfect, so that nonrational choice processes, which were not explicitly incorporated into the analysis, could also be at work.

UNFAIR LABOR PRACTICES

Following the analysis of Greer and Martin (1978), the decision of an employer to engage in unfair labor practices to defeat a union organizing effort may be treated as a rational choice, in which expected gains are weighed against expected costs. Several empirical studies model unfair labor practices in this fashion, though their findings are somewhat mixed.

Flanagan (1987) proposes a rational choice model of the propensity of employers to engage in unfair labor practices (as well as the tendency of unions to file charges against employers). His model suggests that employers will act strategically to commit unfair labor practices should the incentives exist. For example, increases in the union-nonunion wage differential are argued to promote illegal action to forestall unionization in order to avoid the costs of a union contract. Time-series analysis of charges of unfair labor practices supports his argument. Freeman (1986) reports similar results in a study focusing specifically on section 8(a)(3) violations of the National Labor Relations Act and the allocation of management and union resources in organizing efforts. In particular, the cost of unionization to the employer, as measured by the union-nonunion wage differential, was found to be positively related to 8(a)(3) violations per election.

A study by Kleiner (1984) tells a somewhat different story. Also starting from a rational choice perspective, he analyzes the probability of 8(a)(3) violations at the firm level. In general, however, market factors were not found to be especially strong in differentiating between firms that had and had not engaged in discriminatory employment practices. Conversely, by far the strongest impact was exerted by a dummy variable indicating whether the firm had committed such violations in the past. Firms in industries with relatively low unionization rates were also significantly more likely to be found in violation of the law. These findings taken as a whole are suggestive of a proclivity by certain employers to undertake aggressive union-avoidance efforts regardless of the economic advantage, thus supporting the interpretation of such action as emotionally charged and less than fully rational.

CONCLUSIONS

This chapter has explored various perspectives relating to the manner in which management U/DU strategies are formulated. A central issue has been whether these actions are the consequence of a rational examination of alternatives as these may relate to overall business objectives or poorly considered, at times irrational, reactions to the threat unions could pose to managerial power and status. Much of the contemporary writing on management choice in these matters favors the former interpretation, though the truth may be somewhere in between.

Empirical research on employer U/DU strategy formulation is richer in detail than studies of union strategy formulation, often focusing on decisions made at the bargaining unit or firm level. The employer studies also tend to be of more recent vintage than the union studies. And the work in this area largely deals with choices concerning the forms, not merely intensity, of employer union-avoidance efforts. This is especially the case in the Greer and Martin study, in which employers are presumed to choose from among several alternative courses of action.

In net, the empirical research would appear to favor the rationalist position. Yet most of these studies presuppose rationality and do not test for alternatives. Kleiner's work provides some indication that nonrational forces may be at work and suggests that additional research on this issue is clearly warranted. There are other significant gaps in our understanding of management decision making in this area. All of the studies reviewed deal with a single or limited set of strategic issues. Efforts to consider union-employer strategic interaction over a wide range of matters are completely absent. It would seem that future research in this area should address that larger issue, as the groundwork for more elaborate models has already been laid.

Some comments regarding methodology seem in order. Since strategic decision making is a dynamic process, the unfolding of strategy over time is of more interest than the static analyses that now dominate. Strategic decision making is also an ill-structured process in which tractable a priori choice models are difficult to formulate. Even if this were possible, obtaining complete information on a large number of cases in order to test the model would be close to impossible, since employers and unions tend to be secretive about organizing and counterorganizing efforts. This suggests that conventional regression techniques are of limited applicability in the analysis of these processes. However, the tendency of many writers in the strategic management area to eschew all forms of quantitative analysis in favor of qualitative case studies does not seem appropriate either.

To resolve this dilemma, it seems that we might wish to move toward more simulation studies, which follow in the tradition of Greer and Martin but are of greater complexity. One advantage to this approach is that large amounts of confidential information need not be collected, as Monte Carlo techniques may be used to project outcomes under differing scenarios. In addition, researchers might be able to work intensively with a small number of cooperative union and employer representatives in order to capture the heuristic rules they are apt to use in making these types of strategic decisions. These rules could then be incorporated into dynamic simulations. Techniques used in artificial intelligence research, especially those applied in the development of expert systems (e.g., Waterman 1986; Boden 1977), may be particularly helpful here.

CHAPTER 5

Labor Relations Consultants

Labor relations consultants, particularly those who assist employers in union-avoidance efforts, have become a major force in the labor relations arena.[1] The American industrial relations system guarantees a role for professional advocates of the rights and interests of both employers and unions. Yet there is a distinction between advocacy activities that complement the intent of the law and those that are either patently illegal or designed to circumvent policy objectives. A major concern is that the services that consultants provide are increasingly likely to fall into one of the latter categories, prompting calls for the statutory regulation of consultants.

This chapter explores aspects of consultant activity related to unionization and deunionization, focusing principally on the utilization of consultants by employers. The bulk of consulting activity is clearly on the employer side, and it is that type of consulting that has provoked the greatest controversy and raises the most serious public policy questions. The strategic choice model of the U/DU process (diagram 2.2) posits that consultants impact strategy formulation. Consequently, this chapter examines the types of consulting services available, the prevalence of consultants in U/DU efforts, their methods, and what is known about their impact on U/DU outcomes. Finally, arguments relating to the regulation of consultants are presented and evaluated.

THE EVOLVING ROLE OF CONSULTANTS

The term *labor relations consultant* as used here refers to an outside individual or organization retained by an employer or union to provide professional assistance in relation to unionization, deunionization, or collective bargaining. Although the concern presently is with consulting activities related directly to the U/DU process, it appears as though U/DU and bargaining processes are increasingly intertwined; employers may utilize contract negotiations as an opportunity to force out an incumbent union, and unions may tie contract settlements to employer neutrality pledges in unorganized units. Consultants may work both angles. The analysis here, however, centers specifically on the role of consultants as linked to unionization and deunionization attempts.

Before focusing on the details of consultant activity, it is necessary to have an understanding of the general nature of the labor relations consulting function and how it has evolved over time. Therefore, we shall first look at the basic role of consultants on both the employer and union sides.

CONSULTANTS AND UNIONS

It would appear that consultants historically played little if any role in shaping or conducting union U/DU strategies. Since organizing is a central function of labor unions, virtually all unions have either professional organizing staffs or field representatives with organizing responsibilities, largely negating the need for outside consultants. Indeed, professional organizers have been a part of trade unionism for well over one hundred years. In contrast, small and medium-sized firms, as well as many larger ones, are only infrequently involved in organizing efforts and do not see the need for staff specialists, thus creating a much more substantial market for consultants on the management side.

Although unions, as do employers, require the services of attorneys, there is little evidence suggesting that law firms are as central in formulating and implementing U/DU strategy for unions as they are for employers. Much more significant than consultants as a source of outside expertise for unions would be the various departments and programs of the AFL-CIO that assist affiliates in organizing drives and in countering deunionization efforts (see chapters 3 and 6-8). This was also the case historically.

In recent years there has been a considerable expansion in the use of consultants by unions in connection with U/DU activities, and there are now several consulting firms that cater to unions (BNA 1985a, 19-25). Yet consultant involvement on the union side is far from widespread. For example, Cooper (1984) reports that unions utilized consultants in only about 1 percent of the sample of NLRB representation elections she studied. Unions would seem most likely to call upon consultants when engaged in certain innovative U/DU substrategies, especially corporate campaigns (see chapter 7). Several organizations specialize in that area, most notably Ray Rogers' Corporate Campaign, Inc.,[2] and the Washington-based Kamber Group.[3] The obvious reason is that organizing departments lack the experience or expertise in mounting such programs. Consultants themselves are often either former union staff members or social activists with experience in community organizing. In addition to these kinds of firms, however, union consultants also include advertising and public relations firms, used both by the AFL-CIO and individual unions,[4] and pollsters who conduct surveys of employee sentiments in preparation for organizing drives.

Yet by the very nature of trade unionism, consultants are destined to play but a limited role in the formulation and implementation of U/DU strategy. As already noted, unions generally have the internal competencies necessary to manage most aspects of organizing campaigns and to deal with employer deunionization initiatives. In addition, union officials may be reluctant to use consultants because of the fear that consultant involvement in campaigns, particularly if effective, may undercut the positions of incumbent leaders (BNA 1985a, 23). Objections in some quarters to the use of consultants may also be related to intraunion political conflicts. Pfeffer (1981, 142–146) notes that outside experts are often utilized in political conflicts, either to secure or to realign power relations. The consultant provides legitimacy to choices and may allow certain actions to take place which would be disallowed within the established authority structure of the organization. Hence, those who desire to introduce strategic change within unions may be more likely to promote the use of consultants (who often advocate radical policies), further engendering resentment and opposition on the part of existing leaders who might view a consultant as the weapon of insurgents.

That consultants are often "outsiders" may make them suspect in the minds of many unionists. For example, in an address to a union group Robert Harbrant, of the AFL-CIO's Food and Allied Service Trades Department, characterizes those who would consult for unions in decidedly unflattering terms: "If we had a skylight on the roof, you could see right now on the trade union roof the consultants swarming over you like vultures, because what they tell you is that they have expertise that you don't and that is B.S." (Harbrant 1987, 139). His comments may also reflect competitive pressures, however, as his organization within the AFL-CIO provides services similar to those offered by many of these "swarming vultures."

It appears, then, than union consultants are a growing presence, but little is known about what they do or how they affect U/DU outcomes other than what has been learned anecdotally. This is an area in which the need for research abounds. In addition to assessing the impact of union consultants on U/DU outcomes, studies concerning the interorganizational relationships among consulting firms, unions, and the federation would be quite useful.

CONSULTANTS AND EMPLOYERS

In contrast to unions, employer use of outside experts to assist in handling labor relations issues has been common in the United States since the earliest days of the labor movement (Bernstein 1985; U.S. Congress 1981, 26–29). The first "consultants" were, in effect, the prosecutors involved in the early criminal conspiracy cases; in fact, some of those prosecutions were bankrolled by employer associations (Saposs 1918, 138). Management lawyers have continued to be at the forefront of the consulting business, not only providing legal representation for employers but often devising ways of using the courts to weaken or undermine unions. Prior to the Roosevelt administration and the New Deal, legal strategems were frequently an employer's most potent tools for combating unions. The use of injunctions and "yellow dog" contracts were commonplace. But undoubtedly the most creative accomplishment of employer attorneys was their success in having the courts apply antitrust legislation to unions for nearly forty years, despite apparent congressional intent to the contrary.

Nonattorney consultants have also been on the scene for well over a century. Private detective agencies, which specialized in decidedly aggressive, if not always legal, union-avoidance methods, appeared as early as the 1870s. Employer associations, most notably the National Association of Manufacturers, were active in aiding antiunion efforts by the turn of the century. Employer groups were prominent in promoting welfare capitalism and the "American Plan" during the twenties. Although professionals in fields such as industrial engineering and industrial psychology were not normally used primarily for antiunion efforts, their focus on management interests and worker efficiency resulted in policies threatening to unions (Gordon and Burt 1981; Gordon and Nurick 1981). Private consultants specializing in the use of behavioral techniques to dissuade employees from supporting unions have also been active for decades; provisions of the Landrum-

Griffin Act relating to disclosure of certain forms of consultant activity were the consequence of revelations of abusive conduct by consultants of this type during the McClellan hearings in the 1950s.[5]

Employer consultants have been around for some time, and their involvement in U/DU activities has also created controversy in earlier times. Yet the current level and sophistication of consultant activity seems unprecedented by historical standards. It also turns out that much is known about the nature of consultants who act for employers, and there are some studies concerning their effect on U/DU outcomes. Hence, the remainder of the chapter concerns those types of consultants.

CONSULTING FIRMS: A TYPOLOGY

In order to understand the variety of labor relations consulting services available to employers, a consultant typology is proposed here. Other writers (e.g., Bernstein 1980, McDonald and Wilson 1979)[6] have endeavored to categorize consultant services, and their work serves as a basis for this framework.

ATTORNEYS

Management attorneys represent their clients' rights and interests in legal proceedings related to unionization and deunionization efforts (as well as in negotiations with unions). This function is clearly an integral and legitimate part of an adversarial labor relations process. Serious concerns have been raised, however, in regard to a second level of attorney activity entailing the use of legal ploys as union-avoidance devices.[7] Election delays and procedural maneuvering during representation elections are common techniques, though more sophisticated methods have gained notoriety in recent years (e.g., use of bankruptcy laws to void existing union contracts and corporate reorganization to take advantage of the limited and unclear obligations of a successor employer to honor an existing contract).

Even more troubling is the practice by some attorneys of assisting employers to engage in actions that are clearly illegal or of highly questionable legality. This has been a particular problem in the case of employer discrimination against union activists and supporters, principally discharges in violation of Section 8(a)(3) of the NLRA. Cases of this sort have skyrocketed in recent years and often require two years or more to resolve (Weiler 1983), which seems to have had a distinct dampening effect on organizing efforts. Procedural maneuvering by attorneys in the adjudication of such unfair labor practices is widely viewed as an important cause of this situation. As Bernstein (1980) notes, certain forms of attorney conduct in the union-avoidance area may constitute serious breaches of professional canons of ethics even if not technically illegal.

CAMPAIGN ADVISERS

The inclusion of Section 8(c) in the NLRA as a result of the 1947 Taft-Hartley amendments firmly established the employer's right to present arguments in opposition to unionization, thus greatly expanding the role the employer might assume during a representation campaign.[8] These changes generated opportunities for those specializing in designing and orchestrating employer campaign strategies.

The evolving policy of the NLRB with respect to card-based recognition (versus the election route) would seem to be an additional factor in expanding the market for campaign management firms. In the *Joy Silk* case of 1950,[9] the courts upheld the NLRB position that an employer must recognize a union that had obtained signatures on authorization cards from a majority of those in the unit unless the employer had a good-faith doubt as to the validity of the majority. Under those circumstances an employer could demand an election but had the burden of proof in establishing its good-faith doubt. By the early 1970s the NLRB had moved to its current position, holding that an employer may, in most circumstances, refuse to accept a card-based demand for recognition and insist on an election.[10] Thus, employers enjoy substantial opportunity to confront unions in organizing campaigns. Contemporary NLRB policy clearly provides a ready market for campaign advisers. Employers may also participate in decertification election campaigns, though their rights are more restricted. Again, however, opportunities for campaign advisers abound, with some of firms largely specializing in decertification.

Attorneys frequently serve as campaign advisers, and some have argued that the role of the attorney as management's legal representative is being increasingly supplanted by that of the attorney as management's chief strategist (BNA 1985a, 8). The design of a union-avoidance campaign naturally requires an understanding of the regulations that the relevant labor relations agency imposes on campaign conduct. However, there has been substantial growth in the past fifteen to twenty years in the number of *nonattorney* consultants who act as campaign managers. Nonattorney consultants typically specialize in the use of behavioral management techniques as a means of dissuading employees from supporting unions. Information on the professional backgrounds of these consultants is scant and must often be garnered from biographical profiles included in publications or program brochures, which may overstate their credentials. Most seem to hold advanced degrees in industrial psychology, organizational behavior, communications, industrial relations, or management. Those without advanced degrees but with extensive experience in industrial relations, apparently including some former union officials and staff members, compose another significant group of consultants in this area. The techniques used by attorney and nonattorney campaign advisers often overlap. Although nonattorneys obviously cannot provide legal representation, attorneys are able to apply many of the behavioral techniques.

POSITIVE LABOR RELATIONS CONSULTANTS

Campaign advisers are brought in under crisis conditions to deal with an immediate unionization threat (or to help oust an incumbent union). Yet virtually all consultants argue that maintaining nonunion status necessitates implementing a "positive labor relations" program that emphasizes the use of management techniques both to reduce sources of employee work dissatisfaction and create structural barriers to the intrusion of a union. As with nonattorney campaign advisers, consultants in the positive labor relations area typically have backgrounds in the behavioral sciences or management fields. Advanced degrees, such as a doctorate in management or psychology, add credibility to their operations. Principals in these firms may have some attachment to an academic institution, perhaps as an adjunct faculty member; on occasion the firm will have a name that suggests that it is some type of research foundation rather than primarily a consulting operation.

EMPLOYER AND PROFESSIONAL ASSOCIATIONS

Organizations of this type are long established in the union-avoidance arena, though many groups that have had limited or no involvement in these activities in the past have become quite active in recent years. The National Association of Manufacturers (NAM) is perhaps the most visible employer association active in the union-avoidance field. The Council on Union-Free Environment (CUE) was established in 1977 by NAM to operate the organization's union-avoidance program. CUE has been involved largely in disseminating information and holding seminars for affiliated employers, with another NAM group providing certain union-avoidance services at the local and regional levels.[11] In addition to employer and trade associations, various associations for professional managers (especially those in the personnel area) hold seminars and distribute materials on union-avoidance techniques. For example, the International Personnel Management Association (IPMA), an organization for government personnel administrators, markets a manual entitled *Measures for Avoiding Unions in the Public Sector.* Unlike the other types of consulting services described above, however, most of the associations are involved in information dissemination rather than in contracting to assist individual clients develop U/DU strategies.

SECURITY SERVICES

Once a mainstay of the employer union-avoidance arsenal, private detective and security agencies are still occasionally used, most commonly to provide guards during strikes. Struck firms clearly have the right to protect nonstriking employees and company property from acts of violence, but there is a distinction between reasonable precaution and excessive muscle flexing. The presence of heavily armed security guards, coupled with practices such as photographing nonviolent picketers, would seem to constitute tactics of intimidation associated with a deunionization effort.

Security services are also used during organizing campaigns, where they may act to restrict organizer access to company property and to enforce company rules against the distribution of union materials and the solicitation of support for the union by employees during work time. Some detective agencies also provide undercover operatives to secure information on the activities of union organizers and identify union supporters (U.S. Congress 1981, 2022).

ADVOCACY GROUPS

Certain political and social action organizations, typically backed by business interests or conservative causes, serve to advance the cause of a union-free workplace. Best known is the National Right-to-Work Legal Defense Fund. As with employer and professional associations, these groups are primarily involved in information dissemination and provide limited direct assistance to employers involved in union-avoidance efforts. Sometimes these organizations provide indirect assistance to employers, such as the Right-to-Work Defense Fund's support of litigation by employees challenging aspects of compulsory union membership. Other groups have occasionally engaged in telephone campaigns seemingly designed to generate public hostility toward unions.

EDUCATIONAL INSTITUTIONS

Several universities and colleges have held or sponsored union-avoidance seminars, which has been especially galling to the labor movement (McDonald and Wilson 1979). As noted above, some consultants hold adjunct faculty positions, which may enhance their credibility. A number of full-time faculty members also engage in union-avoidance consulting; at least one advocacy organization apparently specializes in referring potential clients to campus-based consultants. Although the AFL-CIO has protested this involvement by universities and colleges in union-avoidance activity and some institutions have responded by withdrawing sponsorship of certain programs, union leaders may fail to understand that standards of academic freedom preclude most restrictions on these activities of faculty or academic programs. Since some academics also serve as consultants to labor organizations, including those individuals involved in drafting the 1985 AFL-CIO report (see chapter 3), it would likely set an unfortunate precedent if campus-based union-avoidance consultants were somehow restricted or eliminated. Labor extension programs also provide considerable assistance for unions at relatively low rates, another factor compensating for faculty consultants and management programs.

CONSULTING FIRMS:
STRUCTURE AND OPERATIONS

Accurate data on labor relations consulting firms are difficult to obtain. As is generally the case with other types of consulting organizations, these firms have a tendency to be secretive to avoid assisting competitors. Labor relations consultants are also apt to be leery of adverse publicity, which has led to congressional hearings and calls for increased regulation of consultant activity. The authors of a Bureau of National Affairs special report on consultants encountered similar difficulty in characterizing the industry, noting the problems they had in generating even a list of relatively large consulting operations (BNA 1985a, 3–8). Consultant secretiveness is reflected in what is apparently an exceedingly low compliance rate on the part of consultants in filing annual reports with the Labor Department as mandated by the Landrum-Griffin Act (Craver 1978).

The *RUB* (Report on Union Busters) *Sheet*, which has been published monthly by the AFL-CIO since the late 1970s, details the activities and organizational characteristics of many consultants (and also highlights union-avoidance activities by employers). Yet the AFL-CIO reports, along with occasional stories in the labor press, are clearly less than objective sources of data on this topic; union officials are prone to interpret any hint of employer resistance to an organizing effort as full-blown "union busting," so that reliance on union sources may create an exaggerated view of the level and nature of consultant activity. Despite these data problems, available information is used here (and in subsequent sections) to construct a portrait of the manner in which consulting firms operate.

STRUCTURAL VARIATIONS

Although the consultant typology presented above identifies some basic organizational forms of management-oriented labor relations consulting services, many consulting firms are composites of two or more basic forms. As we have already noted, attorneys frequently provide campaign management services to clients, often adopting the techniques of behavioral consultants. In a survey conducted in 1977, Craver (1978) found that in a national sample of labor law firms 65 percent engaged in activities reportable under the Landrum-Griffin Act, most of which were related to campaign management (e.g., communicating with employees to persuade them not to support unionization). Craver's results represent a conservative estimate of attorney involvement in campaign management, since the Landrum-Griffin Act reporting requirements involve only a limited set of activities.[12] Law firms can also have some involvement in the positive labor relations area, especially in drafting personnel manuals and training supervisors in the legal enforcement of rules designed to discourage unionization.

Nonattorney consultants specializing in the use of managerial techniques (henceforth *management consultants*) would often seem both to provide campaign advising and to design positive labor relations programs (though some firms concentrate in a single area). The phases of the U/DU process are interrelated, and managerial techniques used in the various phases involve similar methodologies. The defeat of a union-organizing drive can generally be expected to lead to the adoption of measures to thwart future efforts. The implementation of a positive labor relations program may be supplemented by campaign contingency plans should a union gain a foothold in spite of the program.

Although there are free-lance consultants who operate on an individual basis or through referrals from employer associations and advocacy groups, the field seems to be dominated by large firms that operate nationally. Modern Management, Inc. (née Modern Management Methods), provides a good case study of the size and structural complexity of a major management consulting firm. Founded in the early 1970s, the firm ("3M" for short)[13] gained a reputation for being tough and highly effective, especially in campaign work. In 1979, for example, the firm was reportedly involved in around three hundred organizing campaigns.[14] By 1980, the firm had been reorganized into several specialized groups, many of which were intended to operate primarily in the positive labor relations area.[15] In addition, a founder and principal in the firm left to establish his own consulting operation. More recently, there has been mention of "2M" (as it is now known) developing a cooperative arrangement with a leading union-avoidance law firm (BNA 1985a, 8).

The March 1981 *RUB Sheet* published a list of 83 consultants that had been reported as having been involved in "union busting" activities on at least three separate occasions. Although a rather subjective and possibly biased enumeration, this list does provide some indication of the most active consulting firms.[16] This list has been expanded by the author, using the *RUB Sheet* and other sources of information, to a total of 116 major union-avoidance consultants. Given available information, it is only possible to make qualitative judgments as to what constitutes major firms. Using the consultant typology constructed above, these firms have been classified by principal category (e.g., attorneys who act as campaign advisers are still classified as attorneys). The proportion of firms falling into each group is presented in diagram 5.1. As would be anticipated, most of these organizations are private law firms or management consultants, with attorneys being the dominant group.

CONSULTANT-CLIENT RELATIONSHIPS

The manner in which consulting services are delivered varies considerably, with firms often employing a range of methods. The simplest and least expensive approach is the seminar on union-avoidance techniques (U.S. Congress 1981, 29–31). Some firms specialize in this area, and the activities of various employer or professional

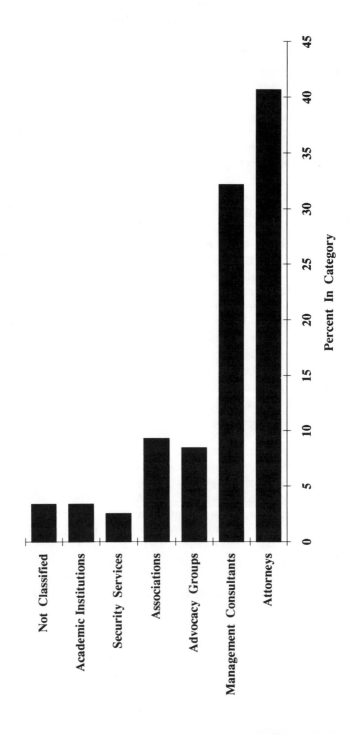

Diagram 5.1. Employer consultants grouped by principal category.

associations and advocacy groups are largely limited to sponsoring seminars. Seminar themes vary and may feature nationally prominent individuals in the union-avoidance field. The seminar serves in part as a vehicle for consultants to showcase skills and develop clients. Some consulting firms have established spin-off operations that conduct seminars, presumably with the intention of generating business for the parent company.

Direct consultant intervention into the affairs of a client organization is certainly more lucrative for the consultant and generally a greater source of concern for unions. Attorneys providing legal representation for employers obviously play a central and visible role in both the formulation and execution of their clients' U/DU strategies. When it comes to campaign management and positive labor relations, however, consultants (including attorneys) often prefer to maintain a low profile. To be sure, consultants not infrequently talk directly to employees, either in small groups or before larger "captive audiences." The tendency is recent years, however, would seem to be for consultants to avoid as much direct contact with bargaining unit employees as possible.

The absence of direct contact with employees limits consultant reporting requirements under Landrum-Griffin (perhaps a minor concern given lax enforcement). More important, it reduces the likelihood of the consultant's presence becoming an issue in a campaign. Unions are often able to exploit the "hired gun" issue when a consultant's involvement becomes known. Maintaining secrecy also reduces the union's ability to predict employer actions during a campaign. Most consultants seem to develop a standard program that they apply, with some modification, in the majority of situations. If union organizers know which consultant is involved in a campaign, then they may know what to anticipate.[17] Consultants therefore may limit their activities to formulating a union-avoidance strategy for the employer and training managerial and supervisory personnel in its implementation in the workplace.[18]

Employers may use several consultants, either in sequence or concurrently. A personnel specialist may be retained to design a new human resource management system to be used after a successful election campaign while the campaign management firm focuses on dissuading employees from voting in favor of bargaining. Should a nonattorney campaign adviser be used, a law firm may also be required for legal representation (unless this is handled by company attorneys). Some management consultants work in tandem with particular law firms, so the employer may be required to contract with both firms. Attorneys may also hire management consultants for some or all aspects of the campaign. Craver (1978) found that about 17 percent of the law firms he surveyed had at times utilized nonattorney consultants in organizing campaigns, though most had not done so on a regular basis.

Although evidence is scant, a consultant-client relationship may sometimes end on a less than amicable note. In at least one case a disgruntled consultant who had lost an account wrote a poison pen letter to the union involved in the case alleging that the employer was planning retaliatory action against union activists. The letter was posted on the plant floor by union supporters, and the union subsequently won the election (the NLRB ruled that the posting of the letter did not constitute election interference).[19]

CONSULTANT FEES

The substantial fees charged by labor relations consultants represent a campaign issue that a union can often use to its advantage, especially if the employer's campaign stresses an inability to meet union demands on financial grounds. Reports of companies paying $200,000 to $300,000 are not infrequent, although these assertions are not always easy to verify. Such large amounts are not unreasonable, however, in light of the customary fees of attorneys and management consultants in general. A fee of around $100 per hour would certainly be close to a minimum for the billable time of most professionals; rates in the neighborhood of $200 to $300 per hour are not uncommon for senior partners of law firms and well-established management consultants. As consultants are frequently involved in a particular campaign for several months, total fees can clearly be substantial. Time spent by clerical and paraprofessional employees, along with expenses, can add significantly to the total. Especially well-known figures in the field may well be able to command substantially higher fees.

Less impressionistic information is also available on consultant fees. Charles Hughes, a leading figure in the union-avoidance field (Hughes 1976) and someone in a position to know, has suggested that consultant fees in a typical representation election are roughly $500 per unit employee (BNA 1985a, 6). Thus, units with several hundred employees could easily generate fees of the magnitude suggested above. Public access to the financial statements of tax-exempt organizations (IRS Form 990) has been used by unions to establish expenses for consultants during campaigns in certain hospitals and other

nonprofit organizations. A graduate student in the author's department was able to cull fairly detailed data on consultant fees in a public
sector decertification campaign from the agency's annual financial
statement. A local government body, the agency spent at least $10,000
for attorney services and about $70,000 on two separate management
consultants.[20] The campaign, which lasted over a year, took place in
1983 and resulted in the removal of the union. The unit consisted of 105
employees, so total fees for labor relations consultants averaged about
$760 per employee, which is somewhat consistent with Hughes'
estimate.

The forms which consultants and their clients are supposed to file
annually with the Labor Department provide an important potential
source of data on many aspects of consultant activity, including fees
and expenses charged to employers, although compliance with the
reporting provisions of the Landrum-Griffin Act have been historically low (see below). What files are available, however, provide some
useful insights. The author analyzed around fifty annual reports filed
by fourteen consultants in seven midwestern states during the period
1972–1979 (Lawler 1980).[21] The consultants involved served an average
of sixty-four clients per year. Although this information is a bit dated,
there is little reason to believe that the nature of the labor relations
consulting field has changed so much as to render results based on
these reports unrepresentative of current conditions.

Not unexpectedly, the fourteen firms differed considerably in size
(table 5.1). The four largest firms accounted for 75 percent of total

Table 5.1 **DISTRIBUTION OF TOTAL REVENUE BY CONSULTING FIRM**

Rank of Firm by Size	Total Revenue 1972–1979[a] ($)	Revenue per Client per Year ($)
1	467,924	38,993
2	363,383	1,566
3	222,665	4,282
4	215,859	3,658
5	158,008	19,751
6	88,334	7,361
7	49,119	1,535
8	47,961	1,262
All others	77,100	1,150

[a]In constant (1979 dollars).

consultant revenues in the sample. There was also some considerable variation in fees across even the largest of the firms. Most firms had annual billings of only a few thousand dollars per client, but two averaged five-digit annual fees. Unfortunately, it was not possible to collect data on unit sizes involved, so expenditures per unit employee could not be calculated. These numbers indicate substantial differences in the focus of consulting firms, however, with some concentrating their efforts on intensive intervention (in presumably larger units) but most providing more limited services. In general, average reported annual fees (not adjusted for unit size) were nowhere near the six-figure amounts that are often cited by unionists. Average fees were under $4000 (1979 dollars) per client per year. Even after adjusting for inflation, the average would be less than $5000 (1986 dollars). In addition, less than 6 percent of the clients had annual billings of more than $10,000 (1979 dollars), with the largest payment being somewhat in excess of $80,000 (table 5.2).

Table 5.2 DISTRIBUTION OF TOTAL REVENUE BY ANNUAL CLIENT PAYMENTS

Client Payments per Year[a] ($)	Frequency	Relative to Total Consulting Revenue[b] (%)
Under 500	147	3
500– 1,000	91	4
1,000– 3,000	143	16
3,000– 5,000	60	14
5,000– 7,000	30	10
7,000–10,000	13	6
Over 10,000[c]	30	47

[a]Real dollar value of consulting services per client per year.

[b]Total within category fees and expenses as percentage of all fees and expenses between 1971 and 1979 (total = $1,702,000 [in 1979 dollars]).

[c]Average equals $27,000 per year.

PREVALENCE OF CONSULTANTS

As with so many other questions regarding labor relations consultants, there are many opinions, but few hard facts, on the size of the industry and the extent of consultant involvement in U/DU efforts. There is general consensus on all sides that consultant use by employers expanded substantially throughout the 1970s and into the 1980s. Although the bulk of consultant activity is in the private sector and involves firms under the jurisdiction of the NLRB, there is considerable activity among consultants in the public sector as well. In fact, consultant intervention had become so extensive in Illinois, especially at the local government level, that the state legislature amended the public sector law to limit the involvement of nonattorney consultants in campaigns (Spizzo 1988). We explore various data sources here to gain at least an impression of the extent and diversity of consultant activity, particularly during the campaign phase.

AGGREGATE ESTIMATES OF CONSULTING ACTIVITY

Estimates of the number of labor relations consulting operations in the United States range from five thousand to less than a dozen "top notch, reputable" firms.[22] In part, this disparity is related to disagreements over what constitutes union-avoidance activity. There has clearly been a proliferation of consulting firms in the human resource management and industrial relations areas over the past ten to twenty years, but this growth is linked in no small part to the expansion of government regulation of the employment relationship.[23] Thus, many consultants are engaging in what might be construed as union-avoidance activities, though that is not really their intention.

Data concerning the annual gross earnings of labor relations consulting firms are likewise wide ranging, running anywhere from $100 million to $500 million (BNA 1985a, 5–6). Moreover, the bases for these estimates are unclear. One approach would seem to be to accept Hughes' $500 per employee figure (see above) as a good estimate of typical consultant fees for union-avoidance activity (conventional legal representation fees are not included in this estimate). Furthermore, the AFL-CIO (1985) asserts that employers use such services in about 75 percent of all elections. Finally, during the early 1980s (the period to which the aggregate activity estimates apply), there were approximately seven thousand certification and nine hundred decertifications per year, with an average unit size of around sixty-five. Multiplying those numbers together generates a figure of around $195 million per year in consultant fees and expenses. Of course, this estimate would not include fees paid in connection with positive labor relations consulting or fees paid in U/DU efforts not involving elections.

Despite the substantial amounts of money involved in campaign management work, there is a sense that activity in that market segment peaked in the early 1980s. The special attention given to campaign advisers by the labor press in the late 1970s has abated to some extent in recent years. This may be the consequence of new confidence on the part of union leaders and organizers in responding to consultant union-avoidance techniques. That is, the standard approaches of the consultants have now become so familiar that organizers are no longer caught off guard. The range of nontraditional organizing stratagems increasingly employed by unions is suggestive of this. Indeed, the AFL-CIO *RUB Sheet* once downplayed the impact of consultants in recent years by running the results of a survey that suggested that union victory chances are about the same with or without consultant intervention. But more important, the number of representation elections held annually has declined since 1980, so that the campaign management market has been dwindling. Yet some in the industry suggest that the new assertiveness of unions in the organizing area has led to an increased demand for consultant services in connection with representation election campaigns. As John Sheridan, a well-known figure in the union-avoidance field, observed in a recent interview: "There was a period in the early 1980s when I wondered if there would be any business because the politics of the country was moving to the right and union activity and membership was [sic] on the decline. . . . But in the last 14 months business has come back strongly because unions are getting their act together."[24] However, whatever the decline might have been in campaign work, positive labor relations work in nonunion settings seemed to have picked up the slack (BNA 1985a, 6–7). Since work in this area cannot be readily benchmarked by measures such as elections held or election petitions filed with the NLRB, dollar estimates of aggregate activity are difficult to develop.

The data collected by the author from consultant Landrum-Griffin reports provide something of an overview of the focus of consulting activity, at least during the 1970s (Lawler 1980). The dollar volume of consulting activity (in constant [1979] dollars) was broken down by the industry of the employer organization and the union involved.[25] Not surprisingly, a large share of consultant revenues (at least for those activities covered under Landrum-Griffin) came from manufacturing firms (table 5.3). More interesting is the substantial amount spent on consultants by firms in the wholesale, retail, and service sectors, which accounted for about 55 percent of total revenue generated over the period 1972–1979. The largest amount was spent by retail establishments, especially grocery stores and restaurants (which provided 26 percent of total consultant revenues). The grocery stores using consultants were generally individual outlets of large

Table 5.3   DISTRIBUTION OF TOTAL REVENUE BY INDUSTRY OF CLIENT[a]

Industry	Total Revenue 1972–1979[b] ($)	Percent of Total
Agriculture	11,119	1
Construction	16,868	1
Manufacturing	412,546	32
Transportation	54,874	4
Wholesale trade	121,997	10
Retail trade	441,200	35
Finance	20,298	2
Services	127,352	10
Public administration	62,414	5
	1,268,668	100

[a]Based on subsample of approximately 400 clients.
[b]In constant (1979) dollars.

supermarket chains, and the restaurants were also typically franchisees or company-operated outlets of national corporations. Service sector clients were most often private hospitals and nursing homes.

These data suggest some interesting patterns. Consulting activity was concentrated heavily in industries characterized by considerable product market competition, relatively rapid growth, small operating unit size, and low existing levels of unionization. Most of these characteristics are associated with strong employer opposition to unionization. Hence, the industrial distribution of consulting activity in this study is consistent with what we would expect. This is also reflected in the distribution of revenue by union involved in the organizing drive (table 5.4). The unions primarily affected by consultants were expectedly those involved heavily in organizing workers in the growth sectors of the economy (e.g., Retail Clerks,[26] Teamsters, Hotel and Restaurant Employees, Service Employees).

CONSULTANT INVOLVEMENT IN ELECTIONS

Although aggregate revenue estimates provide a general picture of the intensity and dispersion of consultant activity, these numbers may not be especially reliable. Moreover, the work done on consultant activity in the Midwest involved organizing efforts that occurred ten to fifteen years ago, so that the pattern of consultant activity may now

Table 5.4 DISTRIBUTION OF TOTAL REVENUE BY AFFECTED UNION[a]

Union	Total Revenue 1972-1979[b] ($)	Percent of Total
Retail clerks	156,615	30
Teamsters	103,410	19
Meatcutters	44,496	8
Auto workers	41,239	7
Electrical workers (IUE)	31,076	6
Hotel and restaurant employees	18,660	4
Carpenters	17,059	3
Paperworkers (UPP)	9,419	2
Service employees (SEIU)	8,204	2
Oil, chemical, atomic workers	7,853	1
All others	92,000	18
	530,031	100

[a]Based on a subsample of 250 clients. Reprinted from Lawler (© Cornell University, 1984).

[b]In constant (1979) dollars.

be different. A number of other studies, some of more recent vintage, reveal a great deal more about the extent of consultant participation, at least in representation elections.

How frequently do employers avail themselves of the services of consultants in representation elections? A study by the AFL-CIO Department of Organization and Field Services of 225 representation elections conducted in 1982 and 1983 found that consultants were used in roughly 70 percent of all certification elections (AFL-CIO 1985, 10). More recent data from the same source suggests that, if anything, consultant participation has increased; labor relations consultants were found to be used by employers in 76 percent of a sample of 189 NLRB elections conducted in 1986 and 1987 (AFL-CIO 1989). In a smaller study, which involved a survey of 52 employers that had recently been involved in an NLRB election, Porter and Murrmann (1983) found that 67 percent of the respondent firms had used an attorney or management consultant as a campaign adviser. However, only 5 percent of the firms gave the consultant full control of the campaign; the other 62 percent used consultants in conjunction with inside managers. Lawler (1984) reports that management consultants (a category that excludes attorneys) were involved in about 18 percent of the 130 certification elections he studied; Cooper (1984) reports a figure of about 23 percent for management consultants in 758 elections. In contrast, consultant involvement in decertification elections does not seem especially high; Anderson, Busman, and O'Reilly (1982) found consultants used by only 7 percent of the employers in a sample of 57 decertification cases that took place in California in the late 1970s.

The author gathered information relating to consultant activity and employer union-avoidance efforts from organizer field reports filed with the AFL-CIO Department of Organization and Field Services. These reports involved certification elections that took place between 1975 and 1982. The reports made it possible to distinguish among several forms of consultant involvement (table 5.5).[27] These results are consistent with the other studies in that consultants were used as campaign advisers in about 73 percent of the elections. They also show that the involvement of management consultants is substantially less than that of attorneys who act in a campaign adviser capacity. This may simply be the result, however, of management consultants being in a better position to disguise their involvement. In addition, as these reports were not filed by impartial observers, the percent of attorneys acting as campaign advisers may be overstated.

WHAT DO CONSULTANTS DO?

The data available clearly depict labor relations consultants as a significant presence. In examining consultant intervention in the U/DU process, we are ultimately concerned, however, with relating the nature of their activities to the strategic choice framework proposed in chapter 2. This suggests we need to consider the impact of consultants on (a) management strategic decision-making processes, (b) the strategic options adopted by management, and (c) the likelihood of a union gaining (or retaining recognition) in a bargaining unit. In the ideal all three of these issues would be considered for each of the major phases of the U/DU process. But this is not feasible within space limitations, nor is the literature sufficiently developed to allow such a complete treatment. Most of the research and commentary that have been published relate to consultant activity during the campaign phase, which shall be the focus here.

CONSULTANTS AND STRATEGY FORMULATION

The strategic choice framework posits the involvement of external consultants to be an important influence on strategy formulation. Research in this area, however, is limited, and we need to rely to a

Table 5.5 **EMPLOYER USE OF CONSULTANTS IN CERTIFICATION ELECTION CAMPAIGNS (N = 201)**

Type of Consultant	Frequency[a] (%)	Employees Affected[b] (%)
Attorney only (as legal representative)	18.9	17.1
Attorney only (as legal representative and campaign adviser)	52.7	56.6
Management consultant only	11.4	5.6
Attorney and management consultant	9.0	13.8
No external consultant	8.0	7.0

[a]Percent of elections in which form of consulting activity reported occurred.
[b]Proportion of all election units in sample in units in which consulting activity reportedly occurred (N = 30,584).

large extent on what union-avoidance specialists themselves write in order to gain at least an impression of their role. The labor press is also vitally concerned with this issue (e.g., Lagerfeld 1981), though obviously from a less than disinterested stance. Although there is considerable need for objective research here, the sensitive nature of client-consultant relationships is apt to make this difficult if conventional survey and data-gathering methods are used.

Although consultants often keep a low profile in ongoing campaigns, many are more than willing to betray at least a few trade secrets in books, seminars, and interviews. While consulting in practice may not be quite the same as consulting in print, the numerous management guidebooks published in the past ten to fifteen years suggest ways in which the essential features of the consultant's thinking process might influence management strategic decision making. Among the better known works are those by Hughes (1976), Myers (1976), DeMaria (1980), and Kilgour (1981). DeMaria focuses considerable attention on legal issues, and the other three write from the perspective of the management consultant. Kilgour deals with both the nonunion and campaign phases, while Myers and Hughes concentrate heavily on positive labor relations during the nonunion phase. Hughes also publishes a monthly newsletter focusing on union-avoidance techniques. DeMaria limits himself largely to representation campaigns, although he has also written a management guide to decertification (DeMaria 1982). Although some authors, such as De-

Maria, take a pragmatic approach, others are much more ideological and occasionally rather banal. Hughes opens with a cartoon in which a hapless traveler (management) is ingested by an insatiable bear (union). For reasons that remain obscure, Myers dedicates his book to the memory of Samuel Gompers ("immigrant, union leader, and statesman").

These authors all seem to share a common concern with creating what they see as a rational framework for addressing the challenge of unionization. They search for a systematic and orderly set of responses to actual or potential union activity. Although this may seem to be a natural approach for any manager, panic may ensue when a union's presence is first detected. Thus, the consultant's first task would seem to be to provide management with a paradigm and overarching strategic mission to guide its action in alien circumstances. They furnish managers with a way of thinking about unions that serves to reduce anxiety and facilitate action. Techniques for responding to the union come later and follow from the strategic framework. This view is shared by Pfeffer (1981, 142-146) in his interpretation of the general role of outside experts in organizational action. He notes that experts can be used to imbue decisions with an "aura of rationality," particularly when those decisions relate to matters of critical importance to the organization and threaten to alter the extant distribution of organizational power (e.g., the threat of unionization).

The critical issue, of course is whether the strategic vision the consultant creates is valid or merely a sophisticated exercise in pulling the wool over the client's eyes. Marketing considerations may supersede scientific merit as the consultant endeavors to find a "hook" that will appeal to potential clients. This would seem to lead to simplified models that tend to coincide with client values and beliefs. The comments of one former consultant suggests this is likely to be the case: "[Consulting] is a very dirty business; it's extremely manipulative.... [Consultants] prey on managers of companies who are obsessed with not becoming unionized. They grossly exaggerate management's concerns."[28]

Simplistic analyses that cater to management fears and biases pervade the union-avoidance literature. Catchy aphorisms abound (e.g., "Any management that gets a union deserves it—and they [sic] get the kind they [sic] deserve" [Hughes 1976, 1]). Both Hughes and Myers base their approaches on concepts drawn from organizational behavior and industrial psychology. Yet their reliance on notions such as Maslow's needs hierarchy and related constructs seem out of place

given contemporary research on motivation and behavior (even allowing for the publication dates). Gordon and Nurick (1981) are sharply
critical of Hughes, noting that aspects of his argument rely on pro-
prietary data sources and research instruments, so that hypotheses
cannot readily be verified by independent researchers. In contrast,
Kilgour has been given higher marks for his attention to published
research and a more objective evaluation of employer options (Donovan 1983). Some of his analyses and recommendations, however,
especially on employee selection and work force composition (as a
means of limiting employee prounion sentiments) appear to come
close indeed to the endorsement of illegal activity. He suggests screening employees with respect to "likely" prior union membership (Kilgour 1981, 98–100) and implies (though does not explicitly state) that
employers may do well to avoid employing women and blacks when
possible. Particularly disconcerting is Kilgour's insensitive portrayal
of the struggles of the United Farm Workers: "The combination of
unionization and racial interest can result in a virulent form of
unionism and collective bargaining, as the recent experience of California agriculture attests" (Kilgour 1981, 98).

CONSULTANTS AND STRATEGY IMPLEMENTATION

Arguments regarding the desirability of regulating consultant
conduct hinge on the extent to which consultant action thwarts the
policy objectives of the NLRA and related legislation. Consequently,
we must pay particular attention to identifying the tactics consultants are likely to promote in the implementation of employer strategy. Fortunately, data concerning union-avoidance tactics pursued in
the presence of consultants are somewhat more readily available than
data on many of the other aspects of consultant activity we have
considered in this chapter. Survey data collected on consultant conduct during representation election campaigns shall be the focus of
the discussion here, with particular attention paid to certain types of
influence, contextual control, and monitoring tactics.

Influence Tactics

Campaign advisers often appear to rely heavily on the use of
influence tactics. The contemporary emphasis is clearly on conversion
rather than intimidation. Campaign themes tend to stress the positive
aspects of management's approach. Some consultants take a different
approach by making statements that acknowledge past failings on the
part of management and make explicit promises of reform. The
inability of the union to obtain favorable settlements in other firms,

the high costs of union membership (e.g., dues, fines), and the possibility of strikes are also common themes. Although overt intimidation does not seem to be employed often, veiled threats relating to possibilities such as job loss and plant closings are widely reported.

Several specific approaches are utilized by consultants. "Captive audience" speeches and distribution of letters and other forms of written communication have long been used by management during organizing campaigns.[29] Consultants would seem to have developed new styles of presentation and message delivery that improve the effectiveness of these methods. But even if consultants are not involved directly in communicating with employees (often avoided for the reasons mentioned above), they typically write employer speeches, letters, and fliers, as well as design and coordinate the overall influence effort. In addition to traditional campaign influence methods, consultants appear to have been quite innovative in the use of group and interpersonal communication techniques. The consultant may meet with small groups of employees or individual employees on a one-to-one basis. Though more time consuming (and thus costly), these methods allow messages to be tailored to the specific concerns of the employees involved. More important, small group and individual approaches are especially powerful for cooptation and gaining worker commitment to management objectives (Salancik 1977).

Information on the extent to which consultants engage in various influence tactics comes from two different sources. Craver's (1978) survey of labor law firms asked respondents the frequency with which they undertake different campaign-related activities for clients. Several of the categories of activity Craver identifies are directly or indirectly related to influence tactics (e.g., preparing employer campaign speeches and written communications, delivering campaign speeches, reviewing the legal propriety of employer campaign material). Respondents were infrequently involved in direct communication with employees (only 15 percent had ever delivered speeches in opposition to a union organizing effort or engaged in informal efforts to persuade employees to vote against bargaining), but a substantial proportion reported occasionally or frequently either writing campaign material (70 percent) or assisting in its preparation (90 percent).

Additional information on consultant campaign activity was derived from the sample of AFL-CIO organizer field reports mentioned above. The data base covers around two hundred elections. As it was constructed using information from several different types of reports, however, certain data are not available for all cases. Information for some of the cases was derived from reports designed by the AFL-CIO with the specific intention of identifying consultant campaign activities. Descriptive statistics for a subsample of fifty-six elections, in which both campaign advisers were used (attorneys or management consultants or both) and consultant activity forms were filed, are presented in table 5.6. That particular form happened to focus on a limited set of consultant activities, mostly those related to influence efforts. As with Craver's findings, it is quite evident that consultants worked largely behind the scenes (at least as the situation was perceived by organizers). Consultants participated in activities involving *direct* employee contact in anywhere from 12 percent to 48 percent of the cases but in 75 percent to 85 percent of the cases for activities in which the consultant had *no direct* contact.

Data from the total sample of 201 campaigns provides additional information on the role campaign advisers play in the selection of tactics. Both narrative descriptions of employer campaign activities and checklists were content analyzed to identify several common types of campaign activities utilized by employers. Because of the nature of the field reports, it was possible to establish the presence or absence, but not the intensity of use, of each activity in a given campaign. The use of each of these activities was correlated with a dichotomous variable indicating the intervention of a consultant as a campaign adviser (table 5.7).[30] Consultant intervention was found to be positively associated with most influence activities, the exception being in the case of activities in violation of Section 8(a)(1) of the NLRA. Although consultant intervention was weakly but positively associated with the use of threatening employer campaign statements, neither a positive nor significant impact was observed in the case of promises and inducements. Thus, consultants would appear to increase the likelihood of influence tactics being used, but the allegation that this results in more coercive or manipulative employer campaigns would be only weakly supported at best by these data.

Contextual Control

Contextual control tactics tend to be more involved and more costly to implement than influence tactics. We might expect, then, that even though consultants may play an advisory role in devising major contextual control measures, management itself would take the lead in the introduction of these changes. Consultants are, however, commonly associated with certain types of contextual control tactics. Programs to train managers (particularly first-line supervisors) in

Table 5.6 **SELECTED CONSULTANT ACTIVITIES IN REPRESENTATION ELECTION CAMPAIGNS ($N = 56$)**

Campaign Tactics[a]	Frequency[b] (%)	Employees Affected[c] (%)
Influence Tactics		
Delivered captive audience speeches	32.1	35.3
Prepared captive audience speeches	75.0	91.8
Discussed issues with individual employees	30.4	30.1
Conducted preemployment inverviews to discuss client's union-free stance	12.5	9.5
Distributed campaign material	48.2	62.7
Prepared campaign material	85.7	91.3
Contextual Control Tactics		
Trained supervisors in union-avoidance methods	78.6	87.9
Used community groups to oppose bargaining	12.5	9.5
Monitoring Tactics		
Obtained information on union activities from supervisors	75.0	90.2
Conducted employee opinion surveys	28.6	33.4

[a]Derived from a sample of elections in which campaign managers were reportedly used and in which organizers completed an AFL-CIO form specifically detailing consultant activities.

[b]Percent of elections in which activity reportedly occurred.

[c]Proportion of all employees in election units in sample in units in which tactic was reportedly used ($N = 6474$).

union-avoidance techniques appear to be a major consultant campaign activity. Union-avoidance guidebooks and articles stress the pivotal role of the supervisor in discerning conditions at the shop floor level, enforcing rules intended to discourage unionization, and convincing employees to vote against bargaining. Among managers it is

Table 5.7 CORRELATION OF CONSULTANT INTERVENTION WITH VARIOUS EMPLOYER CAMPAIGN TACTICS (N = 201)

Campaign Tactics	Correlation Coefficient[a]	Significance Level
Influence Tactics		
Captive audience speeches	.19	.01
Individual group meetings with employees	.20	.01
Written communications	.28	.01
Use of threats	.10	.10
Use of promises or inducements	−.04	ns
Contextual Control Tactics		
Training of supervisors	.35	.01
Excelsior-list irregularities	.03	ns
Discrimination against union supporters (8(a)(3) violations)	.12	.05
Unilateral change in wages, conditions of employment	.07	ns
Directed (vs. consent) election	.01	ns
Election delay (days)	.11	.10
Monitoring Tactics		
Surveillance	.30	.01
Attitude surveys	.18	.01

[a]All Spearman correlation coefficients except for correlation between consultant intervention and election delay (Pearson correlation).

the supervisor who will most likely enjoy at least the potential for developing the best rapport with unit employees (though this is often not realized). The consultant endeavors to develop this relationship in ways supportive of union-avoidance objectives. Supervisor selection is often the first step in this process, with both unpopular and prounion supervisors being replaced. Intensive training of supervisors in union-avoidance techniques then follows.

Empirical findings confirm that consultants work extensively with supervisors in union-avoidance campaigns. Craver (1978) found that attorney instruction of supervisors, in both the lawful conduct of union-avoidance campaigns and techniques useful in discouraging employees from supporting unionization, was among the most common forms of attorney activity, with 75 percent of respondents indicating that their firms frequently provided these services to clients. Data drawn from the AFL-CIO reports of consultant activity (table 5.6) indicate that campaign advisers engaged in supervisory training in the vast majority of cases in which they participated. Moreover, training was significantly more probable in situations in which consultants were utilized as campaign advisers (table 5.7).

Of particular concern from a public policy perspective has been the sharp increase in charges of employment discrimination against union activists and supporters in violation of Section 8(a)(3) of the NLRA (Weiler 1983). Not only does this conduct hold the potential for undermining organizing efforts but it also can have personally devastating effects on the employee or employees involved, especially when discharge is involved. Unions argue that "union busters" encourage conduct of this sort, despite its obvious illegality. The AFL-CIO field report data provide some support for this view, as a moderate correlation was found between discriminatory activity and consultant intervention (table 5.7). In addition, the presence of labor relations consultants appears to be related positively to the period elapsed between the filing of a petition for a representation election and the holding of the election (election delay).

Monitoring

Collecting information regarding the potential actions of an opponent is clearly viewed as an important element of successful employer campaigns in the union-avoidance literature. When used for union-avoidance purposes, certain intelligence-gathering techniques (e.g., the surveillance of employees) are illegal yet often used. Employee opinion surveys are one means used to identify centers of union support to be targeted for action. Specific questions regarding union support need not be included, as this may be inferred from respondent work attitudes, demographic characteristics, and worker values. Consultants used this technique on occasion, but not in most of the cases in which they were involved (table 5.6); the intervention of a consultant, however, did increase the frequency of this approach (table 5.7).

A much more common method of intelligence gathering involves the utilization of supervisors to monitor conditions, discern union activity, and report what they find to employers (or directly to the consultant). Supervisor surveillance in various forms took place in most of the cases for which detailed consultant activity reports were available in the AFL-CIO field reports (table 5.6), and this type of activity was quite strongly related to consultant intervention (table 5.7). This finding is again corroborated by the results of Craver's survey, in which about half of the attorneys responding reported obtaining information on employee organizing activities through supervisors. Of course, other employees and undercover operatives are used to monitor union activity, though specific information on the application of these methods was not available from the AFL-CIO field reports. Craver did ask some questions regarding interrogation of employees, though only about 2 percent to 3 percent of the respondents acknowledged having done this even infrequently.

Conclusion

The data clearly suggest that external consultants acting as campaign advisers increase the prospects that certain tactics will be used during campaigns. Influence tactics are more common, and the content of campaign messages may be more intimidating. Consultants make extensive use of supervisors, both to conduct union-avoidance activities at the shop floor level and gather information on union activities. There also seems to be a somewhat greater likelihood of discrimination against union supporters. These findings most certainly bolster the union view of consultants as "union busters." These observations regarding the impact of consultants on the implementation of employer strategy are, however, based on descriptive statistics and simple correlation coefficients. Thus, we can draw only weak inferences regarding causal linkages between consultant use and the nature of the employer's campaign. An obvious alternative explanation of these findings is that employers who utilize consultants are more aggressive in responding to organizing efforts across the board and would act in these ways even absent a consultant.[31]

DO CONSULTANTS MAKE A DIFFERENCE?

That labor relations consultants seem to promote more aggressive employer union-avoidance campaigns is not a surprising finding. Yet this conclusion does not speak to the more significant policy issue: Is the effect of consultant intervention a reduction in the likelihood of union recognition? Although empirical evidence on the impact of different campaign strategies and tactics will be examined in some detail in chapter 9, research relating specifically to the impact of consultant involvement on election outcomes is considered here.

A relatively limited study of consultant intervention in certification elections in supermarkets and grocery stores (Lawler 1984) found that, after controlling for influences such as labor market conditions and bargaining unit size, consultant intervention reduced the proportion of employees voting in favor of bargaining by perhaps as much as

28 percent. Yet it was also shown that conditions that promoted consultant use also independently contributed to a significant increase in prounion votes. This suggested a kind of backfire effect. That is, the very intense employer motivation to oppose unionization associated with consultant use may encourage the employer to overreact, thus intensifying employee resolve to organize.[32] In its survey of a sample of elections held in 1986 and 1987, the AFL-CIO Organizing Department found the union win rate to be 55 percent for elections in which employers used labor relations consultants, versus about 39 percent for those in which consultants did not participate (AFL-CIO 1989). Porter and Murrmann (1983) report that employers are more likely to win elections in which campaigns are administered jointly by a general manager and consultant than in cases in which only a consultant or a general manager has complete responsibility for the campaign. In contrast, Cooper (1984) found that unions are somewhat less likely to win certification elections in which the company is primarily represented by either a management consultant or an attorney (versus an officer of the company). As for decertification elections, Anderson, Busman, and O'Reilly (1982) found no statistically significant relationship between consultant intervention and election outcome.

The studies mentioned above consider only the impact of labor relations consultants without controlling for other aspects of the employer's response to the organizing effort. But perhaps it is not what consultants do so much as how they do these things that affects outcomes. Both an employer acting independently and one working in conjunction with a consultant may utilize the same influence tactics (e.g., captive audience speeches, small group meetings, letters to employees), yet the effectiveness of these tactics in reducing union support may be greater in the latter case given the consultant's expertise. Conversely, consultants could advocate and pursue union-avoidance techniques that have little impact or may possibly be counterproductive.

Consultant involvement, then, could be expected to exert some direct effect on U/DU outcomes after controlling for other aspects of an employer's union-avoidance strategy. Lawler and West (1985) used the AFL-CIO field report data in this way to analyze consultant effects, along with those of a wide range of employer campaign tactics and contextual factors, in a broadly based sample of 175 certification elections. Differentiating between attorney consultants and management consultants, the authors report that although management consultants acting in the absence of attorneys reduced prounion vote by 10 percent to 15 percent, the joint action of both in a campaign had little impact on election outcomes. Put another way, attorney campaign advisers acting independently had no impact, and their presence seemingly undercut the effectiveness of management consultants. These results are indicative of a backfire effect in the sense that employers engaging in overkill in response to an organizing drive (by hiring both a management consultant and an attorney campaign adviser) may generate union-avoidance policies that alienate workers further and generate greater solidarity on their part. Alternatively, management consultants and attorneys may work at cross-purposes, and their mutual interference may nullify the impact of otherwise effective campaign tactics.

THE REGULATION OF CONSULTANT ACTIVITY

The visibility and prevalence of labor relations consultants have prompted calls for tighter restrictions on the activities of consultants. Expectedly, the labor movement has been at the forefront of this effort, though this initiative has not apparently gained much support in other quarters. Also predictably, opposition has been strong among employers and consultants themselves, who argue that consultant efforts are not inconsistent with public policy, that unions are merely using consultants as scapegoats for the failings of labor organizations themselves, and that increased regulation would serve only to impose another layer of bureaucratic control on management, thus lessening economic efficiency. Employers and managers also maintain that consulting activity is less prevalent than unions would lead us to believe, suggesting that unionists are likely to interpret most forms of personnel and human resource management consulting as "union busting" no matter what its purpose.

The matter of consultant regulation really breaks down into two rather separate questions. The first of these concerns the reporting of consultant activities to the Labor Department under provisions of the Landrum-Griffin Act. The second relates more directly to the sanctioning of illegal or unethical consultant behavior. Here we will look at issues and suggested options relating to the regulation of consultant activity and the formulation and execution of U/DU strategies for employer clients.

MONITORING CONSULTANT ACTIVITY

In addition to revelations regarding corruption and undemocratic practices in unions, the McClellan Committee heard considerable testimony regarding abusive conduct by labor relations consultants.

It was felt that such practices might be constrained if employees in affected bargaining units had knowledge of consultant involvement. Thus, the Landrum-Griffin Act (1959) required both employers and consultants to file reports detailing the nature of the consulting arrangement when certain conditions are met (LMRDA, Section 203(a) and 203(b)).

Reporting Requirements

The law narrowly defines reportable activities, which are limited to efforts to persuade employees in the exercise of their protected rights under Section 7 of the NLRA and the gathering of information on employees and labor organizations in connection with a labor dispute. Moreover, administrative practice and case law have further limited the reporting obligations of consultants and employers. Perhaps most controversial has been the distinction drawn between consultants as "advisers" versus consultants as "persuaders" (Beaird 1986; Bernstein 1980). In essence, consultants who provide assistance to employers but who do not deal directly with bargaining unit employees are exempt from the reporting requirement. As we have seen, consultants are considerably more likely to engage in such indirect action (table 5.6). This would undoubtedly be the case even without the Landrum-Griffin Act, as secrecy is seen to promote consultant effectiveness. Hence, the objective of the Landrum-Griffin reporting requirements—the disclosure to employees of the professional expertise utilized by management in a labor dispute—is effectively nullified.

Compliance and Enforcement

In addition to relatively weak reporting requirements, most consultants apparently choose not to file reports even when engaged in reportable activities. In his survey of law firms, for example, Craver (1978) found that although about 65 percent of the firms indicated having provided some type of service reportable under existing standards less than 2 percent of these law firms had filed reports. Craver also discovered considerable ignorance on the part of attorneys regarding what is reportable; for many firms that had clearly engaged in reportable activity, survey respondents from those firms indicated that they thought these activities were exempt. Of course, Craver's study deals only with attorneys. Since employers typically rely on the advice of their attorneys in these matters, it seems even less likely that employer reports are filed with any greater frequency or reliability. There is also little reason to believe that management consultants or detective agencies are any more conscientious in conforming to the requirements of the law.

That consultants and their clients generally avoid filing legally mandated reports is in no small part facilitated by lax enforcement on the part of the Labor Department. The secretary of labor enjoys considerable discretion in matters of enforcement of the reporting requirements. Although the AFL-CIO and various unions often file complaints, only a handful of actions have ever been brought against consultants, and most of those were in the years following passage of the act (U.S. Congress 1981, 45–47). This has been especially true during Republican administrations. The Nixon administration initiated not a single enforcement action. And during the Reagan years, Labor Department enforcement standards were substantially weakened, as was highlighted in congressional oversight hearings in 1984.[33] The labor movement maintains that reporting rules currently implemented render the law virtually meaningless. However, the federal courts now seem to be acting to tighten enforcement standards to some extent. In a case brought by the United Auto Workers and other labor organizations against the Department of Labor, the District Court for Washington, D.C., recently held that supervisory training involving instruction on how to influence employees to vote against unionization is reportable "persuader" activity (though this seems to be at odds with established precedent).[34] At this writing the case is now before the Court of Appeals and has generated considerable controversy. No less than six national business organizations, including the U.S. Chamber of Commerce, the National Association of Manufacturers, and the American Society for Personnel Administration (ASPA), have intervened on the side of the Labor Department.[35] In addition, diverse appellate court rulings on the extent of reporting requirements may cause the Supreme Court to consider the issue in the near future (Bush 1986).

A Need for Change?

What is to be done, then, with regard to the Landrum-Griffin consultant reporting requirements? Though secretaries of labor have generally chosen not to exercise the option, the Labor Department has broad authority to initiate investigations of violations of the law; criminal charges can be filed against those who do not report (Bernstein 1980). Thus, there is machinery in place to bring sanctions against illegal behavior and to expand the definition of reportable activities, if only it were to be mobilized. Yet there continues to be strong opposition to enforcement of the consultant reporting provisions. Most of the respondents to Craver's survey endorsed repeal of this requirement. Arguments supporting repeal include the apparently high costs of investigating these cases relative to the benefits and the fact that many of what are believed to be the most pernicious forms of consultant activity, including clearly illegal conduct, are not reportable under even the most liberal interpretation of the current law (Beaird 1986).

The argument for increased enforcement is perhaps best articulated by Craver (1978, 628), who asserts:

> Although the complete exemption of lawyers from the consultant reporting regulations would most easily eliminate the problem caused by widespread noncompliance, such a "solution" would be entirely inappropriate. If management attorneys were permitted to engage in anonymous proselytizing during union organizing campaigns or the collective bargaining process, there is a substantial likelihood that many employees would be unfairly influenced by the opinions expressed by seemingly disinterested labor relations experts.

An apparent source of resistance to the law is the requirement that consultants disclose their financial arrangements with the employer and also report all labor relations consulting fees received during the year, even from clients for which they did not engage in reportable activities. Craver recommends amending the LMRDA to exclude the reporting requirement when consultants engaged in reportable activities are identified to employees as management agents; he also suggests elimination of the requirement to report other labor relations consulting income. These changes are posited to reduce the disincentives to compliance.

The Craver recommendations are based on the assumption that somehow "anonymous proselytizing" will have a greater impact on employees than situations in which consultants are clearly identified. But that is purely conjectural as no empirical evidence supports such a position. The empirical evidence we do have suggests that consultant impact is complex and often minimal, especially in the case of attorneys (which are the focus of Craver's paper). Moreover, his proposal does nothing to extend coverage of the reporting requirement to activities other than persuasion and information gathering nor does it seek to eliminate the rather artificial distinction between the adviser and persuader roles of consultants.

ILLICIT CONDUCT

The Landrum-Griffin reporting requirements deal largely with legal action on the part of consultants, and it is not clear that broader reporting standards or more aggressive enforcement of these standards would do much to alter management strategies or affect U/DU outcomes. More to the point would seem to be the issue of containing illegal or unethical consultant activity.

Much of what is asserted about consultant activity is anecdotal, so that the data presented in tables 5.6 and 5.7 represent the only comprehensive description of the variety and frequency of consultant activities. It seems clear that consultant involvement is at least associated with an increased likelihood of certain illegal activities occurring (especially discrimination against union supporters and surveillance of union activities). Although this relationship could be spurious, it seems more likely than not that consultants do promote certain types of illegal activity. Thus, ways of limiting illicit consultant behavior should be a pressing matter. Different avenues have been proposed to address this concern, though an optimal solution is not clear-cut.

Unfair Labor Practice Charges

In general, unfair labor practice charges under Section 8(a) of the NLRA are brought only against an offending employer; consultants are named in complaints only in extreme cases (U.S. Congress 1981, 47–49). This means, of course, that cease and desist orders, as well as any subsequent enforcement actions, apply only to the employer and the NLRB cannot directly restrict the actions of the consultant.

A difficulty in bringing charges against consultants involves establishing the appropriate linkage between a consultant, its operatives, and the actions of the employer. The established standard is one of agency; that is, if the consulting firm is clearly acting as the agent of the employer in the commission of the unfair labor practice, then it may be held liable (Bethel 1984). But that the consultant is generally at work behind the scenes means that it cannot be held accountable under the agency doctrine. In the 1982 *St. Francis Hospital* case, charges were filed against a consultant that had principal responsibility for coordinating the employer's campaign, a campaign in which numerous unfair labor practices had been committed. However, the NLRB ultimately rejected the argument that the consultant was liable as a "coprincipal" (Harvard Law Review 1984). Other legal theories also can be presented as to why consultants should be subject directly to NLRB provisions, but these have not found much favor with the NLRB. An important consideration is that, in the case of attorney consultants, the naming of management's attorney in an unfair labor practice case would intrude on the employer's right to counsel, amounting to "intimidatory and coercive constraint" (Harvard Law Review 1984).

Bethel (1984) suggests several remedies that would perhaps address these problems and still allow the NLRB to impose restrictions on consultant conduct. For example, he suggests greater use of "broad" cease and desist orders, which could be issued against consultants serving as employer agents and which would limit their activities in situations other than the one directly linked to the unfair labor practice. This would be available only in cases in which the consultant's misconduct was clearly extreme and widespread. Bethel also suggests expanded use of contempt proceedings against consultants with established histories of involving themselves in illegal activity; he notes one case in which a federal judge ordered employers not to use the services of a consultant who fell into this category (though this ruling was later reversed).

Alternative Sanctions

In most instances naming a consultant in an NLRB cease and desist order is likely to be more of a symbolic move, as the NLRB has no power to impose punitive damages, and actual damages (to be shared by the employer in any event) will most likely be relatively small. In a perverse sense, unfair labor practice charges may serve to enhance a consultant's reputation in the eyes of potential clients.

There are other, more damaging, sanctions that might be applied to consultants who clearly and continually engage in illicit and unethical behavior (Bernstein 1980; U.S. Congress 1981, 48–50). The NLRB may suspend or disbar consultants from practice before it, though this has been done in only a few cases. This is clearly a more damaging move than merely naming a consultant in an unfair labor practice charge. In some instances consultant actions may constitute criminal offenses, as when consultants submit false statements to federal agencies or commit perjury in hearings. Thus, they could be subject to prosecution. Bernstein (1980) also suggests situations under which unions could initiate liable suits against consultants who interfere with, or cause the employer to breach, an established contract. Finally, attorney consultants are potentially subject to discipline by the bar if they engage in illegal or unethical behavior.

CONCLUSIONS

Although mechanisms exist in principle to impose restrictions on certain forms of consultant behavior and to bring sanctions against outright illegal actions, these approaches are little used in practice. Current litigation may result in more aggressive enforcement of Landrum-Griffin reporting requirements, but they are now virtually unenforced by the Labor Department. Consultants are also largely immune from action taken by the NLRB or from alternative means of controlling their behavior. Even though arguments are strong for applying these measures with greater force, the empirical evidence discussed above does not suggest that the net impact of consultant intervention on outcomes, at least in representation elections, is very substantial. It would not seem that restricting consultants will have much of an impact on union organizing effectiveness, and it is probable that consultants will merely develop new methods to circumvent restrictions and avoid sanctions. Thus, scarce union resources are probably better utilized in developing proactive measures which anticipate consultant action, rather than in seeking to impose restrictions on consultant activity.

CHAPTER SUMMARY

This chapter has explored the roles of both attorney and nonattorney labor relations consultants in the U/DU process. Although consultants are increasingly used by unions, they are still only infrequently encountered and mostly assist unions in implementing nontraditional tactics and strategies. The primary focus here has been on the use of consultants by employers during representation election campaigns. It is this form of consultant activity that has been most controversial and earned consultants the "union buster" nickname. Although consultants are active on the employer side during other stages of the U/DU process and seem to be of increasing importance in assisting unions as well, there is much less information on their participation in such circumstances, and this has not generated the same level of concern in regard to public policy.

The data presented and evaluated in this chapter lead to several broad conclusions as to the part consultants play in organizing campaigns:

1. Consultant involvement is varied in form and extensive, at least in the campaign phase.
2. Attorneys are most common as labor relations consultants, and a substantial proportion of these act as campaign advisers or coordinators for their clients (i.e., they provide significant services beyond legal representation).
3. Management consulting firms are also quite active, though much less prevalent than attorneys.

4. Labor relations consultants are apt to pursue aggressive union-avoidance strategies that substantially differ in the manner in which they are implemented than the strategies pursued by employers acting alone. Many of the tactics apparently favored by consultants are those that, if not illegal, nonetheless seem incompatible with public policy.

5. The impact of consult involvement on election outcomes is somewhat ambiguous. As seen later (chapter 9), many of the tactics they promote are moderately effective in lessening union victory chances. Consultant intervention seemingly coexists with other factors, however, that compensate for or reduce their impact on outcomes, perhaps as the result of some type of backfire effect. In net, then, it is not clear that consultant intervention per se has been principally responsible for the declining organizing effectiveness of unions.

6. The issue of regulation or restricting consultant activity has been raised often in recent years. It seems unlikely that much will be done in this area in the coming years. It is also questionable that this approach would, in principle, do much to enhance union organizing.

CHAPTER 6

Implementing Strategies in Nonunion Settings

Considerable ingenuity is evident in the array of tactical initiatives through which employers and unions implement U/DU strategies. Though labor-management conflict in the organizing arena is intense, refinement and sophistication are the hallmarks of contemporary U/DU strategies, in marked contrast to the blunderbuss approaches typical of earlier times. The process is not, however, totally free of abuses on either side. And even though violence and blatant intimidation may not be so common today, many of the techniques used or advocated are highly manipulative and raise troublesome ethical and public policy questions.

Having examined strategy formulation processes, we turn to the task of identifying and interpreting common U/DU strategies and tactics within the conceptual framework laid out in chapter 2. This chapter deals with strategies common in preunion and nonunion settings. Chapter 7 focuses on the implementation of election campaign strategies. Chapter 8 considers the strategies and tactics used by employers in attempting to dislodge incumbent unions and the responses of unions to such efforts.

EMPLOYER PREEMPTIVE STRATEGIES

The union-avoidance efforts of employers have become increasingly focused on preemptive measures taken long before any employee interest in unionization is overtly manifested or an organizing campaign is under way. Contemporary employer preemptive strategies would appear to be shaped by distinctive managerial ideologies, which, in turn, drive operational strategies.

STRATEGY AND IDEOLOGY

Foulkes (1980, 326–330) argues that effective preemptive union-avoidance policies are typically rooted in a strong view by top management as to the relationship that ought to exist between the firm and its employees. Such managerial ideologies motivate well-articulated strategic missions that generate an integrated pattern of human resource policies. Foulkes (1980, 45–57) proceeds to draw a distinction between *philosophy-laden* and *doctrinaire* firms. The former are companies that have traditionally emphasized the centrality of the individual in the organization and constructed personnel policies accordingly. Union-avoidance objectives were not historically a principal driving force for top management in these firms, though organizational policies succeeded to that end. Conversely, top management in doctrinaire firms developed union-avoidance strategies intentionally and are committed to operating exclusively on a nonunion basis or to containing, and possibly diminishing, existing union influence.

At a more specific level, Kochan and Katz (1988, 190–194) distinguish between two general employer union-avoidance strategies: *union suppression* and *union substitution*. The former, aggressive and coercive in character, dominated employer efforts to contain unions throughout the nineteenth and early twentieth centuries. Yet "welfare capitalism" and human relations management approaches, which emerged in the 1920s, offered an apparently more effective alternative. Employers recognized that union-substitution strategies (often used in conjunction with more repressive techniques as insurance) could be very potent in preventing unionization. With employers once again pursuing union-avoidance objectives with great vigor, it is little wonder these earlier union-substitution techniques have been resurrected and enhanced, with newer methods also being added to the union-avoidance repertoire. Such preemptive strategies, and the "positive labor relations" programs through which they are put in place, emphasize the structuring of sophisticated human resource management systems that provide a wide range of benefits andservices to employees (hence union substitution). Yet they also often contain suppressive elements, though such features are usually disguised.

TACTICS IN PREEMPTIVE STRATEGIES

Having characterized management ideologies and typical preemptive strategic forms, the tactics associated with the implementation of these strategies can be explored and assessed from both behavioral science and policy perspectives. A great deal has been written on the nature of preemptive strategies. Union-avoidance specialists have generated much of this work (e.g., Hughes 1976; Myers 1976). Although the cookbook approach of the union-avoidance literature tends to treat issues in a superficial manner, there is also objective work in this area. In addition to several studies produced by Kochan and his associates, the series of case studies by Foulkes (1980)

Table 6.1 EMPLOYER AND UNION TACTICS IN NONUNION SETTINGS

Tactical Objective	Employer Activities	Union Activities
Influence	Orientation programs	Off-work contacts with employees[a]
	Quality circles (especially for blue collar)	Informal workplace contacts (involving organizer and/or committee members)[a]
	MBO (especially for white-collar or professional workers)	
	Information sharing	Associate membership programs[b]
	Attitude surveys	Community outreach programs[b]
	Structuring of group interaction	Media campaigns[b]
	Empathetic management style	
Contextual Control	Plant location	Internal organizers[a]
	Small plant size	Development of in-plant committee[a]
	Outsourcing and use of flexible employment arrangements	Associate membership programs[b]
	Employee screening	
	Supervisor selection and training	
	Influential HRM department	
	Desirable working conditions	
	High wages, good fringes	
	Job security	
	Career advancement opportunities	
	Grievance program	
	Restrictions on workplace solicitations by union supporters	

Table 6.1 *Continued*

Monitoring	Attitude surveys	In-plant organizers
	Surveillance	Reports from in-plant committee members and union supporters
	Reports from operatives and management loyalists	
		Off-work contacts with employees
	Review of employee complaints	Employee surveys
	Review of personnel records	External data sources (financial reports, press reports, etc.)

[a]Especially in target selection strategies.
[b]Especially in target cultivation strategies.

continues to be a definitive work on the nature of positive labor relations in nonunion corporations. Thus, we have a fairly clearly defined notion of the manner in which contemporary preemptive strategies are conducted. Common employer tactics, along with those that typically compose the initial phases of union organizing strategy in nonunion settings (examined in the next section), are summarized in table 6.1.

Influence Tactics

The use of influence tactics, especially those intended to convert rather than intimidate, is the cornerstone of most positive labor relations programs. In contrast to the rather direct influence efforts encountered during election campaigns, themes and communications processes are much more subtle and complex in preemptive efforts.

Much of what goes on in these programs constitutes what has come to be known as organizational *culture building*, a process that rests on the assumption that organizational "cultures" can be contrived and orchestrated by management. An essential ingredient of culture building, exemplified by the "commitment-based" organization (Walton 1985), is presumed to be the proper design of the human resource management system (Kravetz 1988, 90–108). Compliance is secured principally through the internalization by employees of values consistent with organizational objectives, rather than by means of bureaucratic control and the manipulation of rewards and sanctions. The design of commitment-based organizations is supposed to provide employees with the opportunity to communicate concerns to management and to obtain some feedback. Management open-door policies and the use of employee attitude surveys provide means by which employee concerns can be expressed to management. Formal systems of participation, such as quality circles and related quality of work life

(QWL) programs, employee-management committees, and management by objectives (MBO), are common. Companies may also use employee orientation programs and various types of social events to establish and reinforce organizational values. The Conference Board survey data demonstrate that firms that emphasize union-avoidance objectives are more prone to utilize participative management schemes and to have implemented employee information-sharing programs (Freedman 1985, 16–20).

A crucial public policy issue in assessing the myriad techniques of influencing employees now relied upon by management is not so much whether, but rather by what means, these tactics might work. If it is true, as Walton (1985, 49) asserts, that "increased employee voice, yielding greater *mutual* influence, is a central feature of the new management model" (emphasis added), then management has responded to worker needs in a fair exchange for employee commitment. Unfortunately, serious questions have been raised in the organizational behavior literature on the validity of this presumed mechanism, with research suggesting that commitment may often be secured by means involving more in the way of manipulation and illusion than substance. Salancik and Pfeffer (1978) point to a number of ways in which techniques of this sort may secure employee commitment and compliance absent true mutuality:

1. Managers are more likely to be in a position to control the content and flow of information than employees. Thus, information-sharing and participation programs may be instruments of manipulation and cooptation as managers seek to gain employee commitment by making certain information highly salient and by deemphasizing or hiding other information. Surveys, MBO sessions, and worker-management committees may all be used in this way.[1]

2. Employees are prone to rationalize or attribute to intrinsic motives their behaviors that are not clearly justified by organizational rewards when in circumstances that are *behaviorally committing* (i.e., situations from which they cannot readily extricate themselves). Thus, employees with limited mobility options may have little choice but to come to terms with disagreeable working conditions if the opportunity costs of leaving are high. Behavioral commitment can therefore serve to generate *psychological commitment* to the organization by affecting employee perceptions and values.

3. Management can often shape patterns of interaction among employees so that certain values and perceptions are reinforced. For example, employees with prounion sentiments may be isolated

from potential converts or dispersed among groups with strongly antiunion sentiments. New employees may participate in programs that convey the firm's nonunion view and be assigned to work groups that are likely to provide further reinforcement of antiunion values and perceptions. Thus, the "social construction of reality" is a powerful tool for both building organizational commitment; as we shall see, it is also often linked to certain contextual control tactics.

These arguments do not mean that worker participation and information-sharing programs are invariably used as highly manipulative influence tactics in union-avoidance programs. However, this is a real possibility in certain circumstances. We know, for example, that commitment-generating processes can distort worker value systems (Salancik 1977), that workers can develop a sense of psychological attachment to an organization as a means of rationalizing poor extrinsic rewards (Pfeffer and Lawler 1979), and that symbolic participation in decision making can be a source of commitment and motivation even in the absence of substantive participation (Barczyk 1987). This is a disturbing possibility and one that has often been raised by those within the labor movement critical of what they see as the cooptive nature of participative management programs. The very term "culture building" evokes orwellian images. That the implementation of these programs is often accompanied by considerable gimmickry (Heckscher 1988, 101–103) serves only to reinforce this perception.

Another issue raised by the establishment of worker participation programs in nonunion settings is whether employee committees constitute "labor organizations" under the meaning of the NLRA. The employer unilaterally establishes the rules governing the activities of such committees, which can be seen as employee representatives. Moreover, the employer either appoints employee members of such committees or conducts elections for committee members. Thus, formal participation systems may give rise to allegations of employer domination of a labor organization in violation of section 8(a)(2) of the NLRA. Historically, the NLRB tended to view participative management programs in nonunion settings involving the establishment of employee committees as violations of section 8(a)(2). In recent years, however, the general trend in NLRB and court decisions seems to be toward excluding such committees from NLRA coverage, except under circumstances in which they are overtly used to undercut organizing (Schmidman and Keller 1984; Fulmer and Coleman 1984; Hogler 1984).

Contextual Control and Monitoring Tactics

Preemptive strategies involve more than measures designed to shape worker values and perceptions. A variety of contextual control tactics, both intraunit and external in focus, are utilized. With respect to external tactics, a major consideration, to the extent feasible, is contextual selection. Union-avoidance manuals often devote considerable attention to plant site selection and acquisitions policies as these relate to the potential for unionization (e.g., Kilgour 1981, 31–59), issues directly linked to broader organizational strategy. That firms are purposeful in locating facilities in settings less likely to promote unionization and pursuing marketing and production strategies that also reflect these considerations is observed by Foulkes (1980). As for the frequency of practices such as these, Porter and Murrmann (1983) found that 19 percent of the firms that they surveyed (all of which at some later point had been involved in NLRB representation elections) had purposefully situated plants in nonunion areas to reduce the likelihood of organization.[2]

Intraunit contextual control tactics associated with preemptive strategies include activities related to the design of both organizational structures and personnel policies. Limiting the size of facilities may be necessary to implement the highly interpersonal human resource management systems crucial to discerning and deflecting employee interest in unionization (Verma 1985). Staffing decisions are also of critical importance, since the values and perceptions employees bring to the workplace should affect management culture-building efforts. Pfeffer (1982, 284–293) posits that, in general, administrative control systems are strongly influenced by organizational demographics. Consequently, managers intent on avoiding unionization are apt to select employees with demographic characteristics that are associated with antiunion sentiments and also compatible with a management system devoted to union-avoidance objectives. While demographics provide a general indicator of employee union proneness, management may also seek more immediate measures by utilizing questionnaires to ascertain an applicant's attitudes and values. Grenier (1988), for example, describes in detail how one employer combined highly selective hiring standards (to filter out those with prounion sentiments) with participative management techniques to create and preserve an antiunion work culture.

Numerous employee selection criteria have been suggested by union-avoidance specialists to screen out potential union supporters and activists, a process Dougherty (1974, 44–45) characterizes as "weeding out undesirables." Of course, discriminatory hiring standards are apt to violate section 8(a)(3) of the NLRA. One such author, although acknowledging this, provides comforting reassurance to the would-be discriminator: "as a practical matter it would be difficult to identify and prove such discrimination" (Kilgour 1981, 90). He goes on to recommend that "perhaps the best advice to the nonunion company is to avoid hiring people who have been members of those unions actively organizing in its industry (99)."

Porter and Murrmann (1983) report that 29 percent of the firms in their sample used current or prior union membership as a factor in hiring decisions as a union-avoidance tactic, though none of the firms indicated that psychological tests were used for this purpose. Ten percent of the firms indicated that job applicant sex, race, or age, however, were taken into account for union-avoidance objectives (it is quite surprising that managers of any firm would have admitted to discrimination based on protected class status, even in an anonymous survey). In another study, based on data collected in the late 1960s and thus prior to the intensification of employer opposition over the past decade, Cohen and Pfeffer (1986) found that a firm's degree of unionization was negatively related to hiring selectivity. The authors attributed this finding, in part, to discriminatory employment practices linked to union-avoidance objectives. Congressional testimony (U.S. Congress 1981, 1–12) also provides considerable evidence of the extent and abuse of preemployment data collection and screening techniques to achieve union-avoidance objectives. The purposeful adoption of discriminatory selection criteria such as these, an interesting study in corporate situational ethics, speaks of a real contradiction between the stated and actual purposes of positive labor relations programs.[3]

Even though preemptive strategies may encourage employee commitment, a firm may also minimize its dependence on its work force. Automation and outsourcing have traditionally been used in this way. More recently, there has been a substantial increase in the use of flexible staffing arrangements (e.g., part-time workers, agency temporaries, contract labor, short-term hires) by U.S. firms (Pierce et al. 1989; Nye 1988). These methods are most frequently used by firms with relatively low levels of unionization (Abraham [forthcoming]). Although flexible staffing arrangements allow firms greater latitude in adapting to uncertain business conditions, their prevalence in the nonunion sector suggests this approach also serves union-avoidance objectives. Short-term hires are not likely to have much of an interest in unionizing. Moreover, depending upon the nature of the relationship, individuals working under a flexible employment arrangement may be independent contractors (and thus excluded from protection under the NLRA) or be the employees of a temporary help service that supplies them (and thus be somebody else's problem) (Nye 1988, 170-178).[4]

Supervisor selection and training are major concerns, as these individuals must frequently take the lead in implementing union-avoidance policies (Lehr and Middlebrooks 1987, 65-69). Supervisors need to have strong interpersonal skills and be persuasive in delivering the company line without estranging employees (Dougherty 1974). Perhaps more important, supervisors are seen to be the "first line of defense" in recognizing and deflecting possible organizing campaigns. They are expected to identify possible campaigns in their infancy and monitor conditions without putting the firm at risk of violating NLRA prohibitions against surveillance and interrogation.[5] Training programs often stress, as does the union-avoidance literature, various "danger signs" foretelling a possible campaign and for which supervisors ought to be on the lookout.[6] In addition to influencing and monitoring, supervisors also are quite frequently expected to enforce rules restricting organizer access to company facilities and those limiting employee organizing efforts during working hours. These must be properly enforced, again to preclude unfair labor practice charges (Kilgore 1984).

Another important structural feature is a personnel or human resources department with considerable influence. Those responsible for employee relations may be expected, within limits, to act as "employee advocates," particularly in firms with formal employee representation plans, some of which provide for third-party arbitration.[7] In addition to furnishing representation services to employees and safeguarding the integrity of the personnel system, human resource managers, in conjunction with first-line supervisors, may be responsible for the rather delicate task of screening out potential union activists and supporters, as well as covert union operatives. This can occur when hiring decisions are made by applying the screening criteria discussed above. But human resource departments also monitor conditions on an ongoing basis, identifying potential trouble spots before the situation deteriorates. Job satisfaction surveys are used for such purposes, and supervisors with poor showings in such surveys may be coached or replaced. Human resource departments may also monitor personnel records and review employee complaints to uncover potential or actual problems.[8] More onerous monitoring techniques are used in some companies, although these would hardly seem to encourage a sense of mutuality.

The most salient aspect of a positive labor relations program is the implementation of a set of personnel policies designed to preclude the need for union representation. The most common of these, which are described in various chapters of Foulkes' book, include attractive compensation packages, structured internal labor markets that provide for career advancement, and job security. A grievance procedure, which serves both to defuse employee discontent and provide feedback to management, is typically a central feature in a preemptive effort.[9] Once relatively rare in nonunion firms in the private sector, grievance systems have grown rapidly since the early 1970s. Ichniowski and Lewin (1988) report that approximately 48 percent to 50 percent of the relatively large-scale firms they surveyed now have grievance or employee complaint systems for nonunionized production, clerical, or professional employees (versus around 95 percent in the union sector). In contrast, only about 10 percent of these firms had grievance systems for nonunion employees in 1970. Yet in contrast to union grievance procedures, relatively few of the nonunion systems provide for arbitration of unresolved grievances.

Yet even though these programs may seek to provide a substitute for union representation, they have also created unanticipated problems for companies in some jurisdictions, where courts have held that provisions contained in employee handbooks may be contractually binding. Contractual obligations may also evolve without any written document, should employer statements imply certain worker rights (Forbes and Jones 1986). The resulting challenges to the "employment-at-will" doctrine, which have grown dramatically since 1980 (Hill 1987), may cause firms to be less eager to install such programs in coming years. As observed in chapter 5, attorneys acting as labor relations consultants are often concerned with drafting personnel handbooks that limit their clients' exposure to these types of suits.[10]

There is another limitation on the discretion of nonunion employers, one which derives from the provisions of the NLRA. Employees in nonunion settings enjoy some degree of protection under Section 7 of the NLRA when engaged in "concerted activities" designed to influence wages, hours, and employment conditions. Although these rights are somewhat ambiguous and subject to fluctuating court and NLRB interpretations, it has been suggested that they may become an increasingly important avenue for the exercise of employee power, especially in circumstances in which relatively well educated workers seek job rights but do not wish to unionize (Fox and Murrmann 1986). Heckscher's (1988, 177–191) notion of "associational unionism" anticipates, to some extent, such a shift in industrial relations practices. Thus, nominally nonunion employers might still be subject to many of the constraints they seek to avoid.

Positive labor relations strategies are no longer largely the province of companies with little or no union activity. As Kochan, Katz, and McKersie (1986, 47–80) observe, the current decline of American unions is also linked to increased union-avoidance efforts in firms that already have significant levels of unionization. That unionized firms are more likely to go this route is evident in the Conference Board data discussed in chapter 4. Although these companies sometimes pursue aggressive deunionization campaigns within established bargaining units, the preferred route is through establishing new, and enhancing existing, nonunion facilities. A good example of this process is found in the construction industry, where unions have experienced significant losses. As large numbers of nonunion contractors have entered the market in recent years, established union firms are now more likely to operate on a "double-breasted" basis (i.e., establish nonunion subsidiaries).

PRECAMPAIGN STRATEGIES OF UNIONS

Prodded by the recommendations of the 1985 AFL-CIO report (*The Changing Situation of Workers and Their Unions*), unions have become more aware of the need to develop and consolidate a base of support within a potential organizing target over a period of years rather than weeks or months. Significant tactics related to such efforts are summarized in table 6.1.

Union strategy prior to the initiation of a formal organizing campaign has traditionally been limited but nonetheless critical. *Target selection strategies* are geared toward identifying and developing units thought to be ripe for organizing. Once a target is chosen, the organizer must develop sufficient support within the unit to proceed to a demand for recognition. Some unions are now also experimenting with *target cultivation strategies*, which involve significantly longer-term commitments to units that are potentially, though not currently, viable sites for formal organizing drives. The objective is to activate what might be only latent support for bargaining or to ride out especially hostile management opposition.

Despite the apparent importance of target selection and target cultivation strategies, there is controversy within the labor movement as to the desirability of protracted organizing efforts in the precampaign phase. Some organizers advocate the use of the "blitz" campaign, a highly focused and rapidfire attempt to secure authorization card signatures and move quickly for an election. The approach is intended to catch management off guard, so that it does not have time to mount opposition to the organizing drive. And on the surface, at least, blitz campaigns seem to work. Data collected by the AFL-CIO (1989) indicate that unions win 55 percent of those elections in which the period between initial contact and the filing of an election petition is fifteen days or less; in contrast, the win rate is only 33 percent when the precampaign phase extends over a period of six months or more. Yet there are serious questions raised by blitz campaigns; pressure tactics seem antithetical to the purposes of the labor movement and it is unclear if those organized in this manner will be sufficiently socialized and committed to the union to remain with it in the face of a determined management deunionization attempt. Consequently, elaborate precampaign strategies are apt to continue to be an important aspect of the U/DU process.

TARGET SELECTION STRATEGIES

Organizing efforts are normally initiated either when a group of disenchanted employees approaches a union and requests assistance or when a union targets a particular unit for strategic reasons. Whatever the basis for the organizing effort, the union in question must make some initial assessment of the likelihood of winning the election and, given victory in the election, of achieving an acceptable contract at reasonable cost. Thus, unions rely heavily on monitoring and information-gathering tactics in the early stages of an organizing effort. The organizer may take a job in the firm to see if conditions warrant proceeding, though Reed (1989e) found this practice to be relatively rare. The organizer may visit employees at home or other nonwork locations (e.g., bars or cafes in which employees congregate before or after work) to discern worker feelings regarding unionization.

Once a decision has been made to proceed, the organizer will undertake more substantive contextual control tactics. The most significant of these is building an internal organizing committee, which is intended to carry out monitoring and influence objectives and to mobilize existing support. The process of selecting and developing an effective committee is complex, as the committee must include those who represent important groups within the unit and who are prepared to devote considerable effort to the organizing process (Gagala 1983, 149-153). Secrecy is a key element as the union seeks to identify or build a solid majority within the unit. Should management be alerted, preemptive measures may be instituted to derail the organizing effort and retaliation taken against union supporters. Thus, committee members must be able to maintain secrecy, and care must be taken to ensure that the organizing committee is not infiltrated by management operatives or loyalists. The AFL-CIO urges organizers to pay close attention to committee development and action, noting that unions win a substantially greater proportion of elections in which are active and broadly representative of bargaining unit employees (AFL-CIO 1989).

Customary target selection strategies are described and analyzed by Karsh (1982, 16–28), who provides case studies of both successful and unsuccessful efforts in the same company. Fulmer (1982, 62–65) also proposes a typology of the various stages of union organizing drives. The first four stages of his system—target identification, interest determination, organization development, and interest building— parallel the objectives identified here as pursued in target selection strategies.

The AFL-CIO report urges unions to improve target selection strategies by engaging in more thorough target screening and to be more discriminating in choosing the units in which organizing is undertaken. There are several issues that, in principle, ought to be considered in discerning the organizability of target units. Gagala (1983, 100–140) specifies a variety of target selection criteria and recommends that organizers develop reports on targets assessing current wages and fringe benefits, the firm's market position and ability to pay, existing working conditions, and the likelihood, given union certification, of obtaining a credible initial contract. The AFL-CIO has prepared several documents to aid organizers in the financial analysis of potential targets.[11] One approach involves the use of a checklist of target characteristics. Organizers evaluate potential sites along several dimensions; the target's scores on each of these dimensions generate a recommendation whether to continue with the effort.[12]

Historically, major union organizing drives often focused on critical sectors or market areas within a union's principal jurisdiction in order to strengthen its bargaining position. But given membership decline, organizing for its own sake has become a dominant consideration. Unions are more willing to pursue targets of opportunity, what the AFL-CIO's Charles McDonald terms "ad hoc" targeting (BNA 1985b, 104–105). Although many unions have never been hesitant to organize outside their primary jurisdictions, they are increasingly likely to follow the lead of the Teamsters in diversifying (BNA 1985b, 106).[13] Indeed, United Steelworkers president Lynn Williams has gone so far as to characterize his union's jurisdiction as "the world."[14] Target selection strategies have also been influenced by corporate campaigns and joint organizing projects (see chapter 7) that often focus on a single employer. Finally, the AFL-CIO report urges unions to be more willing to organize smaller units (where union victory rates are generally higher) and to involve the rank and file more directly in the organizing process.

TARGET CULTIVATION STRATEGIES

The AFL-CIO report stresses the need for unions to engage in target cultivation efforts. At one level, target cultivation is tied in with attempts to enhance the general image of unions through a variety of public relations initiatives. More direct efforts involve redefining the nature of union membership through substrategies such as associate membership programs.

Image Management

Organized labor's use of the media to endeavor to influence public opinion is hardly a new tactic. Douglas (1986, 17–47) traces the history of union media use in this century. She notes that public relations efforts were especially pronounced in the 1950s. The focus of those efforts, at least on the part of AFL-CIO, was to effect a positive image of the labor movement on the part of the general public and was not, for the most part, directly related to organizing (which was a low priority objective in any event). To a large extent, these programs sought to identify organized labor with symbol of Americanism and provide the labor movement with credibility as an American institution. As public opinion turned against the labor movement following the revelations of the McClellan hearings, Douglas notes that labor movement communications efforts turned inward during the 1960s and 1970s and were concentrated on influencing existing members; public relations expenditures dropped sharply, especially in the 1970s.

The rethinking of union strategy that began in the early 1980s has led to a renewed commitment by the labor movement in the public relations arena and a significant increase in union expenditures on media efforts. Several unions, as well as the AFL-CIO (through its Labor Institute of Public Affairs ([LIPA]), have initiated fairly extensive advertising programs intended both to attract new members and build public support for organized labor.[15] The ILGWU's (International Ladies' Garment Workers' Union) "look for the union label" television ads in the mid-1970s (Douglas 1986, 53–64) became the model for a series of glitzy media campaigns, often costing several hundred thousand dollars in fees to advertising agencies and television stations. Recently, LIPA has undertaken a multimillion dollar media campaign, which has the dual objectives of enhancing labor's overall image and sensitizing younger workers to the advantages of unionization.[16] As a part of this program the AFL-CIO ran a series of short spots during the 1988 Olympics featuring Hollywood personalities who promoted union membership. Designed in large part by a major New York advertising agency, the "Union, Yes" campaign seems to have been effective in at least attracting public attention.[17]

At a different level, community outreach programs sponsored by labor unions and the AFL-CIO (Craft and Extejt 1983), although not an entirely new concept, have been revitalized in some areas as a means of helping to engender a more positive public view of unions, with the hope that this will increase public support for unions and attract new members. Such programs may also provide a springboard for future organizing drives.

Despite a substantial investment in sophisticated public relations campaigns, questions have been raised about the usefulness of this approach. Craft and Abboushi (1983) examine several union public relations efforts, including media campaigns, which were undertaken during the late 1970s and early 1980s. Their general assessment is that most were piecemeal and not linked to overall strategic plans. Moreover, they argue that union leaders often have an inadequate understanding of why unions often suffer from a negative public image and are thus poorly equipped to design campaigns that address the problem. Illustrating labor's difficulties in building an effective public relations initiative is the AFL-CIO's failure, after a concerted effort, to generate much interest on the part of motion picture studios and television networks in films and documentaries with labor themes.[18] The federation opened a media office in Hollywood to promote this objective, though it was closed after four years and few successes. In general, producers felt "working class" themes have little appeal to mass audiences; moreoever, federation media watchers complain that workers are increasingly portrayed in negative stereotypes.

Associate Membership

Decidedly more controversial, but also much more to the point, is the report's proposal recommending that unions institute associate membership programs, which would establish a special category of membership for employees outside of recognized bargaining units. In the post-NLRA era most unions have limited membership to employees in units where a union is recognized or an organizing campaign is actively under way. The associate membership program would allow those in nonunion settings certain membership benefits, such as group insurance, access to AFL-CIO-sponsored discounts on such things as home appliances, tires, and legal services, and low-interest, no-fee credit cards.[19]

The concept of associate membership is hardly a new idea, of course, as it harkens back to the days of unions as mutual aid societies. It is innovative now, however, in that the technique has not been used widely as an organizing device since the nineteenth century; moreover, the method is now advocated as part of a broader strategic effort to organize members, rather than as an end in itself.

Related to associate membership programs, though more removed from the union organizing process, is the establishment of labor networks and community associations, sometimes in conjunction with nonunion groups, to promote worker issues and provide limited services to members (BNA 1985b, 101). There are also examples of community or interest-group organizing efforts that grew into conventional labor organizations, though these efforts were not necessarily initiated by mainstream labor unions (e.g., Local 925, which is now part of the Service Employees). Some authors argue that to attract workers not traditionally a part of the American labor movement (such as Asians and Hispanics), community-based groups that address broader social concerns are a necessary first step to building union consciousness (Green and Tilly 1987). In general, this technique is little used, and organizers are only moderately convinced of its effectiveness (Lynn and Brister 1989).

One motivation for associate membership programs is to create an enduring union attachment on the part of employees before any campaign for recognition is initiated, thus helping to build and consolidate support. This is necessary because the period needed to establish sufficient strength to seek recognition has increased, as a result of both intensified employer resistance and worker ambivalence toward unions. In addition, organizers recognize that it may take more than a single organizing campaign to gain recognition. Although unions are likely to lose an initial representation election, the conventional wisdom of union organizers holds that the chances of victory increase in subsequent elections. Consequently, union organizing strategy seems to be increasingly viewed as a process of waiting out management, hoping that commitments made to workers by employers in

response to an initial campaign are not carried out, then using unfulfilled promises as ammunition in a subsequent campaign
(McDonald 1987). Associate membership provides a vehicle by which a
union can remain in contact with supporters, serving to maintain
their loyalty and providing a means by which organizers can keep
abreast of development within the unit between campaigns. Thus, this
approach is intended to accomplish several tactical objectives: influence, monitoring, and contextual control (by maintaining a structural
linkage to the unit).

Despite its innovative character, the associate membership program has, to date, hardly proven to be a panacea. There is resistance
within many unions to what is considered an alien concept of union
membership. Union officials seem uncomfortable with the establishment of a special class of members with unclear and potentially
significant rights to draw upon increasingly scarce resources. As a
consequence, only a handful of unions have made the constitutional
changes necessary to allow for associate membership and even fewer
have actually implemented such programs.[20] Yet organizers seem to
be increasingly receptive to this method. Although few organizers
report using it in practice, most of those surveyed by Lynn and Brister
(1989) believe associate membership potentially to be a very effective
organizing tool.

The American Federation of Teachers (AFT), which has been at
the forefront of the associate membership program, is one union that
has claimed considerable success over the past few years, particularly
in efforts centering on Texas and Louisiana.[21] The AFT used sophisticated canvassing and direct mail techniques, often seeking out those
who had been members in the past but who were currently working in
nonunion school districts. Associate membership fees are around $50
per year (versus roughly $250 per year in established units), and those
who join receive benefits such as occupational liability insurance and
access to legal assistance programs. The AFT claims to have recruited
about one thousand associate members in those states and, as a
consequence of the drive, organized three new locals. Since the AFT is
not typical of most unions, especially in that it caters to a professional
elite that forms a natural occupational community, these results may
not suggest how well the associate membership approach might work
in nonprofessional settings. And despite the program's apparent
success, there were apparently many difficulties in its implementation; cost data were not made public, so that a cost-benefit analysis is
not possible.

The manner in which associate membership programs are typically implemented is of somewhat questionable validity from a behavioral research perspective. Studies of commitment-building processes suggest that providing material inducements to encourage people to join and participate in an organization is not very effective in securing a sense of long-term attachment to and identification with that organization (Staw 1983). Individuals are most apt to develop long-term commitment if they must bear some costs that force them to engage in a process of self-justification for participating in the organization. In addition, Gordon, Philpot, Burt, Thompson, and Spiller (1980) have noted the critical role socialization processes play in union commitment, lessons unions have been quite appropriately applying in "internal organizing" programs designed to build commitment among existing members (see chapter 8). In contrast, employer preemptive strategies may be effective not so much because of the substantive benefits they provide workers but rather as a result of cooptation and socialization. Although credit cards and the like may attract individuals to unions, these organizations are going to have to develop techniques that foster an intrinsic and symbolic bonding of the individual to the union.

CHAPTER SUMMARY

This chapter has considered employer and union actions in the nonunion phase of the U/DU process. Employer strategies in nonunion settings, which most typically involve union-substitution techniques combined with a heavy dose of culture building, have been well articulated and appear to be widely used. The anecdotal evidence at least suggests that the bulk of employer union-avoidance effort now focuses on nonunion phase strategies, as opposed to campaign phase strategies, since the employer seeks to ward off election campaigns through preemptive measures.

Union target selection strategies in nonunion settings are becoming increasingly sophisticated in some unions, though it is not clear how extensive these changes are within the labor movement as a whole. Target cultivation strategies (especially the associate membership technique) are much more controversial and involve a fundamental departure from traditional union-organizing methods. Thus, unions have been slow to embrace this approach. Intensive use of the media to condition favorable public perceptions of unions may be effective, but the approach has the drawback of being indirect and quite expensive. Even though the media approach has been used now for some time, there is no hard data linking this technique to increased organizing success.

CHAPTER 7

Election Campaign Strategies

The bulk of writing and research on strategy implementation has naturally centered on the campaign phase. Although the impact of campaign strategies may be diminishing in comparison to strategies pursued in other phases of the U/DU process, the certification election remains by and large the ultimate moment of truth in relation to the ability of unions to build membership. Without changes in the law the principal vehicle for new union growth in the private sector will continue to be NLRA certification procedures, which almost always involve representation elections.[1] Thus, it is important to have a clear understanding of the strategic options available to both sides during certification campaigns, the tactics by which strategies are accomplished, and evolving strategic styles.

ELECTION TRENDS

That union victory rates in representation elections have declined dramatically provides a clear indication of the relative effectiveness of union and employer campaign strategies. Unions now win only around 45 percent of the certification elections in which they participate, compared with victory rates of 60 percent to 70 percent in the 1950s and 1960s. As Dickens and Leonard (1985) demonstrate, decreasing union organizing effectiveness (versus fluctuating economic conditions) seems to have been a major cause of union decline over the last thirty years.

This trend has been especially apparent in the 1980s. Between 1980 and 1985 union membership declined at an average rate of around six hundred thousand workers per year (Troy and Sheflin 1985). The same period saw the number of NLRB certification elections in which unions participated drop nearly in half (diagram 7.1).[2]

Diagram 7.1.   NLRB election: 1977-1988.

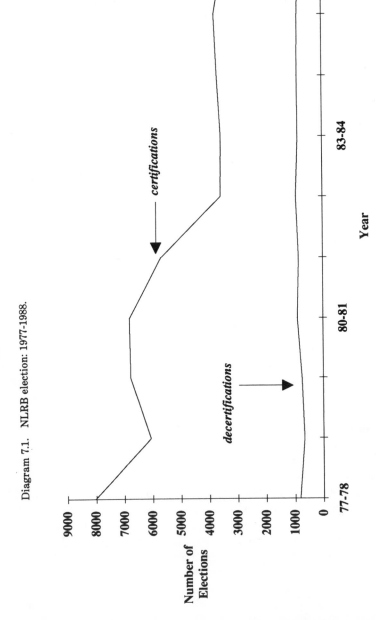

Although decertification elections remained level, this decline in certification elections meant that membership losses through decertification began to approach and, at least in 1983–1984, actually surpass gains through certification (diagram 7.2).[2] More typically over the period, net membership gain through representation elections amounted to only twenty to thirty thousand employees per year, less than 5 percent of total annual membership loss (now that membership decline appears to be abating, this figure is much larger in comparison to membership loss).

Although unions have been faring quite poorly in expanding membership through certification campaigns, this does not mean the trend is irreversible, even in the short term. The new organizing techniques promoted in the AFL-CIO report, which unions may only now be perfecting, offer the promise of enhanced union organizing effectiveness. And there has been informed speculation recently that union decline may be bottoming out, as evidenced by some recent significant victories.[3] Employers and management consultants are also less confident of the labor movement's decline and see signs of resurgence.[4]

EMPLOYER CAMPAIGNS: ELEMENTARY TACTICS

Although preemptive strategies are long-term efforts designed to create organizational climates unreceptive to unionism, employer actions undertaken during formal representation election campaigns (table 7.1) most frequently constitute stopgap measures meant to deflect immediate unionization threats. Hence, campaign strategies on the employer side are often exercises in crisis management that may not address the fundamental sources of employee disaffection.

Although employer strategies vary with circumstances specific to the bargaining unit in question, certain approaches are regularly encountered. The wide selection of management guidebooks available describing what are believed to be effective union-avoidance methods (e.g., Lehr and Middlebrooks 1987; Lawson 1977; Dougherty 1980; Dougherty 1974; Kilgour 1981; DeMaria 1980), coupled with the extensive use of consultants by employers, has generated some relatively common campaign approaches. This section explores strategic forms and elementary tactics often associated with employer campaign efforts. Later on, survey data are used to characterize employer campaign strategies in practice and compare these to what is presumed concerning the nature of employer strategy.

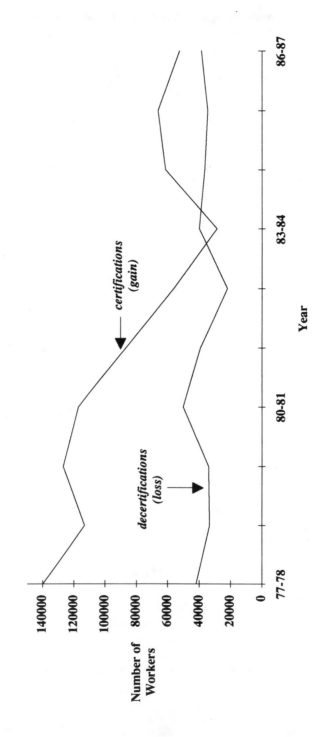

Diagram 7.2 Membership gain/loss through certification/decertification.

Table 7.1 EXAMPLES OF ELECTION CAMPAIGN TACTICS

Tactical Objective	Employer Activities	Union Activities

Influence	Captive audience speeches
	Small group and individual meetings
	Letters, posters, handbills, and other written communications
	Threats and/or inducements
	Films, slide shows
		Intraunit
		  Off-work contacts with employees
		  Leaflets, letters, posters
		  Rallies
		  In-plant committee action
		  Threats and/or inducements
		External
		  Picketing
		  Negative publicity for company or management[a]
		  Harassment or pressure tactics directed toward firm's business partners[a]

Contextual Control	External
	  Use of regulatory agency procedures
	  Election delays
	  Linkages with community institutions (banks, police, newspapers, churches, etc.)
		External
		  Use of regulatory agency procedures
		  Linkages with nonlabor community groups and institutions
		  Boycotts and other financial pressures directed against employer[a]
		  Legal or political action[a]
		  Interunion cooperation

	Intraunit
	  Supervisor training
	  Discriminatory treatment of union supporters
	  Short-term improvement in wages, working conditions
	  Establish or support employee antiunion committee
		Intraunit
		  Network building and in-plant committee development
		  Mobilization of support
		  Strikes

Table 7.1 *Continued*

	Refuse workplace access to union organizers	
	Restrictions on workplace solicitations by union supporters	
	Excelsior-list misreporting	
	Neutrality agreements	
Monitoring	Attitude surveys	Reports from in-plant committee members and union supporters
	Surveillance	
	Interrogation	
	Reports from operatives and management loyalists	Off-work contacts with employees
		Attitude surveys
		External data sources (financial reports, press reports, etc.)[a]
Direct Action	Direct recognition of union	Withdrawal from campaign

[a]As part of a corporate campaign.

STRATEGIC FORMS

As in the nonunion phase, management may, at the one extreme, assume a militantly antiunion stance, pursuing a union-suppression strategy during the election campaign. As in the nonunion phase, suppression strategies during election campaigns involve both employee coercion and aggressive efforts to block a union's ability to mobilize support. During a formal campaign, employers generally do not enjoy the leeway necessary to establish a union-substitution program. Yet in contrast to a suppression strategy, a soft-sell approach may be followed that emphasizes the positive aspects of the employment relationship, downplays the potential effectiveness of collective bargaining, and seeks to promote employee goodwill toward management (*reconciliation strategy*). But an employer may also decide not to oppose the organizing effort vigorously, thus pursuing a *neutrality strategy*. In rare instances, the employer may engage in a *cooperative strategy*, in which it provides direct or indirect assistance to a union seeking recognition (though, depending upon the nature and degree of assistance, this could violate the law). Cooperative strategies are most apt to occur in campaigns involving interunion rivalry in which the employer, accepting the inevitability of bargaining, provides assistance to the least threatening alternative. As with preemptive strategies, employers are likely, in practice, to build operational strategies that combine elements drawn from two or more of these stylized strategic forms.

Should the employer opt for a union-avoidance approach, then an important initial consideration would appear to be designating a group responsible for mounting and coordinating the campaign. Even if a consultant is retained, it is unlikely the consultant will have full responsibility for orchestrating the campaign; more often, the consultant will work through management, which coordinates and implements campaign tactics, at least those that are intraunit in character.[5] The management committee may be formed on an ad hoc basis; in companies with strong union-avoidance policies individuals from an established group within the human resource management unit, who specialize in campaign management, may be brought in to handle the situation. In any event, well-planned strategies demand that a variety of decisions be made on the structure and administration of the campaign coordinating group. Fulmer (1982, 74) discusses this as a process of mobilizing organizational talents and competencies. The union-avoidance literature devotes considerable attention to committee formation. DeMaria (1980, 94-96) likens this process to assembling a general staff for a military campaign, going so far as to recommend establishment of a "war room." Dougherty (1974, 61-62) suggests the need for a committee chaired by an individual with "sweeping authority" to make personnel policy changes. Another writer sees it as akin to political campaigning, suggesting several ways in which managers could utilize precinct-level organizational techniques in administering election campaigns.[6]

INFLUENCE TACTICS

Influence tactics play an even more central role in campaign strategies than in preemptive strategies. Although the employer may succeed in delaying the election, it still has a limited period within which to make a strong case that employees should vote against bargaining. In most instances, the employer will probably assume that it is initially at a disadvantage, since organizers typically do not petition for an election without the support of a substantial majority within the proposed unit.[7]

Information taken from the AFL-CIO field report data base (described in chapter 5) provides an indication of the frequency with which employers utilize various campaign tactics (table 7.2). Based on organizer recall and subject to bias, these data can perhaps best be interpreted as indicating dominant employer campaign tactics, rather than constituting an exhaustive enumeration of all tactics used. Overall these data indicate that employers relied upon at least one well-structured influence effort in about 90 percent of the 201 elections in the study. Most common was the "captive audience" speech, a formal presentation that bargaining unit employees are required to attend in which management (or a consultant) presents arguments on why the employees should oppose implementation of bargaining. Captive audience speeches often feature film or videotape presentations, some of which may be quite inflammatory. Unions consider the captive audience speech to be a particularly potent weapon, since organizers, in most circumstances, are not allowed corresponding access to a mass employee audience in the workplace and on company time.[8] Various forms of written communications (e.g., letters, memos, leaflets, posters) were also quite frequently employed.

In addition to captive audience speeches, managers or consultants may meet with employees on an individual or small group basis. One might expect such personal contact to be more effective in discouraging organization, since management is in a better position to structure and influence group interaction, tailor persuasive messages to the particular circumstances of the individual or group, and take advantage of commitment-building and cooptive personal influence techniques (Salancik 1977). A very important aspect of small group and individual meetings is that it allows management to communicate with employees in isolation from the social support of union backers. Yet the intensive use of supervisors and other managers in individual and small group meetings is more time consuming and costly than other forms of communication, suggesting why it is less frequently utilized than either captive audience speeches or written communications.

Grenier's (1988) case study illustrates the manner in which small group meetings, as part of a quality circle (QC) system, can be used by management to undercut union support during an ongoing campaign. Management facilitators used QC sessions as an opportunity to express management opposition to bargaining. Outside of the QC sessions managers would confront individual union supporters and

Table 7.2 RELATIVE FREQUENCIES OF COMMON EMPLOYER CAMPAIGN TACTICS (N = 201)[a]

Campaign Tactics	Frequency[b] (%)	Employees Affected[c] (%)
Influence Tactics[d]	89.1	90.2
Captive audience speeches	67.2	72.7
Individual and group meetings with employees	36.3	47.5
Written communications	69.7	76.8
Use of threats	10.4	13.7
Use of promises or inducements	4.5	3.9
Contextual Control Tactics[e]	76.6	85.1
Training of supervisors	38.3	46.6
Excelsior-list misrepresentations	9.5	19.7
Discrimination against union supporters (8(a)(3) violations	25.9	22.9
Unilateral change in wages, conditions of employment	16.9	13.8
Directed (vs. consent) election	21.4	27.1
Election delay[f]	31.3	52.3
Employee anitunion committee	6.0	7.5
Monitoring Tactics[g]	36.3	37.2
Surveillance	33.3	35.4
Interrogation	1.0	2.2
Attitude surveys	10.9	8.1

[a]This table was originally published, in a slightly different form, in Lawler and West (© Regents of the University of California, 1985). Discrepancies are the result of a slight difference in the composition of the sample.

[b]Percent of elections in which tactic was reportedly used.

[c]Proportion of all employees in election units in sample in units in which tactic was reportedly used (N = 30,548).

[d]Proportion of cases in which at least one of the following influence tactics was reportedly used.

[e]Proportion of cases in which at least one of the following contextual control tactics was reportedly used.

[e]Defined as elections in which sixty or more days elapsed between the filing of a petition and an election.

[g]Proportion of cases in which at least one of the following monitoring tactics was reportedly used.

attempt to isolate them socially within the workplace (though overt employment-related discrimination was not used).

A particularly interesting finding is that neither the use of threats nor promises or inducements were reported to be especially widespread. Given that these data were derived from union reports, we would expect, if anything, an upward bias in these numbers. Hence, direct managerial influence efforts would not appear, in the main, to be especially coercive. This is understandable, since direct intimidation represents a clear violation of the law and such overt action is typically discouraged in the union-avoidance literature. However, intimidation can also be accomplished in more subtle ways. Grenier (1988) describes ways in which managers encouraged employees to ostracize union supporters during the campaign he studied. Employees came to associate support for the union with potential status loss and social rejection. Discrimination either against union supporters (e.g., discharge) or in favor of union opponents (e.g., raises or promotions) also sends coercive messages to employees who are not themselves targets of discrimination. Although such discrimination is illegal, it is often more difficult to prove than a direct threat or inducement by an employer.

The AFL-CIO survey data provide only broad measures of the frequency of various employer campaign tactics. These numbers parallel to some extent, however, data published elsewhere. Although the categories do not correspond precisely to those used here, Porter and Murrmann (1983) report results similar in terms of the degree to which employers reportedly relied on these techniques (81 percent of the responding firms used speeches, 71 percent sent letters to employees, and 56 percent held small group meetings during the course of the election campaign). Frequencies reported by Getman, Goldberg, and Herman (1976, 85–96) with respect to employer influence tactics also reveal a similar pattern, although their data were collected through employee interviews and also are not strictly comparable to AFL-CIO field reports. Moreover, their sample of bargaining units was relatively small and rather selective. Of approximately one thousand respondents in the Getman et al. study, about 90 percent reported receiving written communications from the employer, and about 82 percent reported attending one or more company-sponsored meetings. Only 14 percent reported being personally contacted by a management representative. Work by Drotning (1965) suggests a somewhat different pattern, however, with individual employee meetings being most common, though such direct contact was much more frequent in relatively small bargaining units. The Drotning study is limited, however, in that it deals with a much earlier period and only examines union postelection objections to employer campaign conduct.[9]

In the case of influence tactics, factors such as timing, content, number of occurrences, and manner of presentation are likely to be critical if the approach is to have any effect at all. Although we do have some data on content (see below), the survey tells us little about those other characteristics. We do know that labor relations consultants frequently prepare written and verbal communications for employers, though the consultants are much less likely to present or distribute the material personally (see table 5.6). The union-avoidance literature typically stresses the unique relationship that can exist between first-line supervisors and employees, urging that employers rely heavily on the use of well-trained supervisors as communicators of management's position. In addition, newspapers or influential members of the community may urge employees to oppose bargaining. Although third parties may speak out on their own, they may also be enlisted by employers or consultants in this effort. Clergymen and respected public officials seem to be frequently used in such efforts.[10]

A variety of themes are developed by employers in influence efforts during representation election campaigns, and we might anticipate that such themes differ in the extent to which they affect outcomes. Campaign themes clearly differ in tone, from highly conciliatory to those that are hostile and consistent with union suppression. Diverse and possibly inconsistent themes may occur within a given campaign; in addition, themes may vary within a campaign depending on the target audience, the state of the campaign, and the response the employer has had to prior themes. For example, in their study of just thirty-three elections, Getman, Goldberg, and Herman (1976, 73–84) identified 35 major employer campaign themes, with an average of 30 themes being used per election. Yet, on average, respondents were able to recall only 10 percent of these themes after the election, though there was considerable variance in this figure. Several demographic and job characteristics were found to be related to respondent campaign familiarity (e.g., gender, job tenure, earnings), but the relationships differed between company and union campaign familiarity and it is difficult to discern any underlying consistency. Drotning (1965) identified a variety of themes similar to those encountered in contemporary campaigns (though with much lower frequency). He was able to relate employer reliance on certain themes to broad contextual characteristics, finding that employers were more apt to engage in intense campaigns that stressed job loss themes in regions characterized by high unemployment. Smaller employers were also found to be more likely to use themes of intimidation than larger employers.

A content analysis of the AFL-CIO organizer field reports identified several common employer campaign themes. Questions in the survey were such that organizers reported only *principal* themes, so we do not know all, or perhaps even most, of the themes actually used. Indeed, in contrast to Getman et al., only 16 themes were encountered with any regularity, with an average of 2.3 themes per election. That these themes were especially salient to organizers suggests, however, that they probably dominated the campaign and would have been the most likely of any themes developed during the campaign to have had an impact.

The themes identified in the survey have been grouped into three major categories (table 7.3).[11] *Antiunion themes* involve messages that attack the institutional credibility of the union involved in the campaign or that of unionism in general. *Procompany themes* endeavor to cast a favorable light on existing conditions and management's willingness to accommodate change in the absence of a union. *Bargaining impact themes* downplay the potential benefits of collective bargaining and emphasize its probable costs.

Although both antiunion and procompany themes were common, the major focus of most employer influence efforts appears to have been the adverse impact of collective bargaining itself, with the most common bargaining impact theme being the personal costs employees are likely to experience under bargaining (strikes, high dues, possible fines and assessments). Such emotionally charged issues (which were prevalent in 24 percent to 40 percent of the elections) would appear to be more likely to make an impression on employees, especially in the short period of a campaign, than more reasoned arguments, such as those relating to the capability of a union to achieve significantly improved conditions (observed as major themes in 5 percent to 15 percent of the elections).

At least one antiunion theme appeared in 35 percent of the elections. No single type of antiunion theme seemed to dominate, as both relatively innocuous statements (e.g., unions as controlled by outsiders) and more damning statements (e.g., unions as corrupt or radical organizations) were equally common. The relatively low frequency of procompany themes (20 percent) is in marked contrast to what we would generally expect to encounter in preemptive efforts.

Does instrum. matter? Er's seem 2 think so.

Table 7.3   RELATIVE FREQUENCIES OF COMMON EMPLOYER CAMPAIGN THEMES ($N = 201$)

Campaign Themes	Frequency[a] (%)	Employees Affected[b] (%)
Bargaining Impact Themes[c]	65.7	78.6
Strikes may occur	39.8	48.5
High union dues	33.3	40.5
Potential for fines and assessments by the union	23.9	36.0
Union cannot guarantee any changes	14.4	22.0
Possible plant closing	13.9	16.1
Bargaining may actually reduce wages, benefits, etc.	5.0	3.2
Antiunion Themes[d]	35.3	30.0
Union will interfere with good worker-management relations	6.5	5.1
Union dominated by "outsiders"	12.9	9.6
Union has failed elsewhere	6.0	3.3
Union is corrupt	9.0	8.1
Union is radical or leftist	6.0	8.8
Union will subject workers to rules	5.5	5.5
Unionism is inconsistent with employee and community values	.5	.3
Procompany Themes[e]	20.4	23.4
Management is a friend to workers	6.5	10.2
Workers already enjoy high wages and/or good working conditions	8.5	10.3
Give company another chance	8.0	4.8

Seems 2 focus on threat = undemocratic

[a]Percent of elections in which campaign theme was reportedly used.

[b]Proportion of all employees in election units in sample in units in which campaign theme was reportedly used ($N = 30,548$).

[c]Proportion of cases in which at least one of the following bargaining impact themes was reportedly used.

[d]Proportion of cases in which at least one of the following antiunion themes was reportedly used.

[e]Proportion of cases in which at least one of the following procompany themes was reportedly used.

This is hardly surprising, since such appeals are apt to have low credibility with already disenchanted workers. Moreover, the culture-building efforts that typically complement the use of such statements are difficult to effect in short periods (and under conditions of conflict). Porter and Murrmann (1983) similarly report that employers place primary emphasis on the adverse consequences of bargaining and, to a lesser extent, portray unions in a negative light. Procompany themes were found in their study to be used much less frequently than the other two.

CONTEXTUAL CONTROL TACTICS

The contextual control tactics typically applied by management in election campaigns differ from those characteristic of preemptive strategies. The latter are time consuming and long term in focus, and many involve increasing wages and improving working conditions, a potential violation of NLRB election standards given an unresolved question of recognition. Hence, employers rely most often on the use of contextual control tactics to create obstacles for the union in its effort to mobilize support. The AFL-CIO field report data revealed a range of common employer contextual control tactics (table 7.2). As with campaign themes and influence tactics, these data are based on organizer recall and are subject to bias.

External

External contextual control tactics revolve largely around the procedures of the NLRB (or relevant agency). The composition of the bargaining unit is an important consideration and employers may seek to reconfigure the unit to dilute union support. The employer may also raise other challenges to an election petition. Such preelection challenges may be costly for the union, signal management's clear opposition to bargaining both to the union and employees, and generate lengthy delays in the certification process. Challenges require preelection hearings and an NLRB determination of the issues raised. Thus, that the election is a directed (versus a consent) election is often taken as an indicator of management opposition and its use of NLRB procedures to forestall unionization (e.g., Cooke 1983). Directed elections also allow considerable leeway in postelection challenges, thus providing greater opportunity to reverse the results of an election should the union win.[12] About 20 percent of the cases in the field report sample involved directed elections, a number roughly comparable with the population as a whole.

Another important consequence of an employer's use of NLRB procedures is that election delays are created.[13] One advantage of an election delay to the employer is that it provides a cooling-off period. Successful organizing campaigns appear to require a building of momentum and solidarity among bargaining unit members that peak just about the time of the balloting. It is unlikely that an organizer will be able to sustain employee fervor at peak intensity for long periods, so there will likely be increasing attrition of support the longer the election is put off. Since employers are often surprised by election petitions, delaying the election provides an opportunity for the employer to formulate a campaign strategy, perhaps bring in a consultant, and fully implement the elements of counterorganizing efforts. Thus, it would seem that election delays generally benefit the employer and rarely the union.[14] A "delayed" election is somewhat arbitrarily defined here as one in which the period between petition filing and the holding of the election exceeded the sample mean (sixty days). About 31 percent of the elections were delayed, a figure that suggests the distribution is actually skewed toward resolving elections rapidly. This result corresponds to the findings presented by Block and Wolkinson (1986), who tend to discount the significance of delays per se in having much influence on union organizing success.

Although directed elections virtually always delay elections for several months, there may also be delays associated with consent elections. Employers rarely agree to simple consent election procedures but generally move for stipulated consent elections (Prosten 1979). In this sample only about five percent of the nondirected cases were simple consent elections; the rest were all stipulated elections. In addition to delaying elections to some extent, stipulation election procedures provide employers considerable opportunity for postelection challenges.[15]

Although the use of regulatory agency procedures may be the principal external contextual control tactic utilized by employers, other external tactics are of significance in some campaign strategies. Most notable are the linkages that employers may be able to build to diverse community institutions. The use of courts and law enforcement agencies extends back nearly two hundred years. Though the excesses associated with the labor injunction have long been curtailed, employers may bring what often amount to no more than nuisance suits against unions. For example, the employer may allege that picketers or others acting as agents of the union engaged in violent or destructive actions in connection with organizing efforts. Damages or injunctions or both may be sought in these circumstances. Local police may be used for security purposes, and there are clear instances of police harassment of organizers and union supporters (Williams 1985, 265–266). Local civic and business organizations may lend support to an employer engaged in resisting an organizing effort, and newspapers may carry stories supporting of the employer's struggle. Union supporters may be blacklisted, making it difficult for them to find jobs elsewhere or to obtain credit from local banks. Unfortunately, the AFL-CIO field reports provide little or no data on the prevalence of these methods. Although we know anecdotally and from NLRB cases that such approaches are used, they are either relatively rare or viewed as not especially significant factors by organizers.

Intraunit

The most common intraunit contextual control tactic mentioned in the AFL-CIO field reports was supervisor training, which supports a variety of tactical objectives (Dougherty 1974; Geissner 1978; DeMaria 1980, 192–211; Gagala 1983, 61–62). As we have noted, the supervisor is frequently the principal conduit for influence efforts, and the appropriate training of supervisors (along with careful selection and assignment) is a major factor in ensuring the success of such programs. Since supervisors are also a primary source of information regarding union activity and employee sentiments, training may often relate to supervisory monitoring techniques. But an assortment of other supervisory functions may be critical to the effectiveness of employer campaign strategy, so that the first-line supervisor is as central an element in the campaign stage as in the nonunion stage. Much of this entails the enforcement of rules restricting organizing activity by employees during working time and preventing external organizer access to the workplace (Dougherty 1974, 64–65; Sullivan 1978; Perras 1984; Kilgore 1984).[16] Although no-solicitation, no-distribution, and no-access rules are perfectly legal, they must be applied within NLRB (or relevant regulatory agency) guidelines in order to avoid constituting election interference or unfair labor practices (Korn 1984). Training programs often focus on acquainting supervisors with the "dos and don'ts" of rule enforcement. In addition, training sessions may be used to sell and establish supervisor commitment to the employer's union-avoidance effort, since it is by no means a foregone conclusion that supervisors will oppose unionization.[17]

Most of the other commonly reported intraunit contextual control tactics are, or border upon being, unfair labor practices or violations of NLRB campaign rules.[18] Unilateral changes in wages and conditions of employment are not reported all that frequently, likely a reflection of the factors mentioned above that limit the short-run effectiveness of such an approach. Employment discrimination against union activists and supporters, a violation of Section 8(a)(3) of the NLRA, is reported much more frequently. The substantial increase in discrimination cases is a major focus of union concern and widely believed to be among the most effective union-avoidance techniques available to management. The ill-fated Labor Law Reform Act (1977) would have allowed the NLRB to assess employers punitive damages in discharge cases, since the present law seems to contain few disincentives to such misconduct. Employment discrimination is another action that can serve more than a single tactical objective. As noted above, it sends a clear message to union supporters or potential supporters (what is termed a "chilling effect" in the case law), thus serving to accomplish influence objectives. More fundamentally, it can act to aid the employer in isolating and fragmenting union support. Kilgour (1981, 235–236) identifies isolation and fragmentation as major strategic thrusts in situations in which union support is relatively localized, noting other tactics useful in such an approach.

Discrimination cases have increased substantially along with the propensity of employers to oppose unionization. The number of 8(a)(3) charges filed per certification election nearly quadrupled between 1955 and 1980 and more than doubled between 1970 and 1980 (Weiler 1984). In addition, the proportion of charges found to be meritorious has increased as well (Weiler 1983). Yet the data do not suggest that employer discrimination is all that widespread; rather, it seems to be concentrated in a minority of cases, with alleged employer discrimination occurring in only about 26 percent of the elections in the AFL-CIO sample. The figure in table 7.2 refers to both employee transfers and discharges (though most were discharge cases),[19] which is roughly comparable to data on Section 8(a)(3) charges in election campaigns reported by Cooke (1985b). He found one or more discrimination charges (both meritorious and nonmeritorious) filed during the campaign phase in about 20 percent of the elections he studied. More recent election survey data reported by the AFL-CIO (1989) reports discharges of at least one union activist in 29 percent of the elections studied. While somewhat higher, this frequency of alleged discrimination is still relatively close to the other figures cited.

Another distinctly repressive tactic deemed problematic in the union literature is employer interference with the NLRB's *Excelsior* rule, which requires the employer to give an organizing union a list of the names and addresses of all bargaining unit employees after an election petition has been filed. These lists are especially critical, since firms generally enforce rules limiting workplace campaigning. If lists contain numerous inaccuracies, presumably attributable in part to employer "mistakes," then union representatives will have difficulty making home visits, a crucial feature of most union campaigns. Yet such problems were only reported by organizers in less than 10 percent of the elections. Employers on occasion also encourage formation of employee committees in opposition to bargaining. Direct support of such committees would clearly constitute an unfair labor practice, though tacit or hidden support is more likely to be used. Again, the field report data do not suggest that this is a common practice.

Certain employer contextual control tactics are consistent with cooperative or neutrality strategies. As suggested earlier, an employer is most likely to provide assistance to a union when two or more unions are vying for recognition and the employer, recognizing the inevitability of unionization, throws its support to the union thought to be less problematic. Such support is apt to be tacit in order to avoid Section 8(a)(2) charges and the appearance of a "sweetheart" arrangement. For example, an employer may support a bargaining unit favorable to the union it would prefer. Some unions have succeeded in obtaining formal neutrality agreements from employers, though frequently as a consequence of union coercion.[20]

MONITORING AND DIRECT ACTION TACTICS

Monitoring tactics in preemptive strategies are mostly intended to alert the employer to incipient or impending organizing drives. When a campaign is in full swing, monitoring tactics serve two principal objectives. First, the employer needs to assess the breadth and intensity of employee support for bargaining. Decisions regarding overall strategy during the campaign will be affected by the concentration of union support and employee commitment to the union. Indeed, the very decision whether to contest the election is apt to depend on management's reading of the union's staying power. Even if the union has obtained the signatures of 60 percent or 70 percent of the bargaining unit employees on authorization cards, management strategy is likely to be considerably different if a significant proportion of the card signers are virtual fence sitters rather than militant union adherents. It is also important to know where support for management may be concentrated, as this must be reinforced and mobilized during the campaign.

A second monitoring objective is the anticipation of union campaign actions so that management will be in position to counter union initiatives. Although union organizers and committee members are prone to maintain tight secrecy in this area, they may also purposefully spread "disinformation." Thus, monitoring techniques will probably be designed, in the ideal, to filter out noise and misleading signals.[21]

The most common monitoring technique discussed in the union-avoidance literature is the use of supervisors to report on the activities of their immediate subordinates. The "special relationship" (assuming the supervisors are not the source of the problem) means that they are likely to be more attuned to workplace conditions, have the most immediate and regular access to employees of anyone in management, and are probably best able to develop subjective estimates of union support and discern union strategy in the workplace. Other means may also be used to monitor employee union proneness and union activity, including reports from undercover security agents and bargaining unit employees loyal to management. Grenier (1988) describes one company's use of quality circle facilitators to identify union supporters during an organizing campaign. The incidents of surveillance claimed in the AFL-CIO field reports were generally linked to supervisor action (table 7.2). Other monitoring tactics were also reported, but much less frequently.[22] Polling to discern employee attitudes was indicated in about 10 percent of the cases, with direct interrogation of employees alleged in only a few cases.[23]

Employers have limited direct action options during election campaigns, the only really significant one being the ability to abandon opposition to the union and grant recognition without proceeding to the election. Though it is a more significant step than assuming a neutral posture, many of the same considerations enter into this choice as do in neutrality decisions. Voluntary recognition, which requires some showing of union majority status within the bargaining unit (usually by means of an authorization card check), has been increasingly promoted by unions in recent years, either in contract negotiations (to obtain accretion agreements covering unorganized units) or as part of a corporate campaign (see below). Consequently, voluntary recognition may assume greater importance as an option for employers in coming years.

EMPLOYER CAMPAIGNS: EMPIRICALLY DERIVED STRATEGIES

So far, we have examined the types and frequencies of various elementary tactics and themes used by employers in election campaigns. Yet strategic action involves something other than pursuing tactics in a piecemeal fashion. Tactics are assumed to be purposefully assembled to create an interlinked set of activities that define the strategic program. Granted, strategy formulation may not always be an objectively rational process. Nonetheless, strategy as a whole, rather than its individual components, may be most relevant in affecting U/DU outcomes, since some tactics may be mutually reinforcing but others may conflict. The objective here is to use the AFL-CIO data to characterize underlying employer strategies as reflected in campaign activities.

SUBSTRATEGIES

Strategies and substrategies can be operationally measured as groups of interrelated tactics (chapter 2). Broadening this definition a bit to include campaign themes and attorney or consultant involvement,[24] it should be possible, given a large number of election campaigns, to identify activity clusters that reflect strategic postures. As described in Appendix A, hierarchical cluster analysis was used to derive such a set of activity clusters from the sample of elections in the AFL-CIO field report data base. Once these clusters were identified, discriminant analysis was used to discern which campaign activities contributed most to differentiating these clusters. Three significant discriminant functions (derived in a manner similar to factor analysis) were extracted. These functions are linear combinations of the campaign activities used in the cluster analysis; the functions are formed so as to differentiate optimally among the clusters. The discriminant functions thus define a reduced space within which the activity clusters are positioned. Each function can be interpreted as an indicator of a given employer's degree of utilization of a particular empirically derived substrategy.[25] Varimax-rotated discriminant function coefficients are reported in table 7.4.

Although the discriminant function coefficients are not tested for statistical significance, their relative values can be used to characterize the substrategies reflected in these functions. Given these results, the three discriminant functions were defined in the following manner:

Vigilance (Function 1)

Firms that are high on the vigilance dimension rely heavily on monitoring tactics and supervisor training. There is also a greater tendency to use management consultants as campaign advisers and individual or group meetings. This approach would appear to equip

Table 7.4 DISCRIMINANT FUNCTION COEFFICIENTS FOR EMPLOYER STRATEGIC PROPENSITIES (N = 177)

Campaign Activity	Function Number[a]		
	1	2	3
Influence Tactics			
Captive audience speeches	.05	−.07	−.28
Individual and group meetings with employees	**.33**	**−.42**	.00
Written communications	−.07	−.18	−.21
Use of threats	.00	.04	.28
Use of promises or inducements	.00	.04	.07
Contextual Control Tactics			
Training of supervisors	**.52**	.18	.14
Excelsior-list misrepresentations	−.04	.09	**.49**
Discrimination against union supporters (8(a)(3) violations)	.04	.03	**.41**
Unilateral change in wages, conditions of employment	−.04	−.12	.13
Directed (vs. consent) election	.14	.09	**.32**
Election delay	−.01	**.87**	.02
Employee antiunion committee	.12	−.10	**.27**
Monitoring Tactics			
Surveillance	**.54**	−.17	.14
Attitude surveys	**.47**	−.24	−.10
Campaign Themes			
Bargaining impact themes	**.24**	.06	−.16
Antiunion themes	**.21**	−.02	.01
Procompany themes	−.05	.09	**.32**
Labor Relations Consultants			
Management consultant	**.32**	−.05	.29
Attorney as campaign adviser	.02	**.40**	−.01

[a]Coefficients in bold exert the strongest impact and are used to define the function.

the employer with the capability of identifying pockets of union support among employees and then applying intensive influence techniques (meetings or supervisor action or both) to endeavor to convince employees of the adverse impact of bargaining and the negative characteristics of unions (given the coefficients associated with those themes).

Legal Maneuvering/Influence (Function 2)

This factor is bipolar, indicating employers make trade-offs between external contextual control efforts (especially election delays) and monitoring or influence efforts. Firms at the positive end of the scale are more apt to use an attorney as a campaign adviser. Those at the negative end are likely to avoid attorneys and delaying tactics, but use an assortment of tactics similar to firms high on the vigilance dimension.

Suppression (Function 3)

Firms that are positive in this factor tend to engage in aggressive and often illegal activities (threats, discrimination, promotion of antiunion committees, *Excelsior*-list violations). Suppression is somewhat bipolar, with firms at the negative end of the scale more likely to favor captive audience speeches and written communications, and tending to avoid highly aggressive techniques.

GENERAL STRATEGIES

Substrategies can be combined in various ways to implement general campaign strategies. That is, one campaign strategy could be high on suppression and low on vigilance, but another might be high on both. The activity clusters, which were identified in the cluster analysis and used to derive the discriminant functions, represent general strategies. Thus, each of the 177 cases is assigned to a cluster containing other campaigns in which employers pursued relatively similar strategies. These clusters are positioned in the three-dimensional substrategy space (diagram 7.3), and the centroid of each group defines the clusters in terms of the extent to which empirically derived substrategies were typically utilized.[26] The scaling of these dimensions is arbitrary but can be used to define strategies in relation to one another.

The most common strategy in the sample is defined by activity cluster 1 ($N = 78$). This approach tended to be relatively low on the vigilance and suppression dimensions and in the negative end of the legal maneuvering/influence dimension. This strategy would seem to be relatively benign, emphasizing three major elementary influence tactics (large-scale meetings, individual and group meetings, and written communications) and seemingly consistent with the reconciliation stance mentioned above. Cluster 2 ($N = 39$) represents a strategy that is quite high on influence efforts, but also involves considerable use of the monitoring tactics characteristic of the vigilance dimension. Cluster 3 ($N = 39$), on the other hand, represents a

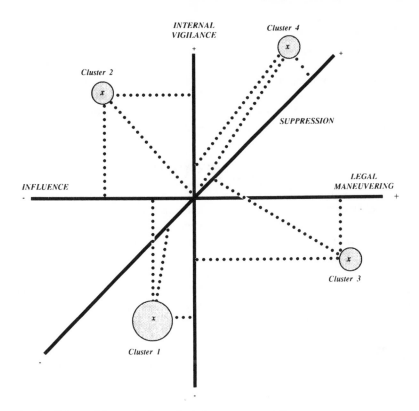

Diagram 7.3. Employer strategy clusters.

strategy that is practically devoid of influence and monitoring efforts, relying almost exclusively on election delays and, to some extent, suppression techniques. Finally, cluster 4 ($N = 21$) is positioned such as to suggest very heavy reliance on suppression techniques and little use of other techniques.

IMPLICATIONS

Discussion of employer union-avoidance strategies in election campaigns has generally distinguished between union-suppression and reconciliation strategies. Most of the cases in the sample involved employer strategies that seemingly would fall into the reconciliation category (clusters 1 and 2), and these employers were not prone to take more repressive measures. Highly suppressive strategies (cluster 4) were relatively uncommon, and the firms engaging in suppression used those types of tactics almost exclusively. Unfortunately, the field reports used focused only on employer opposition, so it was not possible to identify units in which employers pursued cooperative or neutrality strategies. Of course, if the employer agreed to voluntary recognition, no election report would be filed. Yet the very low incidence of consent elections, in both this sample and in the population of elections as a whole, would seem indicative of the limited extent to which such strategies are used.

UNION CAMPAIGN STRATEGIES:
TRADITIONAL AND NOVEL

Union campaign strategy has customarily centered on the workplace. As with strategic decision processes, some unions, prompted by the recommendations in the 1985 AFL-CIO report, are experimenting with new organizing techniques that involve activities undertaken well beyond the focal bargaining unit. In addition, there has been concern with strengthening conventional workplace strategies. This section will explore common union tactics associated with both traditional and more innovative strategies (table 7.1).

WORKPLACE STRATEGIES

Research and analyses extending back to the early 1950s provide insights into the nature of conventional union campaign strategy. In general, authors assume that there must be fundamental job dissatisfaction, rooted in actual working conditions, among a critical mass of workers. That is, dissatisfaction is, in the first instance, spontaneous and not contrived through the actions of the organizer. In addition, employees must view bargaining as having the potential for alleviating job difficulties and believe they have limited alternatives to unionism. Whatever might initially motivate worker interest in the possibility of unionization, the translation of interest into action is seen to depend ultimately on the building of a viable coalition in support of bargaining. Coalition building may take place spontaneously, especially when facilitated by a supportive technology or social climate (Strauss 1953; Dunlop 1948). More often the need arises for a professional organizer to enter the picture.

Although organizers are apt to be involved directly in efforts to convince individuals of the value of collective bargaining, an even more significant aspect of their work would seem to be coalition building and the mobilization of union adherents (Karsh 1982, 106–117; Karsh, Seidman, and Lilienthal 1953). Coalition building and

mobilization may be accomplished by organizers positioning themselves as visible leaders and symbols of the bargaining movement. Yet
given that organizers are normally outsiders, it is more likely that
they will seek to develop, and work through, an internal leadership
cadre. Another aspect of this process is the structuring of social
interactions within the bargaining unit (both within and between
groups) that serve to propagate probargaining sentiments and foster
solidarity. Yet unions are often hampered in this process by a short-
age of staff. Roughly one-quarter of a sample of elections surveyed by
the AFL-CIO (1989) lacked a full-time organizer and an additional 30
percent had only one full-time organizer. Since personal contact
between organizers and bargaining unit employees was found to be an
important correlate of union victory, the implications of these short-
ages are clear.

Influence Tactics

To win an election, the union must hold the attention and interest
of bargaining unit employees by maintaining the pace and momentum
of the campaign and by guarding against peaking long before the
election occurs (Gagala 1983, 190–194). Influence tactics would seem to
be vital to this process, as they are designed to reinforce the support of
current supporters as well as to attract more opponents and fence
sitters to the union cause. Workplace campaign strategies involve a
continuation of many of the activities associated with target selection
strategies, though once the organizing effort is in the open, a wider
range of tactics becomes available.

The in-plant committee continues to be the principal vehicle for
exercising influence. Reed (1989e) reports that organizers involve, on
average, about 21 percent of those in the bargaining unit in committee
activity. In addition, organizers frequently hold open meetings and
mass rallies, distribute handbills, display posters, have supporters
wear union emblems while at work, and produce written communications—all largely precluded during more secretive precampaign activities. Reed's work suggests that distributing literature, personally
contacting bargaining unit employees, and getting employees to attend organizing meetings are all important aspects of the typical
union campaign. In another study organizers report that literature
distribution, small group meetings, and visits to employee homes are
among their most effective, as well as most commonly used, tactics
(Lynn and Brister 1989). A union may also engage in picketing, though
this practice is limited by provisions of the NLRA and seemingly rare
(Reed 1985e).

Union campaign themes have generally tended to vary less than management themes, focusing on compensation, job security, poor management practices, and worker participation (Lynn and Brister 1989; Fulmer 1982, 71–73), as well as countering management arguments. Unions now appear to be giving more attention to broadening their message and soliciting input from potential members (Gilberg and Abrams 1987). In addition, unions that have been giving increased attention to organizing workers outside of labor's traditional mainstream appear to highlight issues such as employment discrimination practices (e.g., the comparable worth issue), health and safety issues (e.g., the health effects of working with video display terminals), and professionalism (Green and Tilly 1987). Some nationally prominent union officials involved in organizing downplay the importance of many of the nontraditional themes, however, noting as an example that female clerical workers are not typically attracted to unions because of feminist concerns (Hurd and McElwain 1988).

In many instances a union's principal opponent during a campaign is not management but another labor organization. Interunion competition was quite common prior to the merger of the AFL and CIO; it is now relatively uncommon in the private sector, with only about 6 percent of all NLRB representation elections involving more than one union (Dworkin and Fain 1989). There are only limited data regarding the campaign tactics and strategies unions utilize in opposition to one another during multiunion elections (Stephens and Timm 1978; Lawler and Walker 1984b).

Just as employers may rely on coercion, intimidation, and inducements during campaigns, so might unions. Some union tactics are relatively benign, such as waiving dues and initiation fees to encourage individuals to join a union that is involved in an organizing effort. Other actions may be quite harmful to the individuals involved, as when union opponents are ostracized or physically assaulted. A crucial issue is whether those committing these actions are doing so at the behest of the union or simply as a spontaneous reaction to frustration (just as intimidation by supervisors may not be the result of company policy). Much of the research on violence and aggression in labor-management relations concerns strikes, but is applicable to organizing situations as well. Thieblot and Haggard (1984), who present some data on union violence in recent years, develop a theory of union-orchestrated violence and the role violence may play in overall strategy. The study is flawed, however, in that the authors only examine violent clashes and do not compare violent and nonviolent situations. An alternative explanation of conflict and violence in labor-management relations (including U/DU efforts), which is based on the nature of human emotion and instinct, is proposed by Wheeler (1985). Wheeler does not see violence in these situations as deriving so much from purposeful union action as from the instincts and frustrations of employees.

Contextual Control Tactics

The employer remains in a dominant position in terms of ability to control the workplace context, though here again the union has more options than prior to the campaign. Organization building remains crucial and, since the organizing effort is in the open, more of this can be done in the workplace. Although employers may limit union activity in the workplace, they cannot prohibit it completely, especially when employees are on break or otherwise not actually engaged in work activities.

Perhaps most important for the union is continuing to sign up new members and mobilizing support as the election approaches. While it is arguable whether campaign influence tactics have any real impact on employee sentiments, ensuring that union adherents vote, perhaps in the face of employer intimidation, is of vital importance, especially in closely contested elections. The processes by which unions (or, for that matter, employers) mobilize support, as well as the impact of support once mobilized on election outcomes, are topics which have only been studied to a limited extent. Florkowski and Shuster (1987) relate several contextual influences to the rate at which bargaining unit employees vote in NLRB elections, although the only U/DU tactic considered is election delays. They find that delays strongly and negatively impact on participation rates. Election delays are normally an employer tactic, yet it appears as though decreased voter turnout serves to increase the probability of union election victory (Florkowski and Shuster 1987; Delaney 1981; Becker and Miller 1981). One argument for this seems to be that union supporters have greater commitment to their cause than employer supporters and thus have greater staying power. In any event, maximizing total voter turnout is not necessarily in the union's best interest; hence, it becomes all the more crucial to union victory for organizers to concentrate on identifying and mobilizing specific groups of union adherents. How this is best accomplished is a significant topic for further research.

A related issue is the nature of the linkage between voter turnout and the winning party's margin of victory. In general, voter turnout is maximized when elections are very closely contested (Block and

Roomkin 1982; Florkowski and Shuster 1987), though the proposed explanation for this is involved and not completely satisfactory. Whether this relationship has any significance for election outcomes is unclear, although it may mean that unions are at disadvantage in closely contested elections (given the relationship between voter turnout and the probability of union victory).

Unions may engage in external contextual control tactics similar to those available to management. Establishing linkages with community institutions (such as churches or other religious organizations) is a central feature of emerging union strategies (Perry 1987, 31–38). Reed (1989e) found that external coalition-building efforts took place in about 21 percent of the campaigns he studied. More important, he observed that coalition building was substantially more commonly utilized by organizers from progressive, as opposed to traditional, organizing departments (see chapter 3).

The use of procedures available under the provisions of the NLRA (or relevant legislation) has traditionally been quite important to unions, particularly the ability to reverse election results when employer conduct constitutes election interference and to obtain NLRB-ordered recognition under circumstances in which employer unfair labor practices are determined to preclude a fair election. That the NLRB has not been a particularly friendly forum for unions over the past several years means that such litigation is not now seen by unionists as a particularly viable tactic in private sector campaigns. Reliance on NLRB procedures may be more beneficial, however, in cases of interunion competition. Unions may seek favorable unit determinations, challenge employer assistance to a competing union, and raise election objections to the conduct of an opposing union. Finally, organizing strikes may be called, though the use of this technique would be restricted prior to an election by the NLRA and would be more likely to be used after union victory in an election should the employer refuse to recognize the union.

Monitoring and Direct Action Tactics

As on the employer side, union monitoring efforts are concerned both with identifying support and anticipating employer actions. The network established through the in-plant committee is the principal source of information, supplemented perhaps by information provided by friendly supervisors and union supporters posing as management loyalists. One monitoring objective is apt to be determining whether, and to what extent, a consultant is involved in assisting management. In addition, knowledge of which consultant the employer has retained can aid in predicting management actions, since many consultants often develop unique core strategies that they apply with limited modification across clients. Indeed, the presence of the consultant can itself be used as a campaign issue. Monitoring tactics also serve to uncover information on the employer that can be used in campaign literature or as part of a broader corporate campaign (see below).

Just as the employer has the option to recognize the union, the union has one important direct action tactic available in connection with election campaigns. It may choose to withdraw from the race. Although a negative option, it may be advantageous when the costs of continuing the organizing effort become excessive relative to the expected benefits of victory.

NONWORKPLACE STRATEGIES

Traditional campaign strategies are increasingly being augmented by innovative strategies that reach beyond the workplace. To be sure, not all unions have adopted these techniques, and like the associate membership program they have stirred controversy and opposition from within the labor movement. Nor will nonworkplace strategies supplant organizing within bargaining units, though these approaches may transform the process by which unions gain recognition. Craft and Extejt (1983) have characterized and explored the use and impact of several of the innovative organizing techniques later endorsed in the 1985 AFL-CIO report. Most prominent of these approaches have been *corporate campaigns* and *interunion cooperation*, both of which fall into the substrategy category.

Corporate Campaigns

"Corporate campaign" is a catchall term applied to an assortment of techniques that involve targeting an employer, either directly or indirectly, for external economic or social pressure.[27] Corporate campaigns (also referred to as "comprehensive campaigns") typically consist of a combination of contextual control, influence, and monitoring tactics. Corporate campaigns are pursued not only in connection with organizing efforts; indeed, unions appear to be more likely to resort to this technique in established bargaining relationships when the employer is engaged in what is seen as a deunionization program (see chapter 8) or is especially intransigent at the bargaining table. Nonetheless, corporate campaigns have a clear and potentially quite significant role to play in union organizing efforts.

The essence of the corporate campaign is that, for the most part, it neither involves bargaining unit employees nor is intended to have a direct impact on their support for bargaining. Rather, corporate campaigns are undertaken to provide leverage in support of workplace strategies. This method, then, encompasses some venerable union techniques (e.g., consumer boycotts), along with newer approaches originally crafted by social activists in other settings, such as the civil rights and antiwar movements. Unlike traditional boycotts, which rely primarily on a single method, corporate campaigns typically employ a multiplicity of devices, applied either concurrently or in sequence and with a high degree of integration (Harbrant 1987).

Craft and Extejt (1983) identify four techniques that have come to be the hallmarks of contemporary corporate campaigns: (a) pressure and harassment directed at a firm's business associates,[28] (b) confrontation with owners and management (often within the context of a shareholders' meeting as a means of embarrassing management),[29] (c) financial pressure, most often through selective investment of union or pension funds,[30] and (d) direct boycotts of the target firm.[31] In addition, unions may seek out information regarding a firm's business practices that may create adverse publicity or be legally compromising if disclosed, parlaying this into employer cooperation.[32] Another approach entails attempts to secure government action, such as disallowing federal or state contracts to an employer with a history of antiunion activity.[33] Unions may initiate suits against recalcitrant employers or encourage investigations of a target firm by regulatory agencies.

Corporate campaigns clearly rely heavily on monitoring tactics to obtain needed information (Harbrant 1987), and units of the AFL-CIO have published several guides to securing business data.[34] Corporate campaigns also involve contextual control tactics (i.e., boycotts, litigation, and financial and legislative pressure) and influence tactics (i.e., harassment, confrontation, and public relations efforts) directed toward the employer and its business associates. Perry (1987, 20–102) provides a much more detailed accounting of these and related activities commonly associated with corporate campaigns.

The model for the corporate campaign has come to be the successful effort directed by Ray Rogers against J. P. Stevens in the late 1970s (Douglas 1986, 199–258). As with other highly visible organizing drives, such as those conducted early by the United Farm Workers in California, a national boycott was initiated. A variety of nontraditional tactics were also directed against Stevens, however, clearly differentiating this effort from a conventional boycott. Following on the success of the Stevens campaign, the Food and Beverage Trades Department of the AFL-CIO (now Food and Allied Service Trades [FAST]) began promoting corporate campaigns in organizing drives.[35] Some national unions independently endorsed the corporate campaign approach in planning documents or goal statements;[36] this was then followed by the highlighting of the corporate campaign as an organizing technique in the 1985 AFL-CIO report. As an outgrowth of the report recommendations, the federation has established the Office of Comprehensive Organizing Strategies and Tactics (COST) to assist affiliates in mounting corporate campaigns.[37] In addition to FAST, the Industrial Union Department of the AFL-CIO and several national unions have staff skilled in conducting corporate campaigns (Mishel 1985).[38]

There have been several major corporate campaigns since 1980 (Perry 1987), with one involving Beverly Enterprises (a major nursing home chain) probably being the most extensive and successful of those specifically directed toward organizing new units. Yet the corporate campaign technique continues to be quite controversial within the labor movement, as evidenced by reactions to Rogers's involvement in the strike by United Food and Commercial Workers (UFCW) Local P-9 against Hormel's Austin, Minnesota plant.[39] Others have noted the limitations of the approach (Mishel 1985), and questions have been raised regarding the legality of certain aspects of the corporate campaign (Perry 1987, 5). Moreover, empirical data suggest that many of the tactics normally associated with corporate campaigns (e.g., picketing of stockholder meetings, pension fund disinvestment, consumer boycotts) are utilized in only a small fraction of representation campaigns (Reed 1985e), with what Reed defines as "progressive" unions apparently more likely to use these techniques than "traditional" unions. In contrast, a sample of organizers surveyed by Lynn and Brister (1989) report a seemingly greater propensity to utilize this technique, though these organizers are also somewhat ambivalent as to the usefulness of the method.

In addition to the reluctance of many unions to undertake corporate campaigns, employers would now appear to be building affirmative defenses to counteract corporate campaigns, which may serve to discourage use of the technique even further. One effective employer approach seems to be simply to "stonewall," thus avoiding appearing to be on the defensive or complicating the issue by engaging the union in a public debate.[40] In contrast, the Associated Builders and Contractors (ABC), the group of nonunion construction firms that promotes the "merit shop," has developed a sophisticated national program (the

"Anti-Intimidation Campaign") that relies upon many of the same public relations and political or legal action techniques central to corporate campaigns.[41]

The AFL-CIO report (p. 21) envisions corporate campaigns in new organizing efforts primarily as vehicles for obtaining neutrality agreements from employers before elections. This was essentially what happened as a result of the Beverly campaign (Perry 1987, 135–144). In another case the Adolph Coors Company, following a lengthy federation-sponsored boycott, signed a formal neutrality agreement with the AFL-CIO in 1987. Among other things this agreement specifically required that ensuing representation elections be conducted under the auspices of an agency other than the NLRB.[42] Yet there are those who advocate the use of corporate campaigns to push employers beyond neutrality agreements. Even with a neutrality agreement, winning an election may be a difficult proposition. By the time an agreement is secured, sufficient damage may have been done by the employer to preclude union victory in an ensuing election. NLRB election standards are viewed by many as stacked against organized labor. Hence, corporate campaigns may be used to circumvent election procedures altogether by pressuring an employer into granting recognition voluntarily. This avenue has been followed, for example, by the UFCW in a corporate campaign mounted against IBP, Inc., a major meat packer. The UFCW succeeded in obtaining a variety of Occupational Safety and Health Administration (OSHA) and Labor Department investigations of IBP for violations of safety and overtime pay regulations. The fines and resulting embarrassment apparently led IBP to grant direct recognition to the UFCW in one plant (and soften its bargaining stance in an already organized plant) in order to avoid future controversy.[43]

Interunion Cooperation

As resources of organized labor have dwindled, the efficient utilization of those resources that are available is of paramount importance. Yet this does not always occur. Diversification and a greater willingness by unions to organize outside of their principal jurisdictions have often generated internecine conflict as unions compete for the same workers. Conflict over organizing rights has intensified in recent years, even among AFL-CIO affiliates.[44] To lessen such problems, interunion cooperation in organizing efforts is encouraged by a number of practices advanced by the AFL-CIO, including mergers, multiunion agreements, and joint organizing efforts.

There have been several union mergers in recent years (Chaison 1986; Dunlop 1990, 45–50), a policy advocated in the AFL-CIO report, especially for smaller unions that are in decline. One AFL-CIO survey found that a substantial majority of the 130 or so unions with less than 50,000 members now support mergers, at least in principle.[45] Although many potential benefits may derive from union mergers, the consolidation of resources and an expanded base of operations have the most significant implications for organizing. In addition, these smaller unions apparently see merging as a means of protecting themselves from raids by rival unions.

Despite advantages, mergers create political difficulties within the unions involved and have not always been especially effective. Chaison (1986, 113–117) concludes that mergers, particularly those that involve the absorption of a small union by a larger union, may actually decrease new organizing. Furthermore, the rank and file may become disaffected, perhaps generating membership loss, as occurred in the wake of the Cement Workers/Boilermakers merger in 1984. Failing to nullify the merger, a dissident group within the Cement Workers formed an independent union that proceeded to win lopsided victories in a string of representation elections, pulling nearly 50% of the old Cement Workers' membership away from the Boilermakers.[46] More recently, an attempt to merge the National Union of Hospital and Health Care Employees (formerly District 1199) and the Service Employees, a move linked to the initiation of a major organizing drive in the health care industry, has been blocked by internal opposition and the intervention of AFSCME, which is also proposing to merge with the union. The conflict by and large revolved around competing political interests.[47]

Less extreme than merger are various interunion pacts and joint organizing projects. There is, of course, a "no raiding" agreement among AFL-CIO affiliates that predates the merger of the two federations. Despite this, raiding has been a concern in recent years, especially raids initiated by the Teamsters against AFL-CIO unions. Now that the Teamsters union has reaffiliated with the federation, this problem may dampen. Yet raiding among AFL-CIO unions has also generated controversy. For example, shortly after affiliating with the AFL-CIO, the National Union of Hospital and Health Care Employees (NUHHCE) became embroiled in a dispute with AFSCME over organizing rights in a relatively large unit of state employees in Ohio. Though the unit had not previously been certified, AFSCME was able to establish jurisdiction under the no-raiding provisions of Article 20 of the AFL-CIO charter.[48] The NUHHCE persisted in its campaign, though it subsequently lost the election. The NUHHCE was ultimately placed under AFL-CIO sanctions (eliminating its own protection against raiding), and AFSCME sought $700,000 in damages from the union.[49] The union was later barred from participating in a multiunion campaign to organize Blue Cross/Blue Shield employees.[50]

A more frequent problem is interunion competition in unorganized units in which the no-raiding pact does not apply. This has led recently to adoption of a new accord among AFL-CIO affiliates that, like the Article 20 procedures, provides for mediation and arbitration of disputes over organizing rights when two or more unions seek to represent the same group of workers (Dunlop 1990, 59–60).[51] If certain conditions are met, then one of the unions may be given sole jurisdiction over the unit for a period of at least one year.[52] For example, shortly after reaffiliating with the AFL-CIO, the Teamsters Union was awarded organizing rights at the Coors brewery as the result of an arbitration of its dispute with the Machinists (which had originally been awarded such rights).[53]

Beyond reducing current interunion competition, the federation's Organizing Responsibilities Procedures system would seem vital should target cultivation strategies become widespread. A union committing considerable resources over a long period to organizing a particular unit would want to be assured that it would not be undercut at the last minute by an opportunistic competitor. Yet the plan is not without its drawbacks. In his decision in the first case brought under the accord, Douglas Fraser expressed concern that since these situations involve ongoing organizing efforts, dispute resolution procedures may unintentionally aid the employer by disclosing organizing plans and strategies.[54]

The most significant move in the direction of promoting interunion cooperation has been the AFL-CIO's encouragement of, and assistance in conducting, coordinated multiunion organizing drives. As with some of the other approaches unions are now pursuing, it is not that this technique is unprecedented, but rather that it is now assigned much higher priority than in the past. For example, the AFL-CIO's Industrial Union Department has conducted major multiunion organizing efforts in the South for decades (Gagala 1983, 287), and another program, credited with organizing 400,000 workers, began in the Los Angeles area in 1963 (Kistler 1984). But the AFL-CIO report highlighted joint organizing efforts as an innovative technique that should be given greater attention by unions.

There have been several highly publicized joint efforts in recent years. Many have been regional in focus, such as the flagship Houston Organizing Project, which involved some thirty unions, primarily in construction.[55] Others, such as the Beverly and recently inaugurated Blue Cross/Blue Shield campaigns, have centered on a particular employer. Industry-specific campaigns include a number of efforts in the semiconductor and computer industries.[56] Perhaps most intriguing of all joint efforts, and unquestionably the most heroic, is a program initiated by an international consortium of unions seeking to organize IBM on a worldwide basis.[57]

Unfortunately for the labor movement, the record to date for cooperative campaign efforts is mixed at best. The joint campaign by the Service Employees and the United Food and Commercial Workers directed at Beverly Enterprises was, by all accounts, highly successful, with union win rates in certification elections of around 70 percent.[58] Yet the effectiveness of the Beverly effort is generally attributed to the corporate campaign that was pursued rather than the joint venture. The results of the Houston program were quite disappointing compared with expectations, though this may have resulted from the onset of depressed economic conditions in Texas that coincided with the program (BNA 1985b, 96-97). After about three years of operation, the Houston project had organized little more than 1 percent of the estimated 700,000 "organizable" workers in the Houston area.[59] The high-tech campaigns yielded no appreciable gains, and union organizing success in Atlanta actually declined to a significant extent after a joint campaign was initiated there.[60] The ambitious "Blues" campaign, directed against Blue Cross/Blue Shield, was fraught with conflict as the participating unions struggled with the issue of organizing rights.[61] No elections nor organizing successes had been registered fully two years after the program began.

On the positive side for unions, however, have been recent gains resulting from an AFL-CIO joint organizing program operated by the Industrial Union Department in several southern states. Though the union victory rate in the South for the period 1985-1987 was only about 45 percent the Cooperative Organizing Program, involving some twenty-five unions, claimed a 63 percent victory rate.[62] A significant feature of this program is that by involving organizers from so many different unions, it is possible to pick individuals for a particular situation who have the most appropriate set of skills. Hence, program coordinators may have worked out ways of handling some of the initial institutional impediments to interunion cooperation and joint action.

CHAPTER SUMMARY

This chapter has considered the manner in which both employers and unions implement election campaign strategies. Data relating to the frequency of specific tactics, particularly on the employer side, have been presented and strategic types identified.

Employer union-avoidance strategies during campaigns may be directed toward a reconciliation between workers and management and/or the suppression of union organizing efforts by means of assertive contextual control tactics designed to create obstacles for the union in mobilizing support. In either case, they are generally intense stopgap measures that do not incorporate the more subtle, culture-building features found in preemptive strategies. Empirical analysis of employer campaign strategies in practice revealed a tendency of employers to adopt either very suppressive *or* relatively benign strategies, with little intermixing of approaches.

Traditional workplace campaign strategies of unions, which are designed to secure recognition through victory in certification elections, are now being supplemented in many unions with more innovative techniques. Corporate campaigns and programs of interunion cooperation are the most visible of these new approaches, but neither is without problems and detractors.

CHAPTER 8

Deunionization Strategies and Union Countermeasures

The hardening of managerial attitudes toward unions has introduced the term "deunionization" into the industrial relations vernacular. Clearly it is not the case that employers are only now discovering that they may act to recapture the joys of a union-free world. The American Plan of the 1920s and other earlier employer offensives had just such a purpose. But following passage of the NLRA, even those employers that strenuously opposed collective bargaining during organizing campaigns tended to accept unionization—albeit only grudgingly—once a labor organization had been certified. Though the relationship might be stormy, purposeful efforts to dislodge incumbent unions were rare, especially among firms in major union sectors.

With such acceptance of unions no longer so widespread, deunionization as a strategic approach is not only tolerated within management circles but, in fact, strongly legitimized. A panoply of methods designed to return firms to nonunion status has emerged. These techniques, though related to earlier approaches, have been adapted to contemporary conditions. This chapter explores the implementation of some common deunionization techniques and the methods unions have been developing to respond to such employer initiatives.

A clear problem is a dearth of hard data regarding the extent of deunionization activity, so what is often believed to be an upward trend is rather impressionistic and may be misleading. For example, decertification election activity is often taken as a measure of deunionization activity. Yet even though decertification elections jumped markedly from the late 1940s to the late 1970s (Dworkin and Extejt 1980), the rate has been relatively flat over the last decade (see chapter 7, diagrams 7.1 and 7.2), suggesting that employer de-unionization activity may be historically high but is not now escalating. Unfortunately, decertification data provide a rather poor index of deunionization efforts, since not all—perhaps not even most—NLRB decertification elections result from employer deunionization efforts. Consequently, the actual intensity of employer deunionization activity remains somewhat obscure.

EMPLOYER DEUNIONIZATION STRATEGIES

There are several clearly defined strategies and substrategies open to employers who would seek to deunionize. As with preemptive and campaign strategies, attorneys and management consultants provide assistance to employers seeking to deunionize, and various management guides have been published (e.g., DeMaria 1982; Kilgour 1981, 304–315). Common tactics used as part of deunionization efforts are listed in table 8.1.

Table 8.1 EXAMPLES OF DEUNIONIZATION TACTICS AND UNION RESPONSES

Tactical Objective	Employer Activities	Union Activities
Influence	Speeches, distribution of literature, meetings, and related techniques (see table 7.1)[a]	Leafletting, letters, posters, rallies, meetings, and related techniques (see table 7.1)[b]
		Picketing
		Negative publicity for company or management and related techniques (see table 7.1)[c]
Contextual Control	"Hard" bargaining[d]	External
	Surface bargaining[d]	Boycotts and other financial pressures directed against employer[c]
	Establish or support employee decertification committee	Legal or political action[c]
	Petition for decertification (RM) election	Intraunit
	Utilize strike replacements	Strikes
	Lockouts	Establishment of internal "solidarity" committee[e]

Table 8.1 *Continued*

		Slowdowns[e]
		Sick-outs[e]
		Working to rule[e]
		Overloading grievance system[e]
Monitoring	Attitude surveys	Attitude surveys
	Surveillance	Use of external data sources (financial reports, press reports, etc.)[f]
	Interrogation	
	Reports from operatives and management loyalists	
Direct Action	Plant closure	
	Disinvestment in unionized facilities and simultaneous expansion of nonunion facilities	
	"Double-breasted" operations	
	Plant relocation	
	Outsourcing union work	
	Voiding union contract through bankruptcy proceedings	
	Refusal to negotiate	
	Withdrawal of recognition	
	Reorganization and "alter-ego" transactions	

[a]During decertification elections (either RM or RD cases).
[b]Both in connection with decertification election campaigns and to build solidarity during in-plant campaigns and strikes.
[c]As part of corporate campaign.
[d]As part of an aggressive bargaining strategy.
[e]As part of in-plant campaign.
[f]Both in connection with corporate campaigns and in-plant strategies.

DIRECT ACTION APPROACHES

Certain deunionization methods rely primarily on direct action tactics in which the employer unilaterally severs the bargaining relationship, either abruptly or gradually. Management's opportunity to determine U/DU outcomes in this manner is probably greatest in the representation phase, though strategies of this sort may expose the firm to substantial legal risk. Deunionization strategies based on direct action tactics are potentially quite powerful (if undertaken with sufficient finesse to avoid legal complications), however, since incumbent unions can often do little to affect the process once it has begun.

Elimination of Union Jobs

Closing a union facility and relocating work to a nonunion facility is a time-honored deunionization ploy. Although "runaway" shops have traditionally been moved to southern states, it now seems that developing countries with low wages, weak labor movements, and friendly dictators are preferred as relocation sites. Two provisions of the NLRA are potentially applicable in plant relocation cases: (a) relocation may constitute discrimination (8(a)(3)), and (b) the employer may be required to negotiate over the decision to relocate (8(a)(5)) (Miscimarra 1983; Irving 1984; O'Keefe and Touhey 1984). The law is complex, and evolving standards generally seem to favor management. Critical considerations revolve around the impact of the move, employer intent, and business requirements. If an employer can construct an argument justifying the relocation decision in terms of bona fide business necessity, then it will not be held liable for violations of 8(a)(3). And even if antiunion animus is established by the NLRB, the firm can defend itself against unfair labor practice charges by demonstrating that the decision would have been warranted on grounds of business necessity absent antiunion animus. The employer may still have to negotiate to impasse the decision to relocate but only if the move does not represent a major shift in the character of the organization.[1]

There are some close relatives to plant relocation that can also achieve deunionization objectives. A unionized facility may simply be closed (without relocation of the work to another facility) in order for the company to avoid dealing with the union. Under the *Darlington Mills* doctrine,[2] this is permissible only if the company goes completely out of business. If not, then the issue may be raised as to whether the facility was closed to create a "chilling effect" on union organizing in the firm's other facilities, thus violating section 8(a)(3). Subcontracting and outsourcing have received considerable attention in recent years; automation also may serve as a means of reducing work force requirements. None of these approaches strictly constitute deunionization in the sense that the bargaining relationship is severed for the unit, but the effect is as if the employer lopped off a part of the bargaining unit. These practices are also constrained by standards similar to those that apply to relocation, but, again, firms using these techniques are generally able to mount defenses based on business necessity.

Another means of deunionization through the elimination of union jobs is related to plant relocation but is effected through a longer-term process of simultaneously expanding nonunion facilities while allowing unionized facilities to decline. This approach is characteristic of firms in which unions are long established and management wishes to avoid an abrupt split. As described by Kochan, Katz, and McKersie (1986, 66–75), firms open parallel nonunion facilities, where capital improvements are concentrated and positive labor relations programs implemented. The flip side of developing nonunion "greenfield" sites is likely to be disinvestment, either rapid or gradual, in unionized facilities, as work shifts to the nonunion plants. In the long term this results in a lessened dependence of the firm on organized workers and sets the stage for phasing out increasingly inefficient unionized facilities.

Verma (1985) presents case studies illustrating both rapid and slow disinvestment processes that he argues are linked to union-avoidance objectives. He suggests a number of characteristics of firms most likely to pursue such a course of action (e.g., ingrained union-avoidance cultures, the necessary human resource management expertise to institute positive employee relations programs in the new plants, multiple unions with little coordinated bargaining). These properties are hypothetical, however, and not empirically tested in his study.

Yet another method involves the redefinition of bargaining unit jobs to remove them from coverage under the NLRA. Gale (1981) provides a detailed case analysis of the implementation of a cab-leasing system by Chicago taxi companies. As a consequence of that action, drivers were no longer direct employees of the taxi firms but independent contractors and thus exempt from the NLRA. The existing bargaining relationship with the Seafarers' Union was terminated, a move ultimately sustained in the federal courts. Although many issues entered into the decision of the cab companies to go the leasing route, Gale (1981, 131–132) suggests union-avoidance objectives, although not strongly articulated by management, were still present and an important motivator.

Attempts by employers to deunionize through plant closings, relocations, and other techniques that result in substantial job losses for organized workers may be inhibited by legislation passed in 1988 requiring advance notification to employees and unions of plant closings and major layoffs (Worker Adjustment and Retraining Notification Act [WARN]). Although earlier versions of the law would have required employers to engage in "good faith" consultation with unions and local government, the version ultimately adopted requires only a sixty-day notice in case of either a plant closing or "mass" layoffs (Susser 1988).

Although WARN was intended primarily to lessen the impact of economic restructuring on areas such as the "rust belt," the law could have significant implications for deunionization activity. The sixty-day notice provides an opportunity for unions to mount an offensive against a closing or relocation[3] and perhaps develop a case that the action is motivated by antiunion animus rather than by business considerations. Management argues against the notification requirement in that it could serve to hamper delicate negotiations if the potential action were made public. Moreover, sixty days is seen as an inordinately long period that may also preclude certain deals from going through. But unionists say that it is not the art of the deal that causes employers to maintain silence in these situations so much as it is the desire to catch the union off guard and rapidly effect a closing or relocation. At this point, however, it is too early to tell to what extent the law will have an effect or whether the Bush administration will vigorously enforce it. The law is replete with ambiguities, and considerable litigation is expected. Indeed, the AFL-CIO has expressed concern that lax enforcement could result in "abusive notice," in which employers might circumvent NLRB provisions regarding threats during election campaigns or negotiations by filing sham closure notices.[4]

Nonrecognition

Another direct action approach an employer may pursue is to deny or withdraw recognition of an incumbent union on the grounds that the organization does not hold majority status under the provisions of the law. Since the union almost assuredly will file unfair labor practice charges, the employer will have to justify its actions to the NLRB or federal courts or both.

In a newly established bargaining unit an employer may refuse to recognize the certified union and refuse to engage in negotiations. Although on the surface a per se violation of 8(a)(5) of the NLRA, this approach is often used to gain access to the courts to review NLRB certification decisions. Unlike unfair labor practice cases, representation cases cannot be directly appealed to federal courts, so that an employer who objects to the bargaining unit determination or other NLRB decisions must force an unfair labor practice charge (termed a *technical refusal to bargain* [Williams 1985, 20-23]). The court may then side with the employer and nullify the certification.

Even if an employer has previously recognized and bargained with the union, it may withdraw recognition if it can demonstrate a good faith belief that the union no longer represents a majority of those within the bargaining unit. In addition, the employer may file an RM with the NLRB petition, which is, in effect, an employer-initiated request for a decertification election (DeMaria 1982, 40-57). These actions, however, are not trivial matters, and the basis for the employer's beliefs and its motives in withdrawing recognition or seeking decertification are subject to close NLRB scrutiny. Although data on withdrawal of recognition are not readily available, it would appear that RM petitions are relatively rare. Only slightly more than one hundred such elections took place annually between 1977 and 1981 (Lynch and Sandver 1987), in comparison to slightly less than one thousand decertification elections per year. The propensity of employers to use this option does, however, appear to be growing, as more than two hundred such elections took place in 1985, with employers winning in about 80 percent of the cases (Kilgour 1987).

Bankruptcy

A ploy that seemed to be gaining popularity in the early 1980s was the use of the Chapter 11 procedures of the federal Bankruptcy Code to abrogate labor contracts, the most notable example being the case of Continental Airlines (Curtin 1986). Although not terminating union representation, the trustee or debtor on possession could act unilaterally to change personnel policies without first negotiating such changes with the union (Chilton and Penoyer 1984). Besides undermining a union's bargaining position, organized labor saw this as a means of ultimately ushering out the union, especially given that companies seemed to be filing for Chapter 11 protection based on projected rather than actual bankruptcy.[5] For example, an employer could use Chapter 11 to terminate a contract, then take the opportunity of an ensuing strike to secure deunionization much as in the case of an aggressive bargaining strategy (see below).

Conflicts between the NLRA and the Bankruptcy Code were resolved by the Supreme Court in the *Bildisco* case in a manner generally favorable to management. Even though there were fears of a flood of deunionization efforts involving the pretext of bankruptcy, this did not occur. Under pressure from organized labor, Congress acted to change the bankruptcy law to limit the ability of employers to abrogate labor contracts without first engaging in good faith negotiations with the union and then only with court approval (Pulliam 1985). Even without changes in the code, however, it is obvious that there are many drawbacks to a financially sound firm declaring bankruptcy. For whatever reason, the bankruptcy strategy is, by and large, no longer a viable option.

Alter-Ego Transactions

Should a firm be sold, then the successor owner, although not bound by the terms of any existing contract, may be required to recognize and negotiate with an incumbent union. The successor is obligated to bargain if, after the sale, there is substantial continuity in the "employing industry" (Bernstein and Cooper 1985; Miscimarra 1983, 186–189). The NLRB has established a number of tests that are used in establishing continuity, which revolve around factors such as changes in the nature of business operations, the physical location of operations, the work force, the equipment used, and the product made.[6]

The deunionization potential inherent in the rules governing successorship has been exploited by some employers, but it is not clear how extensively this approach has been used. Of particular significance would seem to be what are known as *alter-ego transactions* (Miscimarra 1983, 181–183). Derided as the "name game" by unions, alter-ego transactions seem most likely to be used by smaller-scale firms that are either proprietorships or closely held corporations.[7] In alter-ego transactions nominal ownership of the firm changes, though neither the nature of the business nor controlling interests in the firm change appreciably.

One condition necessary for a successor to be exempt from the requirement of recognizing an incumbent union is that the original owners actually relinquish control of the business. But a number of devices exist by which owners may shift a business or corporate identity without really giving up control. Holding companies can be used or new corporate entities created; operations may terminate for a period of time then start up again at the same or a new location under a different name and with ostensibly different owners. Existing owners may sell the firm to a front but retain control over the organization by financing the nominal owner's purchase. Under those circumstances rules apply that would be similar to a plant relocation. And if the apparent ownership change is simply a ruse to avoid union representation, then the existing contract still holds and the employer is in violation of section 8(a)(5) of the NLRA and, depending upon the manner in which employees were treated, section 8(a)(3) as well. Yet as with many other aspects of contemporary labor law, the NLRB and courts have created an environment that allows management more leeway with regard to these criteria. Although voiding a bargaining relationship through a sham reorganization remains illegal, proving that a change is truly an alter-ego transaction would seem more difficult.

CONTEXTUAL CONTROL AND INFLUENCE EFFORTS

The strategies and substrategies outlined above result in deunionization through the unilateral action of management, though additional tactics may be used in support of these direct action measures. Other strategies and substrategies are multifaceted and involve efforts to shape the actions of other entities (e.g., employees, unions) and affect outcomes through the use of influence, contextual control, or monitoring tactics. Although more time consuming, these strategies and substrategies may expose the employer to less in the way of legal risk than some of the more overt direct action techniques.

Aggressive Bargaining

That a union is certified as a bargaining agent does not, of course, guarantee that it will be able to negotiate (or renegotiate) a contract. The union itself may be hampered by internal discord and negotiator inexperience. Despite good faith efforts on both sides, an agreement may never be reached because of imperfect information, mutual distrust and hostility between the union and management representatives, or other situational factors. Management may intentionally create barriers, however, that preclude meaningful bargaining as part of a deunionization strategy. The employer pursues negotiations but in such an aggressive or superficial manner as to preclude settlement (e.g., "hard" bargaining, "surface" bargaining).

If this approach is successful and renders the union ineffective, then one of the following outcomes is likely to occur: (a) the union may tire of dealing with an intransigent employer and effectively withdraws from the unit; (b) employees may tire of paying dues without obvious benefit and file a decertification petition; or (c) the employer may be able to establish a good faith basis for doubting continued union majority status after the appropriate contract or election bar has elapsed, leading to withdrawal of recognition or the filing of an RM petition. And even if, failing to oust the union, the employer ultimately signs a contract, it may do so on extremely favorable terms. Thus, the employer may have few of the burdens of a conventional bargaining relationship; moreover, "concession bargaining" may so weaken the union institutionally as to make it highly vulnerable to future deunionization efforts.

In what seems to be an increasingly common scenario, an employer either forces or takes advantage of a strike to secure deunionization (Balanoff 1985; Gagala 1983, 221–229). The employer proceeds to operate during the strike using supervisory personnel or replacements (Perry, Kramer, and Schneider 1982). The conventional wisdom of industrial relations suggests, all other things being equal, that employers have more staying power than employees (though this probably depends on various market and organizational factors). Thus, in a protracted strike in which the employer holds fast to its position, discord is apt to build among the striking employees, leading some to return to work; the employer may also hire permanent replacements for the strikers. This then sets the stage for a decertification effort (in which permanent strike replacements may vote), an RM petition, or withdrawal of recognition (DeMaria 1982, 52–57). The strategy pursued by the Reagan administration during the 1981 air controllers' strike is often cited as the definitive model for this approach (Hurd and Kriesky 1986).

The union may file unfair labor practice charges against the employer, forcing management to assume a more reasonable bargaining posture if successfully litigated.[8] Whether the union will win is another question. The NLRA only requires that each party engage in a good faith effort to reach agreement (section 8(d)). Should the process fail and an impasse be reached, then the employer is free to act unilaterally in establishing or changing personnel policies that are mandatory topics of negotiation. Although NLRB case law has generated standards of conduct that define good faith bargaining, an aggressive and assertive stance on the part of management, sometimes termed "hard bargaining," does not in and of itself constitute bad faith bargaining. A reading of the employer's intention, as with most unfair labor practice charges, is critical in determining if the law is violated. If the employer avoids revealing its deunionization intention, then it will not be found to be in violation of the NLRA. As Kilgour (1981, 307) advises his readers: "refusing to bargain or engaging in surface bargaining is illegal and will have to be done with tact and skill."

Aggressive bargaining leading to deunionization seems most common in newly established units in which the union has yet to negotiate a first contract. Although there is some question as to the reliability of estimates of success in negotiating initial contracts, there seems to be little doubt that the success rate has declined markedly over the last twenty years. Weiler (1984) reports that approximately 63 percent of all newly certified units won contracts in the late 1970s, versus around 78 percent in the late 1960s. In another study Cooke (1985) reports initial contracts negotiated in 77 percent of units newly certified in Indiana in 1979–1980. AFL-CIO data suggest that the contract attainment rate may be improving; while unions achieved first contracts in 63 percent of a sample of units surveyed in the early 1980s, units certified in elections held in 1986 and 1987 secured contracts 73 percent of the time (AFL-CIO 1989). Nonetheless, the contract attainment rate was found to be less than 40 percent in larger units (more than 150 employees), suggesting the impact to be more widespread than the overall average indicates. Whatever the figure, it is clear that unions fail to obtain initial contracts in a substantial proportion of those units in which they win certification.

Employee-Initiated Decertification

Although employers may file petitions for decertification elections (RM cases), the employer's motives and basis for its belief that the union no longer holds majority status will be subject to strong tests by the NLRB (DeMaria 1982, 43–48) and may well be rejected. In any event, RM elections, though increasing, are relatively infrequent. RD cases, which occur much more frequently, involve employee-initiated petitions for decertification. Employer involvement in employee-initiated decertification cases is a delicate matter. Although union-avoidance specialists view this as a viable option (e.g., DeMaria 1982, 58–89; Kilgour 1987), they generally urge employers to act cautiously. Union proponents, on the other hand, are apt to view the growth in decertification elections as the consequence of management intrusion (Gagala 1983, 197).

In addition to decertification elections, employees may also petition for an election to deauthorize the union from negotiating union security clauses (UD cases). Petitions and elections for UD cases are handled like RD cases, except the limited window of opportunity for RD cases created by a contract bar does not exist. Although the outcome of a deauthorization election may fall far short of the goal of deunionization, it is seen as a means of weakening the union, much as in the case of statutory restrictions on union security clauses in right-to-work states. DeMaria (1982, 8–9) suggests four principal advantages for the employer resulting from deauthorization: (a) reduction in union income from dues, (b) reduced ability of the union to socialize ("brainwash") new employees, (c) decreased control by the union over the membership through internal discipline procedures, and (d) diminished services for members. Besides weakening the union at the bargaining table, deauthorization may also set the stage for a subsequent RD petition to be filed by disgruntled employees. Despite these apparent advantages to management, UD cases are relatively few and have not grown much over the past decade; the NLRB typically conducts 120–140 deauthorization polls per year, with unions losing about 55 percent of the time.[9]

Neither employee-initiated decertification nor deauthorization can be accomplished by management through direct action tactics. For management openly to orchestrate such a move will clearly constitute an unfair labor practice. Employers may work covertly (albeit still illegally), however, to encourage employees to seek decertification or union shop deauthorization. There are several ways in which employers might involve themselves in decertification or deauthorization efforts. As observed above, an aggressive bargaining stance by the employer may generate employee frustration that leads spontaneously to a decertification effort. Many of the interpersonal influence techniques discussed in the preceding chapters may also be used to undercut employee support for established unions. As an example, the author is familiar with one instance in which an employer forced the union to go to artibration in a large number of cases, virtually all of which were won by the union. The cost of these arbitrations virtually bankrupted the local union; the employer, with the aid of a consultant, then surreptitiously encouraged members to seek decertification as a means of avoiding an assessment of several hundred dollars per member to pay the arbitration bills, a ploy that was successful.

Not all employer action in UD and RD cases is illegal. Although an employer may not instigate employee decertification (or deauthorization) campaigns, it may provide what is termed "ministerial assistance" (limited help, such as the address and phone number of the NLRB office, language that could be used on the petition, etc.) to employees who request information on undertaking a campaign, and once a campaign is under way the employer may participate as in a certification election (Lewis 1986). In a survey by Fulmer (1978) employers reported relying primarily on four tactics: the use of meetings, the use of legal consultants to advise employees of their rights, letter-writing campaigns, and improvements in working conditions. Campaign themes were generally similar to those encountered in certification campaigns. Anderson, Busman, and O'Reilly (1982) report employer influence tactics as most common, especially meetings. Others argue—usually anecdotally—that employer tactics often go considerably beyond the bounds of the law, with employers providing substantial assistance in promoting the decertification effort, possibly organizing antiunion committees. Moreover, respondents in the Anderson et al. survey cited employer tactics most frequently (47 percent) as the cause of the decertification election.

THE UNION RESPONSE

Union countermeasures to deunionization efforts have often appeared to be rather diffuse and ad hoc. It is probably true that unions were initially caught off guard by contemporary deunionization strategies. Employer deunionization and negotiation strategies may be intertwined and difficult to disentangle. When an employer takes a strong position against unionization during an organizing campaign or implements a preemptive strategy, its intentions are normally quite evident, and union representatives are likely to have a fairly clear notion as to how they ought to be responding. In contrast, employers have every reason to be secretive regarding deunionization activity, as attempts to undermine an established union are clearly illegal. Moreover, it seems that employers have often stumbled onto viable deunionization strategies quite by accident. That is, what might have begun as a very aggressive bargaining stance may have led to deunionization as the consequence of a failed strike, though this may not have been the employer's original objective.

As unions have come to understand the dynamics of deunionization attempts, their responses have become increasingly structured and well defined (table 8.1). Unionists often suggest that organizing must be viewed as an ongoing process, since employer deunionization initiatives may occur without warning. Hence, union countermeasures have naturally grown out of techniques that are also designed to respond to employer aggressiveness not related to deunionization attempts. As a consequence, union bargaining approaches are often indistinguishable from strategies and substrategies designed to avoid deunionization.

INTERNAL ORGANIZING

Gaining in popularity, *internal organizing* utilizes many of the commitment and culture-building techniques characteristic of employer preemptive strategies. Internal organizing efforts seek to reinforce member loyalty to the union and to garner the support of employees who are either apathetic or antiunion. The premise is that the union should not cease its efforts to sell itself once recognized and follows widely expressed concerns regarding the apparent estrangement of union leadership and rank-and-file members (including those contained in the AFL-CIO report [AFL-CIO 1985, 24–25]). Thus, the technique is clearly preemptive and intended to be used prior to an active deunionization effort. By bolstering rank-and-file loyalty through internal organizing, unions seek to deflect or discourage deunionization attempts early on.

Internal organizing campaigns make use of many of the union socialization techniques identified as effective by Gordon, Philpot, Burt, Thompson, and Spiller (1980). As an example, Terry (1987) indicates ways in which the Communications Workers of America (CWA) have utilized national conferences to build internal solidarity. Internal organizing efforts also tend to rely extensively on influence tactics that include considerable work on the part of union officials in communicating with, and attending to the problems of, rank-and-file members. These programs are often supplemented by attitude surveys and attempts to expand member participation in the affairs of local unions (Gagala 1983, 247–284). Since not all workers in established bargaining units are union members, internal organizing efforts may also include efforts to bring these individuals into the fold. As another aspect of its internal organizing program, CWA has established its "Local Organizing Network" with that objective in mind, as it represents some sixty thousand nonmembers.[10]

To a very large extent, internal organizing seeks to accomplish outcomes we might normally expect to occur when member interests are well represented by a union (e.g., rank-and-file loyalty, solidarity, militancy). The extensive use of influence tactics seemingly central to most internal organizing programs suggests, however, that unions may place greater emphasis on form rather than on substance. As has already been argued (see chapter 3), the organizational nature of labor unions may promote biased or distorted interpretations of reality by participants. This tendency, in turn, can be used to shape perceptions by those wishing to secure or maintain power. Thus, internal organizing may, at times, be little more than an image-management technique in which propaganda, cooptation, and manipulation are utilized to build favorable member impressions of the union and its leadership without truly increasing rank-and-file participation and influence or improving representation. To the extent this is so, then the same criticisms apply as were raised concerning the commitment-generating and culture-building techniques central to employer preemptive strategies.

The corporate campaign is an increasingly important component in union responses to perceived or actual deunionization efforts. Corporate campaigns are best viewed as substrategies, as they are virtually always undertaken as part of a broader program of action. The components of a corporate campaign, discussed in detail in chapter 7, are varied and largely external (rather than intraunit) in focus. Campaigns largely revolve around attempts to coerce management through adverse publicity, litigation, pressure directed against business associates, and related techniques. The corporate campaign serves as one alternative to striking, both as a defense against deunionization attempts and during conventional negotiations (usually in response to substantial concession demands by the employer), hence one reason for a blurring of U/DU and bargaining strategies. Strikes are seen as "passé," since employers who so desire are widely viewed by unionists as readily able to prevail in strike situations (Harbrant 1987). And as observed above, a determined employer may welcome a strike as a means of ousting an established union (Gagala 1983, 221–229).

Although employed in organizing campaigns to secure voluntary recognition or neutrality pledges on the part of an employer, corporate campaigns are often seen to be most effective in counteracting aggressive bargaining strategies by management that are designed either to frustrate initial contract negotiations or precipitate a strike with little chance of union success. A campaign directed against Litton Industries grew out of stalled contract negotiations in a newly organized unit but ultimately developed into a general attack on Litton's alleged antiunion posture (Perry 1987, 156–177). The action by the Airline Pilots and Machinists against Texas Air and its subsidiaries, which led to the filing of a $1.5 billion suit against those unions by Eastern Airlines,[11] is probably the most spectacular of recent or ongoing efforts of this type. Several other corporate campaigns, undertaken in response to threatened plant closings or employer refusals to bargain, have been pursued over the past few years, with apparent success in several cases.[12]

IN-PLANT STRATEGIES

Another alternative to the strike is what has come to be known as the "in-plant strategy." Like corporate campaigns, in-plant strategies rely on a variety of tactics. As the name implies, however, the focus of the effort is the workplace rather than external targets. Virtually all in-plant programs to date have occurred in established bargaining units in which employers either have demanded what unions felt were excessive concessions or have undertaken full-fledged deunionization efforts. Balanoff (1985, 8) explains the concept of in-plant strategies in the following way: "The in-plant strategy is based on the premise that organized, conscientious and disciplined workers can have a high degree of control over a workplace. Through a combination of work practice and concerted activity on-the-job, workers can wield control over a company's ability to run a plant the way it would like to run."

In-plant strategies are undertaken in lieu of strikes and fully implemented after a contract has expired (or an impasse has been reached in initial negotiations). Employees continue to work, minus a contract, but pursue job-related actions designed to pressure management into moderating its position (and abandoning efforts to weaken or eliminate the union). Essentially, the union takes advantage of the protection afforded to workers engaged in "concerted activities" under Section 7 of the NLRA. Concerted activities include, but are not limited to, strikes. Examples of protected concerted activity include techniques such as the slowdown and "working to rule." Contractual clauses may bar such actions, just as they normally bar strikes. Absent a contract, however, or upon expiration of an existing contract, these restrictions no longer apply.

A significant advantage of the in-plant strategy is that workers do not, in general, lose employment while applying pressure to management. Furthermore, the employer is not able to use a strike situation to secure deunionization. Although management may lockout employees engaged in an in-plant campaign, only temporary replacements may be hired. Although unfair labor practice strikers are always entitled to reinstatement, it may be difficult to establish that a strike was occasioned by an employer's illegal efforts to deunionize. As economic strikers, union supporters could be permanently replaced. The riskiness of the in-plant campaign is clearly less than that of striking.

Nonstrike concerted activities, such as slowdowns, are often pursued spontaneously by informal work groups. In-plant strategies differ in that they involve the formally coordinated use of a variety of these methods. As with corporate campaigns, different techniques are used at different times. By varying the mix and intensity of tactics, unions seek to catch employers off guard. The level of conflict may be escalated or reduced, depending upon the employer's response.

Since in-plant strategies serve as an alternative to the strike, the methods used to ready the rank and file for such a campaign often parallel strike preparation procedures and other activities associated with conventional negotiations. Indeed, the union leadership will probably wish to keep management in the dark about its response in an impasse. In general, the effectiveness of in-plant strategies would seem to derive from the union's ability to keep management uncertain of what to expect next.

A pamphlet prepared by the Industrial Union Department (1986) of the AFL-CIO identifies the general steps and possible job actions, as well as pitfalls, associated with in-plant campaigns. Initially, campaigns revolve around team building and information acquisition. In addition, employee support for the proposed action must be consolidated. Hence, influence and monitoring tactics, as well as contextual control tactics related to team development, predominate up front. For example, formal sueveys of rank-and-file attitudes toward the employer and union may be administered, and union representative and committee members may visit employees in their homes.

Once under way, the essence of the in-plant campaign is controlling the context of employee-management relations to exert pressure on the employer to accede to the union's bargaining position. In addition to slowdowns and working to rule, concerted activities may include "sick-outs," the filing of mass grievances, and refusing overtime work (Tucker 1987). Another common ploy is to involve outside regulatory agencies (other than the NLRB) through the filing of complaints and by demands that the company comply rigidly with various government regulations. Especially significant are charges brought in regard to health and safety violations (Balanoff 1987).

The in-plant campaign is apt to be used in combination with other substrategies to define an overall strategy of resistance for the union. Maintaining membership involvement and commitment, as well as demonstrating that commitment to management, are accomplished through the actions of entities such as "solidarity committees" (Metzgar 1985) and by the use of other internal organizing techniques. Involving external agencies, such as OSHA, in the effort blurs the distinction between corporate and in-plant campaigns. Indeed, broad-spanning corporate campaigns may effectively complement in-plant strategies (Tucker 1987).

ELECTION CAMPAIGNS

Both employee-initiated and employer-initiated decertification elections (RD and RM cases, respectively) normally involve formal campaigns that are similar in character to those that take place prior to certification elections (RC cases). Unions (as well as employers) use a range of influence, contextual control, and monitoring tactics to influence election outcomes. Election campaign strategies may also be used in association with corporate campaigns, in-plant strategies, or internal organizing.

Decertification election campaign tactics would seem to be similar in many respects to those used in certification elections. Anderson, Busman, and O'Reilly (1982) report that influence tactics dominate a union's response to a decertification effort, which is consistent with findings reported by Fulmer (1978). Both studies only consider individual tactics, however, and fail to identify overarching strategies. Moreover, these data derive from surveys conducted over a decade ago and therefore may not reflect changes resulting from contemporary pressures for innovative U/DU strategies and tactics.

CONTRACTUAL PROVISIONS

In organizing campaigns, unions may secure neutrality agreements or voluntary recognition by the employer. Unions may also negotiate clauses in existing contracts ensuring employer neutrality or providing for automatic recognition in new facilities (accretion agreements). Both methods can be used to combat employer disinvestment strategies. Clauses may also be included binding successor employers to honor existing contracts and recognize the union, a practice that both lessens the probability of an employer pursuing an alter-ego successor strategy and protects the union in case the firm is acquired by another company.

CHAPTER SUMMARY

Several deunionization strategies are now being increasingly adopted by employers, most of which seem to rely principally on direct action tactics that allow the employer to sever a bargaining relationship unilaterally. When undertaken purely with the intent of eliminating an incumbent union, such activities are clearly illegal. In some instances deunionization is likely to be the outcome of managerial action conditioned by a variety of factors other than antiunion animus (e.g., changing markets, increased competition, technological change), as in the case of automation, corporate restructuring, and so forth. In other instances, such as decertification elections, deunionization appears to be linked principally to rank-and-file disaffection with the performance of the union. Yet it is equally clear that many, perhaps most, deunionization efforts are orchestrated by employers primarily for the purpose of ridding themselves of the bargaining obligation. Management's ability to do this would seem to derive from recent NLRB and court rulings that have greatly reduced the range of employer activities viewed as illegal under the NLRA.

Unions are responding to the deunionization movement, with corporate campaigns, in-plant strategies, and internal organizing being the principal innovative defenses. Unfortunately, our understanding of these techniques to date is informed almost exclusively by descriptive and anecdotal material. Detailed and objective academic research relating to the implementation, as well as impact, of such measures is very much needed. For example, researchers might want to explore factors related to the receptivity of rank-and-file union members to internal organizing methods, which could build on research concerning union commitment (Gordon, Philpot, Burt, Thompson, and Spiller (1980). However, there are serious difficulties in doing such research. Although extensively publicized, there are relatively few instances of the use of innovative defenses against deunionization efforts, at least for purposes of statistical sampling. Thus, initial research is probably going to have to be limited to in-depth case studies, along the lines of Perry's (1987) book. Another difficulty is apt to be the hesitancy of unions to cooperate in such studies, as there will probably be concern that research results could aid employers. However, unions do seem to be increasingly willing to allow academic research on U/DU activities.

CHAPTER 9

Strategic Choices and Unionization/Deunionization Outcomes

The debate continues whether management and union actions ultimately have any discernible effects on the outcomes of unionization and deunionization efforts. Several issues have been explored in the preceding chapters: possible linkages between U/DU strategies and other factors thought to have an impact on union growth and decline, the nature of U/DU strategy formulation, and strategy implementation. Yet the acid test—whether union and employer strategies and tactics matter much—is ultimately an empirical question.

There is now a rather extensive body of literature devoted to estimating and assessing the effects of U/DU strategies and tactics. Unfortunately, this research does not always provide complete or unambiguous answers. This is to be expected if the strategic choice perspective is accepted. By explicitly recognizing that both sides enjoy considerable latitude in selecting from among many options, discretionary strategies are likely to impact differentially depending upon contextual conditions. In a strategic choice framework U/DU outcomes are not the only criteria for selecting a course of action, so certain strategies may be pursued that do not optimally fit a particular setting. Perhaps more significant, strategy formulation may not always be an objectively rational process. Information may be distorted (intentionally or unintentionally), alternatives ignored, and nonoptimizing choice rules invoked. Thus, unions and employers may at times implement ineffective and even counterproductive strategies.

This chapter reviews and assesses relatively recent empirical studies that deal with the impact of strategy and tactics on U/DU outcomes. The studies cited here, which constitute a fairly exhaustive sampling of the literature since the mid-1970s, are summarized in

Appendix B. Studies are arranged according to level of analysis (individual, bargaining unit, organizational, and aggregate) and are classified both by the phase of the U/DU process and the dependent variable or variables studied. The results of some additional empirical analysis by the author are also presented in order to expand upon and clarify themes in the existing literature. A prime objective of this chapter is to state in fairly definite terms what we do—and do not—know regarding the impact of these factors. This would seem to be a particularly compelling objective since the debate concerning the causes of the decline of the labor movement often involves arguments that draw from this literature in highly selective and self-serving ways.

THE NONUNION AND REPRESENTATION PHASES

Chapters 6 and 8 discuss aspects of employer and union strategy in, respectively, the nonunion and representation phases. Although both phases seem to be of increasing importance in determining union organizational strength, there is much less empirical research dealing with the impact of strategies associated with these two phases than there is on election campaign strategy. Hence, the discussion of research related to nonunion and representation phase strategies is combined in this section, with the remainder of the chapter focused on the impact of campaign strategies.

THE NONUNION PHASE

How effective are employer preemptive strategies in nonunion settings? Unfortunately, quantitative studies on this topic are quite limited. In addition, research to date examines only the effects of employer initiatives, so we have no hard data regarding the effects of either target selection or target cultivation strategies. As the nonunion phase is rapidly becoming the principal arena in which labor and management compete for the hearts and minds of potential union members, there is clear need for more research here. This is especially true on the union side, where researchers should pay particular attention to nontraditional methods such as the associate membership program.

Kochan, McKersie, and Chalykoff (1986) use data generated in the Conference Board survey to examine the impact of the extent to which a firm utilizes innovative personnel practices in its nonunion facilities in the likelihood that nonunion employees will subsequently organize. The authors include several control variables in their analysis (e.g., market conditions, company expansion) and two principal independent variables: the number of workplace innovations in the firm's nonunion facilities and the priority attached by the firm to union-avoidance objectives.[1] In various specifications of the model, which explained 30 percent to 40 percent of union growth in the firms sampled, Kochan et al. found that both workplace innovations and a strong union-avoidance emphasis contributed substantially to reducing the chances of union organization.

The Kochan et al. study focuses on evaluating the effects of a general union-avoidance strategy rather than those of substrategies and elementary tactics. That is, an index of positive employee relations techniques is constructed that measures the intensity of employer commitment to this approach. The innovation index is somewhat limited, since it is composed exclusively of indicators of personnel policies; factors such as site and employee selection criteria and monitoring tactics are not included (though the union-avoidance emphasis variable presumably controls for this to some extent). In contrast, Fiorito, Lowman, and Nelson (1987) utilize the same data to assess the impact of specific tactics human resource management policies) on the likelihood of unions ultimately winning elections in the company and the proportion of nonunion facilities successfully organized. In both instances a variety of techniques were found to have significant independent effects, generally in the expected direction of reducing union success. Particularly strong effects were noted for the presence of participative management systems and employee communications programs, clearly indicating the effectiveness of influence tactics. Unfortunately, these data tell us little about the nature of these participation and information-sharing programs, so we are not in a position to discern whether these effects result from "true mutuality" or their potentially manipulative character.

Evansohn (1989), in a research note which leaves much to the imagination, utilizes individual level data from the 1977 Quality of Employment survey to explore arguments drawn largely for radical analyses of labor market structure (e.g., Edwards 1979). In particular, he argues that (a) union members can be differentiated from nonunion workers in that the former are subject to a greater degree of managerial bureaucratic control and (b) nonunion workers expressing the desire to remain nonunion are likewise subjected to greater control than those who wish to unionize. The definition of bureaucratic control employed in this study unfortunately intermixes notions drawn from traditional bureaucratic theory (e.g., rules, procedures, formality) with notions of management generally associated with commitment-based organizations (e.g., flexibility). In any event, his findings support the view that personnel practices similar to those described by Foulkes (1980) (e.g., rationalized reward system, high job security, employee involvement in decision making) significantly decrease employee union proneness. Yet the study rests largely on the self-reports of participants in the survey and their interpretations of organizational conditions may reflect preexisting sentiments; consequently the direction of causation is unclear.

Although results reported by Porter and Murrmann (1983) relate primarily to employer tactics during the campaign phase, some of the activities examined were undertaken long before campaigns were initiated and are really preemptive measures. Again, the small sample size that the authors report only simple correlation coefficients limit the usefulness of this study. Nonetheless, relationships are suggested that bear further study. The authors report negative correlations between union victory and the use of employee hiring criteria designed to weed out potential union supporters (especially discrimination based on past employment in a unionized setting). Close monitoring techniques, both by supervisors and personnel departments, were also found to be negatively related to union victory chances. Union-avoidance considerations in plant siting, in contrast, had only a weak effect on election outcomes. Porter and Murrmann did not consider, however, linkages between these preemptive measures and the likelihood of a campaign ever being initiated. Discouragement of campaigns is really the primary objective of preemptive strategies, and it is not clear that tactics associated with these strategies will have much of an effect on election outcomes, as the existence of a campaign implies failure of the preemptive effort.

THE REPRESENTATION PHASE

As with the nonunion phase, only a handful of empirical studies examine the impact of employer and union activities on deunionization outcomes. Moreover, this research is limited to analyses of decertification elections and contract negotiations.

In a study of union success in negotiating initial contracts, Cooke (1985a) demonstrates that employers who engage in aggressive and illegal bargaining strategies are more likely to be successful in precluding unions from obtaining a first contract. Both outright refusals to bargain and discrimination against union supporters (occurring after the election) substantially reduced the likelihood of obtaining a contract. Discrimination, however, with its potential for demoralizing the rank and file and decimating the union leadership cadre, was found to have a much stronger impact. Cooke also found post election procedural maneuvering, which served to delay certification, negatively affected the likelihood of successful contract negotiation, a finding he attributes to the erosion of union resources and rank-and-file support.

Research by Thomas Reed provides some indication of the impact of union, as well as employer, actions on contract attainment. Reed (1989c) develops a typology of general union organizing strategies, differentiating between "progressive" and "traditional" organizing departments (see chapter 3). His research links campaign phase strategy to successful contract negotiation, suggesting that progressive organizing strategies increase the likelihood of contract attainment (Reed 1989d). In another study (Reed, 1989b) he examines the impact of specific campaign tactics and organizer characteristics on contract attainment. A significant feature of that study is that Reed controls for both employer and union tactics; as with Cooke's study, employer unfair labor practices reduce the likelihood of contract negotiation. On the union side Reed links certain organizer personality characteristics to contract attainment, finding, for example, that inflexible and highly manipulative organizers are more apt to fail in securing a first contract. Another important finding of this study is that organizers who stress building coalitions with external groups during the campaign phase (characteristic of unions with "progressive" organizing departments) increase the probability of contract attainment.

In a study that relied on both case analyses and survey data, Anderson, Busman, and O'Reilly (1982) found that a variety of employer influence tactics used during decertification election campaigns (e.g., captive audience speeches, leaflets, house calls) did not increase the likelihood of decertification. To the extent management tactics have any effect, it would seem that they serve to promote the probability of union victory through some type of backfire effect. In contrast, the authors found that similar union influence tactics were somewhat effective in reducing the probability of decertification.

As discussed in chapter 7, election delays are presumed to reduce the likelihood of a union winning a certification election, since the employer is afforded additional time to resolve grievances and undercut union support. The converse argument would seem to hold for decertification elections, so we might expect to see incumbent unions seek delays to solidify their positions. Similarly, unions would seem to be likely to engage in various forms of preelection procedural maneuvering, reducing the likelihood of a consent election taking place. Neither ploy would seem to be very beneficial, however, from the union's standpoint. Dickens, Wholey, and Robinson (1987) found that agreeing to a consent election had no significant impact on prounion vote in decertification elections and that election delays significantly decreased, not increased, prounion vote.

WHAT DO WE KNOW?

Although there is a growing body of literature relating to the impact of U/DU strategies and tactics in the nonunion and representation phases, it remains rather limited. Unlike the research dealing with campaign activities reviewed below, however, which often utilize archival data collected in the 1970s, many of these studies rely on more recent data generally collected by authors through their own surveys. Consequently, there is less of a tendency for authors to substitute proxies of sometimes dubious validity for direct measures of important constructs. What, then, in our state of knowledge concerning strategic and tactical effects in these two phases of the U/DU process?

Union Effects

The published empirical findings do not allow us to draw firm conclusions about the impact of either target selection or target cultivation strategies pursued by unions in nonunion or preunion settings. Thus, claims regarding the effectiveness of methods such as associate membership programs are quite speculative and rest largely upon anecdotal evidence. This should be a very fruitful research area in coming years, as unions are increasingly emphasizing these aspects of the organizing process.

Some research relates to union actions undertaken in the representation phase to avoid deunionization. Union influence tactics apparently can make a difference in decertification elections, although those union contextual control tactics that have been studied do not appear to influence decertification election outcomes. Yet it would appear that most decertification efforts derive from intraunion politics and various contextual forces, so work in this area may not really be concerned with aggressive deunionization efforts by employers. Reed's work concerning contract attainment indicates that the personal characteristics of the chief organizer are perhaps as important as union strategies and tactics in determining whether an initial contract will be obtained. Hence, it is not only *what* unions do that matters but also *who* does it. Research is clearly lacking, however, on the impact of innovative union substrategies, such as in-plant and corporate campaigns, on deunionization outcomes.

Management Effects

As for employer deunionization strategies, it would appear that something of a backfire effect may result from aggressive decertification efforts, since increased employer activity seems to be associated with a decreased likelihood of the removal of the union.[2] It seems clear that decertification is a complex process, and although it may not infrequently be linked to employer deunionization efforts, many other factors are at work. In contrast, employer policies very much influence the ability of a certified union to consolidate its power through the successful negotiation of a first contract.

Only a few studies assess the impact of employer strategies and tactics in the nonunion phase. The studies of Kochan, McKersie, and Chalykoff (1986) and Fiorito et al. (1987), although the best developed of these, examine only certain types of positive labor relations policies and use the same data base. The Conference Board survey involved a substantial number of important companies, however, and can be treated as representative of a major sector of the American economy. The panel study design has allowed researchers to make stronger statements regarding causal order. Results to date would lead us to believe that employer preemptive strategies can substantially reduce the likelihood of unionization.

THE CAMPAIGN PHASE: WORKER ATTITUDES AND VOTING BEHAVIOR

Most of the empirical research dealing with the impact of U/DU strategies and tactics concern certification election campaign activities. Given the extent of this literature, our discussion is divided into two sections. Although the strategic choice model posited in chapter 2 focuses on bargaining unit processes and outcomes, the attitudes and decisions of individual employees are central in determining collective choice in an election campaign. Hence, this section examines the impact of U/DU strategies and tactics on individual employee support for bargaining and voting behavior in certification elections. The following section will deal with campaign effects at the bargaining unit level.

RESEARCH ON VOTING BEHAVIOR AND EMPLOYEE UNION PRONENESS

Several studies have examined behavioral factors related to employee support for collective bargaining and the proclivity of employees to vote for unionization in representation elections. Although these studies do not explore the possible effects of campaign strategy, they nonetheless provide a conceptual basis for research that does. The initial empirical work in this area was not especially sophisticated.[3] Job satisfaction measures and other variables were correlated with actual or intended vote in a representation election (or some proxy for vote). Thus, causal linkages were poorly identified and untested. Fortunately, researchers soon became more sensitive to theoretical concerns, and multivariate models of employee support for bargaining were proposed and empirically tested (e.g., Kochan 1979; Walker and Lawler 1979; Youngblood et al. 1984; Zalesny 1985). Most of these studies propose models based on the expectancy theory (e.g., Fishbein and Ajzen 1975; Brief and Rude 1981) and, taken as a whole, suggest that worker support for collective bargaining will increase with worker job dissatisfaction,[4] the perception that collective bargaining improves employment conditions (union instrumentality), the degree of social supportiveness for bargaining, and the extent to which employees have limited alternative employment opportunities. Studies of this type take worker cognitive structures as given and assume rational decision-making processes to predict voting behavior and related outcomes. The manner in which perceptions and values form and change is not addressed.

GETMAN, GOLDBERG, AND HERMAN: RATIONAL CHOICE VERSUS REALITY

The Getman, Goldberg, and Herman (1976) study, although clearly the seminal work in the analysis of campaign effects, has been controversial and subject to considerable criticism since its publication. The authors' principal concern was that NLRB election rules relating to misrepresentation of fact, which could result in the nullification of election results and an election rerun even in the absence of any unfair labor practice, were untested and based on faulty assumptions regarding the manner in which bargaining unit members make voting decisions.[5] They were also concerned that remedies imposed for such unfair labor practices as threats and promises may have been extreme relative to the impact of these actions.

Getman et al. start from the position that NLRB election rules are rooted in certain implicit assumptions regarding the manner in which employees decide how they will vote. These assumptions hold that employees are rational information processors and decision makers; the NLRB's "laboratory conditions" standard is presumed necessary to protect free choice in a setting where employees might be easily misled or intimidated. The authors test the validity of these assumptions by studying the impact of union and management influence tactics on both worker belief systems and voting behavior. They limit their analysis to such direct communications activities of unions and employers as the use of letters and posters, mass meetings, and small group or individual discussions. Certain employer unfair labor practices relating to influence efforts were also investigated. The authors used a panel study design in which bargaining unit employees were interviewed at the beginning of formal certification election campaigns and again just after the election. They were asked questions on how they voted (or intended to vote), job and union attitudes, the campaign tactics to which they had been exposed, and their general level of familiarity with themes developed by both sides during the campaign.

The results of the study suggested that campaign influence tactics have little impact upon the way employees vote. In general, employees tended to be surprisingly unfamiliar with campaign issues, though campaign familiarity was found to be correlated with exposure to influence tactics. Despite intense activity by both employers and unions, however, the vast majority of employees in the sample seemed to be unaffected by the information presented to them, with about 80 percent voting in the elections as they had said they would before the campaigns began. Those who did change by and large did so for reasons unrelated to influence efforts. Even those who had been uncommitted in the first wave of interviews, but who had made a choice by the election, were only marginally swayed by campaign communications. The only significant campaign effects were those exerted by some union influence tactics.

Getman et al. (1976, 141–146) propose a revised model of information processing and choice in organizing campaigns based on behavioral decision theory concepts. Although they did find campaign familiarity to be related to exposure to campaign tactics, they attributed this to individuals intentionally choosing to be exposed to campaign messages supportive of preexisting intentions. Furthermore, employees may distort messages received so that established belief structures are not disrupted.[6] Thus, employees are argued to be predisposed to vote in a certain way, and the campaign serves to reinforce rather than alter these intentions.

Despite the fact that the study has been faulted on methodological and conceptual grounds, there has been only limited follow-up research related to the Getman et al. book. One clear problem with the study is that the underlying model was never rigorously specified (Flanagan 1976), and the statistical analyses presented are limited to simple correlations and cross-tabulations. Dickens (1983) reanalyzed the Getman et al. data using a probit model in which numerous control variables were included. His work tends to demonstrate a negative impact by employer influence tactics on the likelihood of employees voting in favor of bargaining. Although considerable stability in voting intentions is still observed, simulation results suggest that even small shifts in employee voting behavior occasioned by employer actions could substantially alter the distribution of election outcomes. But the Dickens study is flawed by its failure to also include measures of union campaign tactics in the mode, which we would expect to be correlated with employer campaigning. Noting this and other problems with Dickens' paper, Goldberg, Getman, and Brett (1984) reaffirmed the conclusions presented in their book (Getman, Goldberg, and Herman 1976).

Walker and Lawler (1986) partially replicated the Getman et al. study in the multicampus faculty election held in the California State University system.[7] A panel study design was also used, though the period between the first and second waves of the survey was five years (the second wave was administered at the time of the election). Their results were similar to Getman et al. Despite an active and vigorous campaign involving two competing unions over the five years between the first and second waves of the survey, nearly 70 percent of the respondents voted as they had originally intended. In addition, union influence efforts were found to be unrelated to the changes in voting intentions that did occur.

EMPLOYEE SUPPORT FOR BARGAINING: A REVISED BEHAVIORAL MODEL

Limited research on the impact of campaign activities on employee attitudes toward unionization clearly restricts our ability to draw strong conclusions regarding the extent to which influence and other tactics may shape voter preferences. Despite Dickens's reanalysis, the most significant finding of the Getman, Goldberg, and Herman study remains unchallenged: employee choices regarding union representation change little over the course of a campaign. The Walker and Lawler study suggests that attitudinal stability may extend over an even greater period, despite considerable contextual change and campaign activity. Both results are consistent with more general research that suggests individuals may be predisposed to certain work attitudes (Staw and Ross 1985; Staw, Bell, and Clausen 1986).

Given these findings and the alternative choice model suggested by Getman et al., an enhanced behavioral model of information processing and attitude formation in representation elections is proposed here. Data from the California State University (CSU) study of Walker and Lawler (1986) are used to test the model. A path diagram with standardized regression coefficients (diagram 9.1) illustrates the model and summarizes the findings. Although specific to the CSU settings, this framework could be generalized.

Data and Study Setting

The CSU election was somewhat different from most representation elections (certainly those in the private sector) in that the principal contestants were two unions. Though the CSU administration opposed faculty bargaining, it did not take an active role in the campaign, since victory for one of the unions was a foregone conclusion. Yet interunion rivalry was intense, and even though we may not be able to draw conclusions on how employees react in situations characterized by strong employer opposition, this model provides a basis for informed conjecture.

The data were collected through mail surveys of the same faculty members, spread throughout seventeen of the nineteen campuses, in 1976 and 1981. The original survey was conducted in anticipation of an election within the CSU system in a year or so. The election was put off for several years, however, because of a delay in passage of enabling legislation and procedural maneuvering by the parties once the bargaining law had been enacted. The unions involved were the California Faculty Association (CFA) (essentially a coalition of the California Education Association [CEA] and the American Association of University Professors [AAUP]) and the United Professors of California (UPC) (an affiliate of the American Federation of Teachers [AFT]). These organizations continued to campaign extensively throughout the period 1976–1981. The CFA ultimately won the election in 1981, though by a slim margin. This took place against a backdrop of considerable change within the CSU system, both at the campus and departmental levels. Some campuses and departments expanded, others experienced retrenchment pressures. Campuses varied in terms of the power exercised by the campus administration.

Hypotheses

The model (diagram 9.1) incorporates features of conventional motivational models (e.g., expectancy theory), as well as models that assume various nonrational cognitive processes (e.g., Salancik and Pfeffer 1978; Staw 1977).[8] The core of the model consists of endogenous variables that measure individuals' current support for bargaining and their expectations of the impact of bargaining. In this analysis there are expectations variables for each of the unions (UPC_{81} and

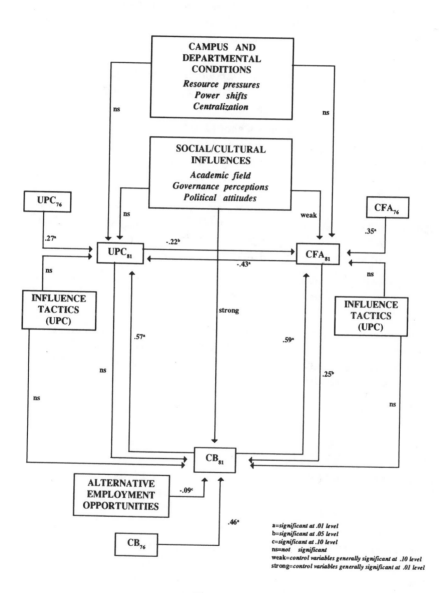

Diagram 9.1 Determinants of faculty support for collective bargaining.

CFA_{81}) and for the general level of support for collective bargaining (CB_{81}). CB_{81} was measured using a five-point Likert scale, and UPC_{81} and CFA_{81} were generated through factor analysis of a series of expectations items (both are scaled so that higher values indicate more positive expectations for bargaining).[9]

Hypothesis 1   *The expected impact of bargaining (UPC_{81} and CFA_{81}) will positively affect support for bargaining (CB_{81}).*

Rational information processors should base their evaluations of the expected impact of collective bargaining in part on current campus and departmental conditions, several of which are included in the analysis as control variables. In addition, social and cultural influences may both affect beliefs and constrain choices; these factors are typically included in rational choice models and are also used here as control variables. Also within a rational choice framework the decision to support bargaining would be anticipated to decline as opportunities for more favorable alternative employment increase.

Hypothesis 2   *Support for bargaining (CB_{81}) will positively affect the expected impact of bargaining (UPC_{81} and CFA_{81}).*

The behavioral literature suggests that actions and intentions may also be used to rationalize expectations. That is, individuals become committed to a position and alter their cognitions to support that choice (as argued by Getman et al.).

Hypothesis 3   *UPC_{81} and CFA_{81} will negatively affect each other.*

As the competing unions provide alternative and conflicting views of collective bargaining, we might expect individuals also to seek to form consistent perceptions of the two organizations.

Hypothesis 4   *Current expectations and attitudes (i.e., UPC_{81}, CFA_{81}, and CB_{81}) will be positively affected by their corresponding lagged values (i.e., UPC_{76}, CFA_{76}, and CB_{76}, respectively).*

The principal exogenous variables in the analysis are campaign tactics and the lagged values of the endogenous variables. A behavioral interpretation would suggest that attitudinal and perceptual predispositions strongly affect current levels of these perceptions and attitudes. Hypotheses 2 and 4 represent similar, but clearly distinct, processes. Hypothesis 4 suggests that current beliefs are anchored to preexisting beliefs; that is, individuals may rationalize what they now believe in terms of what they believed in the past. Once a behavioral intention is formed, however individuals may be prompted to reconcile contemporary beliefs in terms of contemporary intentions, either through rationalization and dissonance reduction or through self-attribution and sense-making efforts (hypothesis 2).

Hypothesis 5 *The influence efforts of the parties to a campaign will increase the degree to which the employees positively evaluate that party.*

Campaign tactics were measured in terms of the intensity of use of different influence tactics (personal contact, written communications, meetings and rallies) by each union on each of seventeen campuses in the CSU system. A rational choice perspective would hold that the information provided employees through the various influence efforts should affect related expectations.

Hypothesis 6 *The influence efforts of the parties will positively affect support for bargaining (CB_{81}).*

Influence tactics might also exert a direct effect on support for bargaining. The messages from the parties may generate the impression that support is socially desirable; the messages and manner of presentation may elicit an emotional or affective response to the union that goes beyond a cost-benefit evaluation.

Results

The model as developed is a system of three simultaneous equations (one for each endogenous variable). Parameter estimates were obtained using three-stage least squares, and the standardized regression (path) coefficients from this analysis, along with significance levels, are reported in diagram 9.1.[10]

The results clearly indicate that certain rational choice processes are at work. Both UPC_{81} and CFA_{81} positively affect CB_{81}, though only the latter is statistically significant (hypothesis 1). Yet the reverse relationship (hypothesis 2) is clearly much stronger. Most of the control variables (campus or departmental conditions and social or cultural influences) exert at best weak effects, and most were found to be statistically insignificant.[11] Hypotheses 3 and 4 are also strongly supported by the results. As would be anticipated from the original analysis of this data, neither hypothesis relating to the impact of influence tactics on expectations or support for bargaining (hypotheses 5 and 6) were supported.[12] This result is a bit at odds with the Getman et al. study, which demonstrated some impact associated with union influence efforts. That study relied on self-reports of exposure to influence efforts, but the approach here was to develop exogenous measures of the campaign environment through interviews with union representatives on the campuses in question. Thus, an endogeneity problem in the Getman, Goldberg, and Herman study is avoided.

Implications

Unlike either the Getman et al. book or the original Walker and Lawler paper, this analysis takes advantage of a panel study design to explore the dynamics of attitude formation and change within the context of an active organizing campaign. It would seem that expectations and attitudes have a strong predispositional character. Although we do not have information regarding the manner in which predispositions are established, that is not really an issue here. What is important is that processes are such that commitment to a particular position on collective bargaining tends to be reinforced over time. Moreover, employees appear relatively unaffected by influence tactics. We must recognize, of course, that the influence tactics studied here were exclusively of the conversion rather than intimidation variety. More aggressive and threatening influence efforts, particularly if undertaken by an employer, could have more pronounced effects.

WHAT DO WE KNOW?

Two separate panel studies have explored the role played by campaign influence tactics on voting in union representation elections. To be sure, both studies are lacking in certain respects, and additional work is clearly warranted. Yet two results suggest that influence efforts are not very important in shaping individual choices regarding bargaining. First, both studies demonstrate little change in support for bargaining over extended periods. Second, the results generally indicated that influence tactics are not strong nor, for the most part, statistically significant. Although it is true, as Dickens (1983) notes, that lack of statistical significance does not mean these factors have no effect on support for bargaining, prudence would suggest that, absent contradictory evidence, it is more probable than not that influence tactics at the individual level have little or no impact on behavior. In contrast, there is little information on the impact of contextual control or monitoring tactics on voting behavior.[13] These techniques could well affect employees attitudes but in a more indirect manner than influence tactics. Hence, we would not expect much of an effect on attitude change resulting from such activities.

THE CAMPAIGN PHASE: ELECTION OUTCOMES

Campaign strategies and tactics may impact election outcomes in a variety of ways: employee attitudes and voting intentions may be changed, the consolidation of existing support enhanced, the mobilization of an opponent's support undercut, the composition of the bargaining unit altered. Various studies have explored the effects of campaign activities on election outcomes at the bargaining unit, organizational, and aggregate levels of analysis (Appendix B).[14] The principal findings of the existing literature are first reviewed and evaluated. Additional empirical analysis is then presented in which the indexes of employer strategy developed in chapter 7 are related to election outcomes. The results of this analysis suggest that strategic effects involve an interplay among tactics that is not evident in the research that centers on the effects of individual tactics.

RESEARCH FINDINGS: UNION CAMPAIGN ACTIVITY

Virtually all of the research dealing with union campaign efforts and election outcomes considers the effects of the level, rather than the form, of union campaign activity on election outcomes. Several different indicators of the commitment of union resources to campaigning have been used, including campaign expenditures, campaign activity relative to the union's resource base, and interunion competition. There are, however, some recent studies which explore, at least to some extent, the impact of variations in the nature of union campaign activity on outcomes; one of these studies examines the personal characteristics of organizers while another reports the associations between certain union campaign tactics and election outcomes.

Campaign Expenditures

Voos' (1983) work on the relationship between union investment in organizing activity and subsequent union success, though somewhat dated, is the leading study in this area. She found that the commitment of union resources to organizing significantly bolsters organizing effectiveness. Depending upon the specification, her results suggest that the probability of organizing nonunion workers increases to 66 percent from 20 percent per $100 (1967 dollars) spent

per organizable worker; put another way, the marginal cost of organizing an additional worker ranged between $375 and $1235 (1980
dollars). But since resources that cannot be readily evaluated in
pecuniary terms are not included in the investment measures, these
results undoubtedly overstate the true return on campaign effort to
unions.

Campaign Activity and Resource Base

Following Block (1980), some authors have constructed indexes of
organizing effort derived from measures of election activity in relation to the number of potentially organizable workers; in addition, the
size of a national union (measured by total membership) is used as a
proxy for the resource base of the union. But such studies have
generated mixed results in relating these indexes to election outcomes
(e.g., Dickens, Wholey, and Robinson 1987; Maranto and Fiorito 1987).
And one study (Elliott and Hawkins 1982) argues that increased union
effort in organizing new units leads to higher decertification rates,
presumably because union resources are diverted from servicing established units. That such measures of union organizing effort have
generated poor results is not surprising, since these variables are
rather remote indicators of resource expenditure at the election unit
level and are subject to the same criticisms as were raised in regard to
Block's study (see chapter 3).

Interunion Competition

Although somewhat common in public sector elections, it is
relatively rare for a private sector election to involve more than one
union, especially given the AFL-CIO organizing accord (see chapter
7). Trade unionists generally disparage interunion competition as
self-defeating, which suggests that competition decreases the likelihood of union victory in an election. Yet arguments can be made that
the opposite is true (Dworkin and Fain 1989). If union rivalry en-
hances the vitality of the labor movement, increases worker free
choice by providing more options, and concentrates greater organizing resources in those units in which competition occurs, then interunion competition could be expected to increase the probability of
union victory. But there is also an endogeneity issue here. Since we
would anticipate that unions will be more likely to attempt to organize
units in which the chances of success are relatively high, a positive
relationship between competition and union organizing success may
be somewhat spurious.

Dworkin and Fain (1989) present aggregate data regarding interunion competition that clearly demonstrate that unions both win
substantially more of the multiunion elections and gain a much larger

share of the vote. Since some multiunion elections are raids on certified units, these numbers may be misleading, as such elections are not new organizing efforts. However, Dworkin and Fain demonstrate that these results hold for nonraid elections as well.

Although there are several multivariate analyses of the impact of interunion competition on election outcomes, results are divergent. Only one study suggests that interunion competition reduces union organizing success and that was found to be the case only in blue-collar units (Maranto and Fiorito 1987). Other studies have typically found interunion rivalry to be positively associated with union organizing success, though researchers are split on whether the effects are significant (Hurd and McElwain 1988; Seeber 1983; Stephan and Kaufman 1987; Maranto and Fiorito 1987 for white-collar units) or insignificant (Becker and Miller 1981; Delaney 1981; Lawler and Walker 1984a). Unfortunately, none of these studies tackles the endogeneity issue.

Resource Mobilization

Jenkins and Perrow (1977) provide yet another perspective on the relationship between the resources available to unions and organizing effectiveness. Their work involves an extensive case analysis of farm worker organizing efforts in the 1940s and again in the 1960s. The earlier campaign, waged by the National Farm Labor Union, was unsuccessful, but the later United Farm Workers effort was at least successful for a significant period. Jenkins and Perrow argue from a resource mobilization perspective that the major factors differentiating the outcomes of these two campaigns were the relative abilities of the unions involved to secure the financial and other resources necessary to mount sustained campaigns and to build bridges to outside organizations and political entities to support campaign tactics (e.g., boycotts). The argument also states that unions, like other reform-oriented social movements, arise not so much from constituent discontent, which is said to be endemic, as from organizational efficacy in assembling and utilizing resources. Such a perspective sees strategic action, rather than contextual forces, as the principal determinant of organizing outcomes.

Organizer Characteristics

Reed (1989a) analyzes union organizing activity in a rather different fashion, concentrating primarily on the relationship between organizer characteristics and election outcomes. His study involved a survey of a number of organizers working for several national and international unions. In addition to obtaining data on their personal

and psychological characteristics, he also queried respondents regarding their experiences in a total of more than three hundred
elections. Since he examines over a dozen organizer characteristics
and certain hypotheses posit curvilinear relationships, a complete
discussion of his findings is not possible here. In general, both the
personality and demographic characteristics of organizers affect the
probability of union victory and the extent of prounion vote in an
election (though not always in ways predicted by Reed's hypotheses).
For example, organizers are more successful the greater their level of
self-esteem and desire for control over situations, but generally less
successful the greater their proclivity to be manipulative ("Machia-
vellianism"). Social mobility (in either direction) and increased educational level both enhance organizer effectiveness. Interestingly,
female organizers were found to be more successful than their male
counterparts; moreover, previous experience at organizing and having
been a rank-and-file union member actually reduced effectiveness.
The relevance of these findings to the themes developed in this book
would seem to be that they lend support to the notion that idiosyn-
cratic strategic choices, reflected in the individual differences among
organizers, have a strong impact on U/DU outcomes. In addition,
though the same strategies and tactics may be used in similar settings
by different organizers, their abilities to implement these actions
effectively may be substantially different.[15]

Campaign Tactics

The AFL-CIO's Department of Organization and Field Services
continually surveys organizers in federation affiliates and occasionally reports the results of these surveys. The most recent of these
reports (AFL-CIO 1989) contains cross-tabulations relating a variety
of bargaining unit characteristics and campaign tactics (both union
and employer) to election outcomes (union win or loss); one hundred
and eighty-nine elections involving units of fifty or more workers, all
of which took place between July, 1986, and April, 1987, were examined. Unfortunately, as only bivariate relationships are presented, it
is not possible to generate very strong statements regarding the
impact these tactics.

The AFL-CIO survey suggests the need for the union to have a
strong base of support prior to petitioning for an election, as a union's
changes of winning an election do not exceed 50 percent unless three-
quarters or more of the unit members have signed authorization
cards. This would lend credence to the argument that successful union
campaigns are largely concerned with mobilizing existing support

rather than winning converts; if the support is shallow when the election campaign is initiated, then the union is apt to lose. The survey also suggested that precampaign support required to give a union a better than even chance of victory has increased since the early 1980s.

Specific tactics examined in the survey include forms of personal contact utilized during the campaign, the use of mass meetings, and the campaign themes developed by the union. Thus, the survey was principally concerned with fairly traditional influence tactics and did not explore more innovative and nonworkplace tactics. Personal contact was found to be strongly related to election outcomes, but in situations in which unions relied on relatively impersonal means of contact (e.g., letters, telephone calls), the union lost ground. Mass meetings, while effective in cases in which substantial numbers of workers attended, were found to have an adverse effect when attendance was off. Finally, the survey suggested that rather traditional campaign issues (e.g., improved working conditions, the establishment of a grievance procedure) were most effective is gaining worker support.

RESEARCH FINDINGS: EMPLOYER CAMPAIGN ACTIVITY

There is a greater abundance of research concerning the impact of employer campaign activity on election outcomes, and studies focus mainly on the form, rather than only the intensity, of employer opposition. Yet this research is still often rather narrow, as most examine only a few of the many possible actions an employer might pursue in the course of a certification election campaign.

General Employer Opposition

A few studies have evaluated the effect on election outcomes of management's overall proclivity to oppose unionism. This approach is somewhat akin to that of assessing the impact of the level of union resources devoted to an organizing effort, although these opposition measures reflect managerial sentiments rather than actual resources expended on the union-avoidance program.

The assumption in these studies is that employer union-avoidance activity increases with the general level of employer opposition to bargaining, although that activity is not directly observed. Maranto and Fiorito (1987) use an industry-specific index of employer opposition derived from the Conference Board survey data. Their results indicate that unions are considerably more likely to lose elections in industries in which management expresses a strong commitment to union-avoidance objectives. The adverse impact of managerial opposition was found to be quite a bit stronger in white-collar than in blue-collar units.

In his study of consultant effects in organizing campaigns, Lawler (1984) constructed an index of the employer's propensity to use a consultant, which was taken as a general indicator of employer opposition to bargaining. Contrary to expectation, he found the opposition measure was significantly and positively related to the likelihood of union victory. Why did this happen? One explanation would seem to be the existence of what might be termed a "backfire" effect. That is, intense employer opposition to unionization might encourage the employer to overreact, thus intensifying employee resolve to organize. There is theoretical justification for this view, especially in research dealing with what is known as *reactance* (Staw 1977). In addition, the more intense the motivation of the employer to resist unionization, the greater would be the perceived undesirable ramifications of failing to defeat the union. The enhanced stress generated by the anticipated consequences of failure, coupled with the complexity of managing a union-avoidance program, could decrease employer effectiveness in formulating and implementing union-avoidance strategies.[16] Some research suggestive of an employer-generated backfire effect has been discussed above (Anderson, Busman, and O'Reilly 1982), and other studies lending support to the backfire hypothesis will be noted later.

Influence Tactics

Measured at the bargaining unit level, influence tactics may exert multiple effects. Besides impacting employee preferences for bargaining, as assumed in the analysis of the voting behavior of individuals, influence tactics could also have an impact upon group solidarity (often a prime objective) and the decision to participate in the election. Block and Roomkin (1982) analyze factors underlying the decison to vote in an election, implying that the intensity of influence activity could affect the decision of ambivalent individuals to vote in the election. Thus, collective as well as individual action could be conditioned by influence tactics.

Lawler and West (1985) estimate the effects of several different influence tactics at the bargaining unit level. Results are mixed, though most influence tactics examined (captive audience speeches, small group meetings, threats and promises) were found to exert negative effects on the proportion of employees voting in favor of bargaining. Each of these tactics, when used, reduced the prounion vote by 1 percent to 4 percent. An exception was the distribution of antiunion literature, which was estimated to increase the prounion vote by perhaps 5 percent, another finding consistent with the existence of a backfire effect.[17] Relying only on simple correlations, Porter and Murrmann (1983) also report significant influence effects, all in the direction of lowering the likelihood of union victory. A composite index of influence activity has a strong correlation ($r = -.45$) with union victory. Employer campaign themes also relate negatively to union victory, with messages emphasizing the cost of bargaining exerting the greatest impact.

Contextual Control Tactics

It is in this area that research is most extensive, with the majority of the studies concerned with election delays and procedural maneuvering (usually indicated by election type). Prosten (1978) and Roomkin and Juris (1979) first noted the apparent negative impact on union organizing effectiveness of factors such as increasing election delays and the growing number of stipulated and directed elections. Cooke (1983) found that unions receive about 8 percent more of the vote and have roughly a 15 percent greater chance of winning in simple consent versus stipulated or directed elections. Florkowski and Shuster (1987) report a somewhat lower impact, estimating that consent elections increase the probability of union victory by about 7 percent. Several other studies point to a negative impact on union election victory chances or prounion vote resulting from stipulated or directed elections (Hunt and White 1985; Dickens, Wholey, and Robinson 1987; Stephan and Kaufman 1987; Hurd and McElwain 1988). While some studies have found election type to be insignificant (Lawler and West 1985; Stepina and Fiorito 1986), the preponderance of research results suggest this factor is of considerable importance in determining election outcomes.

Some studies have examined more direct measures of procedural maneuvering. For example, Hunt and White (1985) found that the frequency of post election objections filed by management (which are intended to nullify election results and cause election reruns) is negatively related to prounion vote. Yet Cooke (1985b) reported that employer success in altering the composition of the bargaining unit prior to the election inexplicably increases union victory chances (a result that is also not strongly suggested by the backfire hypothesis).

There is far less consistency in research findings concerning the impact of election delays. For example, although Cooke (1983) found delays to be statistically significant in reducing the likelihood of union victory in certification elections, delays did not prove to be substantively important in Cooke's study, since the probability of union victory was found to decrease by only 1 percent per month of delay. Although other studies demonstrate strong, as well as statistically significant, delay effects (Dickens, Wholey, and Robinson 1987; Stephan and Kaufman 1987), some authors question whether delays, after controlling for election type and other procedural maneuvering indicators, matter much (Cooke 1985b; Hurd and McElwain 1988; Lawler and West 1985). Moreover, after analyzing election delay patterns since the 1940s, Block and Wolkinson (1986, 48–55) conclude that "delay as a weapon may not be as pervasively wielded as unions believe it to be. Moreover, there is no indication that employers are intentionally or strategically attempting to prolong the process to take advantage of the presumed benefits of so doing."

Florkowski and Shuster (1987) assessed the effects of election delays by including a nonlinear term (inverse of days between petition filing and the election); their results suggest that delay effects drop off rapidly and are negligible after about twelve days. Since elections are rarely held in so short a period, the increase in delays in recent years is not likely to be important in explaining declining union victory rates. Yet their findings would provide some support for Weiler's (1983) proposal to hold "instant" elections (conducted within five days or so of the election petition), since the probability of union victory is substantially enhanced if the delay is only a few days.

Unfair labor practices, especially discriminatory discharges, are widely believed to be among the leading causes of declining union victory rates (e.g., Weiler 1983). Studies that look exclusively at employer unfair labor practice measures report strong effects. Cooke (1985b) estimates that discharges associated with an election campaign reduce the probability of union victory somewhere between 17 percent and 24 percent; Freeman (1986) similarly reports a strong unfair labor practice effect on aggregate union organizing effectiveness. This effect is not stable, however and quite sensitive to model specification. The inclusion of other employer tactics in the analysis substantially reduces, and even reverses the sign, of the unfair labor practice effect (Stephan and Kaufman 1987; Maranto and Fiorito 1987; Cooper 1984; Stepina and Fiorito 1986; Hunt and White 1985; Lawler and West 1985). Of course, a positive unfair labor practice effect may indicate a backfire effect.

Most of the other employer campaign phase contextual control tactics mentioned in chapter 7 (e.g., supervisor training, rules restricting organizing activity during work time, improved wages and working conditions) have not been examined by authors other than Porter and Murrmann (1983) and Lawler and West (1985). Some are quite important (e.g., *Excelsior*-list violations and no-solicitation rules), but others seem to have no impact (e.g., supervisor training). Clearly, further research is required to discern whether these tactics are truly related to election outcomes.

Monitoring Tactics

Monitoring tactics, which may have a chilling effect on bargaining unit employees, also could affect election outcomes by providing employers with advance warning of union campaign activities and by identifying pockets of union—and management—support. If management uses this information to tailor its campaign to current conditions, then we should expect more effective campaign moves and a reduced likelihood that the union will prevail.

Research findings are here again limited to those reported in the Porter and Murrmann and Lawler and West papers. The latter study found that direct surveillance of employee activities has a weak negative effect on union victory chances, but attitude surveys had a pronounced negative impact. Union concerns with the use of surveys during campaigns would seem to be well founded. Porter and Murrmann also found that several different monitoring techniques are associated with reduced union victory probabilities; they also found, not surprisingly, that the earlier the employer detected that an organizing drive was under way, the less probable the union would win.

EMPLOYER STRATEGIES: AN EMPIRICAL ANALYSIS

The research considered above largely evaluates the individual contributions of one or more campaign tactics without exploring the interrelationships that might exist among tactics. In chapter 7 the AFL-CIO field report data were used to construct indices of campaign substrategies. The dimensions that were identified suggest how organizations combine tactics in the real world. Tactics may be combined in certain ways since some tactics may be seen by managers to be complementary and others as mutually incompatible. Thus, the interplay among tactics composing a strategy could have more to do with election outcomes than the individual tactics would in isolation from one another.

Although elections were grouped according to general strategic tendency in the analysis in chapter 7, employer actions across elections within clusters can deviate considerably from the central tendency of the group. For each election separate scores were computed for each of the three substrategy dimensions identified (vigilance, legal maneuvering/influence, and suppression). These scores, which represent the extent to which management pursued each substrategy during the campaign, are used to determine the impact of substrategies on election outcomes. This analysis extends that reported in an earlier study (Lawler and West 1985) using the same sample of elections.

Control variables used in the analysis are the rates of change in earnings and employment in the county in which the election took place and the logarithm of the size of the bargaining unit. As in the original paper, weighted least squares are used to regress a logit transformation of the percent of votes cast in favor of unionization against the independent variables.[18] Parameter estimates are converted to first derivatives of the probability function, which express the impact of variables on the proportion of employees voting in favor of bargaining (table 9.1).

Table 9.1 **LOGIT ANALYSIS OF IMPACT OF SUBSTRATEGIES ON PROPORTION OF EMPLOYEES VOTING IN FAVOR OF COLLECTIVE BARGAINING ($N = 177$)**

Independent Variable	Coefficient	Derivative
Log of unit size	$-.07^a$	$-.02$
Annual rate of change in employment in county	$.96^b$	$.24$
Annual rate of change in total earnings in county	2.26^b	$.56$
Vigilance	$-.01$	$.00$
Legal maneuvering/influence[c]	$.02$	$.00$
Suppression	$-.07^d$	$-.02$
Constant	$.85^b$	
$R^2 = .25$	$F = 9.39^a$	

[a]Significant at .01 level.
[b]Significant at .05 level.
[c]Legal maneuvering is the positive end of the scale, and influence is the negative end.
[d]Significant at .10 level.

The results of this analysis suggest that only the suppression dimension exerts a relatively strong and statistically significant negative effect on the proportion of votes cast in favor of unionization in representation elections. Recall that increasing levels of suppression are characterized by an employer relying to a greater extent on threats, discrimination, improperly drawn *Excelsior*-lists, management consultants as campaign advisers, and so forth. Hence, a somewhat different picture emerges than when individual tactics are considered in isolation (Lawler and West 1985), in which case the impact of suppressive efforts appears less pronounced and some influence efforts seem to be more important. Repressive measures used in conjunction with one another appear to represent a powerful management instrument for the defeat of unionism.

The impact of varying levels of suppression activity on election outcomes is simulated in diagram 9.2.[19] In the sample of cases studied, the supression index ranged between a low value of approximately −2.0 and a high value of about 3.0. In the cases as observed, unions garnered an average of about 51 percent of the vote and won about 45 percent of the elections, thus successfully organizing around 28 percent of the eligible voters (since union victories are concentrated in smaller units). These results can be contrasted with what would have occurred under two different scenarios.

High Suppression

Assuming all employers had pursued strategies involving levels of suppression equal to the highest cases in the sample, then, all other things being equal, the proportion of the votes cast in elections in favor of unions would have declined by only a few percentage points. However, the impact on union victories and employees organized would have been quite pronounced. Unions would have won less than 40 percent of the elections and, more dramatically, would have organized only about 18 percent of the employees in the bargaining units.

Low Suppression

Assume, in contrast to the high suppression condition that all employers had pursued low suppression strategies. Unions would then have won 6 percent to 7 percent more of the elections than they actually did, successfully organizing 8 percent to 9 percent more of the bargaining unit employees.

WHAT DO WE KNOW?

Research concerned with the impact of campaign activities on election outcomes is extensive, though there are clear limitations on the extent of work in this area. Moreover, research designs and the methods used to analyze data are such that findings cannot always be interpreted in an unambiguous manner.

Diagram 9.2. Simulated election outcomes.

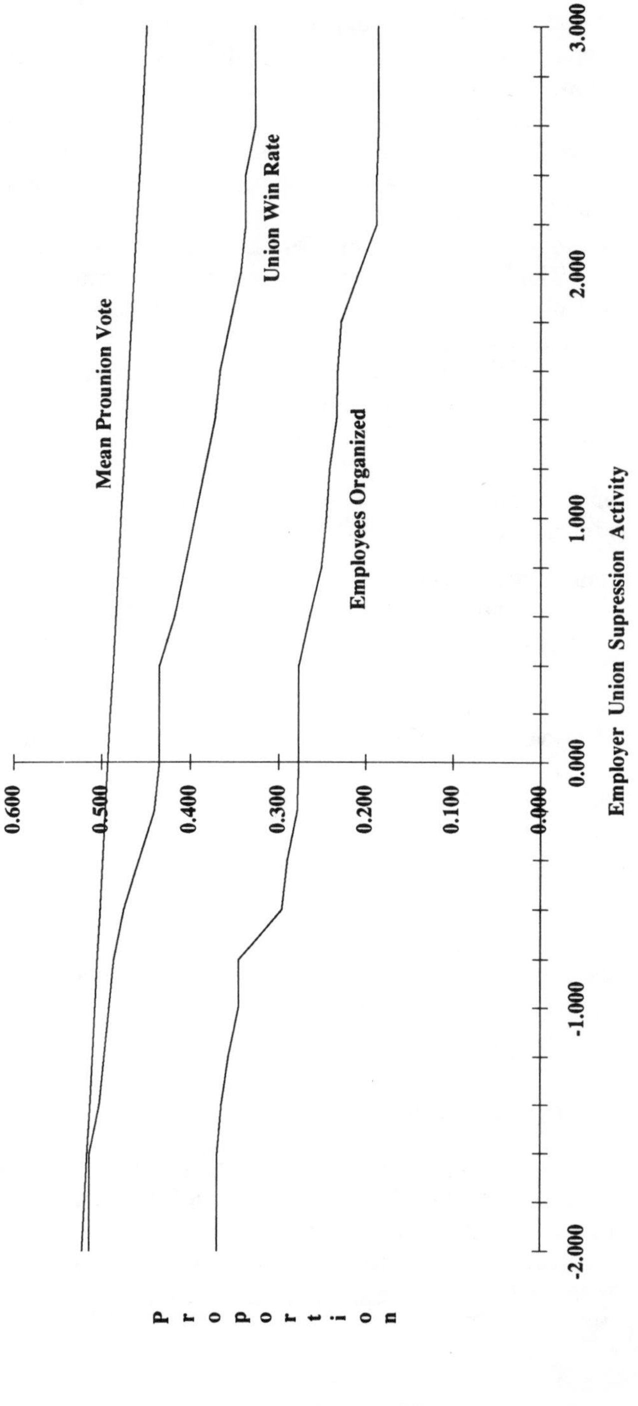

Research tends to be tactical rather than strategic in focus, dealing with only selected sets of campaign activities rather than considering the broad array of actions typically utilized by both sides. Moreover, most studies are concerned exclusively with employer conduct during campaigns, so there is much less analysis of either the direct impact of union conduct or the interplay of union and employer actions. And since many of these studies rely heavily on archival data sources (e.g., NLRB tapes, industry and state averages for various market and social influences), direct measures of important constructs are often missing. Since proxy variables are apt to be measured with greater error, the results may be less reliable than had direct measures been used. Another problem with such heavy reliance on archival data is that the range of campaign activities investigated is often restricted to factors contained in data tapes. Studies of the impact of election delays and election type are numerous, but those dealing with other tactics (e.g., influence efforts, supervisory training, surveillance) are few in number.

As for union campaign activity, most of what we know concerns the intensity of union organizing effort, rather than strategies and tactics, in relation to organizing outcomes. Research by Voos (1983) is the most thorough investigation of this issue. Other studies link intensity of organizing activity to election outcomes, though there are some conflicting findings; none of these other studies, however, employ direct measures of resource investment, as does Voos. A problem with virtually all of the research in this area is that studies rely on data from the 1970s or earlier. That these studies are somewhat dated is especially significant given the innovative organizing techniques promoted by the 1985 AFL-CIO report and utilized by several unions. Hence, we cannot be sure that structural relationships have not substantially changed because of the new directions in strategic thinking that, if not pervasive in the labor movement, certainly have made their mark.

Reed's (1989a) more recent work fills many gaps and is especially novel in the manner in which it demonstrates the effects of organizer characteristics, particularly those associated with "progressive" rather than "traditional" organizing strategies, on election outcomes. But what is still lacking is a close examination of the effects of a wide range of union tactics, strategies, and substrategies on organizing success. Of particular interest would be studies that contrast conventional and innovative organizing tactics (or progressive and traditional strategies) and are able to make strong statements regarding, for example, the relative efficacy of corporate campaigns.

Although there is more research on the employer side, results are frequently contradictory. What has been lacking in most of the literature on employer campaign activity is a strategic focus. This is largely a case of a familiar problem—specification error. If employers design overall campaigns to achieve strategic objectives in representation elections and choose tactics with those strategic objectives in mind, then empirical analyses ought to consider the various elements of employer strategy as a whole. Examining one or two tactics at a time is bound to generate biased results. The dimensions of employer strategic action empirically determined in chapter 7 have been used here to provide a partial remedy for this problem. The findings of this analysis reinforce, in part, what several other studies have found. However, new insights into employer campaign processes also follow:

1. Campaign strategies that emphasize suppressive and often illegal tactics have strong, negative effect on union success in elections.

2. Campaign strategies that emphasize aggressive, but generally legal, tactics would seem, in practice, to have little discernible impact on election outcomes.

This research is still, however, limited. In the ideal, election outcomes should be analyzed in terms of both employer and union strategies. A completely specified model would also take into account employer and union strategic interactions and the simultaneity apt to exist among the endogenous variables in the system.

CHAPTER 10

Strategy, Tactics, and Outcomes:

An Assessment

We have examined a range of topics related to unionization and deunionization activity, the principal focus being employer and union strategic action at the bargaining unit level. The theoretical core of the book is the strategic choice model developed in chapter 2; this model is used to explore several aspects of the U/DU process. Prior empirical studies, along with analyses of data collected by the author, are used to illustrate the model and investigate some of the implications that derive from it. The book does not provide, nor was it intended to provide, a complete test of the model. Rather, it has been designed primarily as a conceptual exercise in which diverse research and writing are integrated in the tradition of institutionalist analysis. Thus, it is intended to provide a framework for future research on the topic of unionization and deunionization processes.

This chapter summarizes the major issues raised in the book, noting areas in which further empirical or conceptual work is most needed. Significant policy implications that follow from the analyses and findings that have been presented are identified and discussed.

THE STRATEGIC CHOICE FRAMEWORK

Contemporary research stresses the importance of employer and union action (or inaction) in affecting union growth and decline. Yet this literature has not generated a comprehensive theory to explain: (a) the manner in which employers and unions develop action plans in connection with U/DU efforts, (b) the techniques utilized in implementing these plans, or (c) the impact of actions on U/DU outcomes. This study adapts the strategic choice perspective to these ends, building on the assumption that the discretionary actions of managers and unionists impact outcomes independently of contextual influences and to a substantively important degree.

There are different views of the strategy formulation process. On the one hand, the extensive normative literature in the strategic management field proffers that strategic choices emanate from the conscious and rational evaluation of options in relation to organizational objectives and capabilities. But there are other perspectives as well, most notably arguments that derive from behavioral decision theory that posit that strategic choices may be based on distorted information, nonoptimizing decision rules, emotional responses, and even random selection. In any event, strategy formulation is inexorably linked to organizational political processes and the influence of dominant organizational coalitions. Moreover, in the case of U/DU strategy formulation, it is necessary to take into account the role played by outside consultants, particularly on the employer side.

Strategies can be characterized in terms of several observable features. The strategic mission is a unifying theme that may be formally stated. There are targets of strategic action, which may be within or external to the bargaining unit. Unionization and deunionization strategies may vary in terms of degree of integration with other strategies and aspects of organizational action. Tactics, which constitute the most visible aspect of strategic action, are of greatest significance for the purposes of this book. The value of the strategic choice perspective in the analysis of U/DU efforts is that it provides a means of categorizing the many tactics employers and unions use and helps us to understand how these tactics are interrelated. Employer and union U/DU strategies can be decomposed into a series of elementary tactics. A typology of the most common elementary tactics (influence, contextual control, monitoring, and direct action) is proposed, and the defining characteristics of each tactical category are set forth.

The model as presently specified (diagram 2.2) could be enhanced in several ways. The role of regulatory agencies and political entities could be incorporated more directly. Indeed, if Dunlop's approach were followed regarding the "actors" in the industrial relations system, governmental bodies could be viewed as relevant strategy-formulating units on a par with unions and employers. This was not done here for two reasons. First, the active intervention of government into the U/DU process is not now as it was thirty to fifty years ago. Governmental bodies are largely passive participants (except, perhaps, in the public sector). Thus, it seems acceptable to treat the

NLRB and other governmental units as contextual elements rather than as vital participants in the process. Second, to have incorporated government into the model would have substantially complicated the analysis and diverted attention from the book's major objectives.

Another element that could be given greater attention is the role of bargaining unit employees in the overall process. The strategic choice model posits employee union proneness to be a central feature in the U/DU process, though the nature of that role is not explicitly developed. Although the analysis of employee support for unionization presented in chapter 9 does this to a considerable extent and could be incorporated directly into the strategic choice model, group processes would have to be treated as well.

STRATEGY FORMULATION IN PRACTICE

The strategic choice approach taken here is distinct from the static analyses that constitute the bulk of the research relating to U/DU processes. Strategies are dynamic in character; how they are initially implemented and how they play out over time depends on the manner in which key decision makers conceptualize problems, assess potential solutions, and make choices. To understand how U/DU strategies come about and why they may vary across like settings, it is necessary that we have a firm understanding of the nature of strategy formulation processes. Research that examines either U/DU strategy formulation directly, or casts light on the process indirectly, was taken up in chapters 3 and 4; the role labor relations consultants play in this process was dealt with in chapter 5.

UNION STRATEGY FORMULATION

Studies of union decision making, as well as union administration in general, have declined considerably since the 1950s, making it more difficult to understand the contemporary strategic choice processes of unions. The research that is available on the allocation of union resources to organizing activity does not provide strong evidence suggesting that these decisions reflect objectively rational considerations. The overall fit of rational choice models is poor, and results are mixed on the impact of principal independent variables. Moroever, qualitative analyses of union governance typically emphasize the highly politicized nature of union administration and presence of institutional inertia.

Given these considerations, a behavioral model of strategy formulation is proposed that accounts for rigidity and stagnation in American unions. Although the model is pertinent in general to the analysis of union decision making, it is applied here specifically to U/DU strategy. But there is reason to believe that those institutional forces that have generated strategic rigidity in unions are abating. The 1985 AFL-CIO report is discussed in terms of what it suggests concerning strategic change, particularly in the organizing arena. Recent studies relating to union strategy formulation in U/DU are also considered; these suggest that, despite continued resistance to change, many national unions have put in place mechanisms designed to improve the quality of strategic decision making.

External consultants are playing something of an increasing role in union strategy formulation, especially in efforts that involve innovative tactics and strategies. Yet they are nowhere near as pervasive a presence as is the case on the employer side. Agencies of the AFL-CIO are much more significant in providing these types of services to unions. Union consultants have also engendered considerable resentment in some quarters within the labor movement, as they are seen as intrusive and may threaten political interests.

The proposed union strategy formulation model is not tested here, and it would seem that there is opportunity for empirical work in this area. In practice, a variety of decision-making processes are apt to be encountered within and across unions. Contextual and situational contingencies are apt to affect the extent to which choices are made in an objectively rational manner, versus the fashion outlined in chapter 3. Identifying those contingencies that favor rationality and realism on the part of union decision makers could serve to promote union effectiveness in the organizing arena. The AFL-CIO report makes a number of policy recommendations related to structural and administrative change in unions that are presumed to enhance the quality of union decision making (merger, interunion cooperation, leadership and staff training and development, increased rank-and-file participation). Many of these proposals are largely untested and could also be evaluated within this framework.

MANAGEMENT STRATEGY FORMULATION

In contrast to studies of union strategy formulation, there is a much more extensive literature on this topic. Prompted by a hostile and turbulent environment, management is typically portrayed as more sensitive to the need for well-planned strategic action in all facets of organizational administration. In respect to U/DU strategies specifically, several trends have been noted in recent years. First, employers have become decidedly more hostile to unions. Second, there is a tendency toward greater centralization of decision making with respect to labor issues. Third, human resource management specialists have become much more influential in the corporate world, often supplanting labor relations specialists, who are not seen as sufficiently antiunion by upper management. Fourth, organizations are emphasizing strategic planning in the human resource management and labor relations areas to a much greater degree. Union-avoidance considerations are an increasingly significant component of these plans.

The assumption that employer U/DU strategy formulation is a well-ordered process in which managers realistically appraise problems and opportunities has been challenged in some quarters. Even though market forces would seem to encourage greater rationality in business organizations, strategic choices may also be influenced by the same behavioral processes that are argued to engender ill-conditioned decisions in unions. In addition, some writers have argued that antiunionism on the part of management is less a response to the tangible costs possibly associated with collective bargaining than an emotional response prompted by a fear of lost power and status.

Several empirical studies utilize different methodologies to investigate managerial choices relating to unionization or deunionization activity. Most studies lend support to the rational choice perspective, though there are some contradictory results. In addition, there have not been any studies that specifically investigate U/DU strategy formulation from a behavioral or social dominance perspective. Thus, there is clearly opportunity and need for research here.

Another aspect of management strategy formulation is the role played in the process by labor relations consultants. There are several different types of consultants, with attorneys and behavioral specialists being by far the most common. The evidence suggests that consultants strongly influence employer choices in U/DU efforts, though the quality and impact of this assistance is not always clearly beneficial to the employer. And, at least in respresentation election campaigns, consultant intervention may be counterproductive, actually serving to increase union victory chances under some circumstances. Even the AFL-CIO, which was quite agitated by the upsurge in consultant activity in the late 1970s, now seems inclined to downplay the significance of consultants.

POLICY IMPLICATIONS

It is important to have an understanding of the processes under-lying U/DU strategy formulation in order to anticipate how changes in organizational and public policies might affect U/DU outcomes. For example, that research suggests managers are relatively rational in choosing to engage in certain union-avoidance actions suggests that unions that pursue initiatives generating significant costs for em-ployers (such as corporate campaigns) are likely to succeed in lessen-ing employer resistance. The same would hold for public policy. The imposition of substantial penalties for illicit activity by employers, such as those proposed as part of the ill-fated Labor Law Reform Act, would be expected to reduce the likelihood of rational managers purposefully engaging in such conduct, unless methods are devised for getting around such prohibitions.

Yet there is another side to the story. To the extent union-avoidance policies are ideologically or emotionally driven (and there is some support for this view), employers would be less prone to respond to high opportunity costs associated with aggressive anti-unionism. It is not clear, then, that the implementation of governmen-tal policies that attach high costs to engaging in antiunion activity will have effects to the extent anticipated. The penalties necessary to dissuade employers from such strategies may be too high to be socially acceptable, especially given the prevalent views of the broader com-munity regarding the usefulness of trade unions. And if the most intense forms of opposition are most apt to be rooted in managerial emotionalism or nonrationality, then punitive action may have vir-tually no meaningful effect on improving union organizing success.

Employers and their consultants seem quite skillful in circum-venting or avoiding statutory restrictions on their actions. Thus, even if we accept the argument that management union-avoidance efforts are rooted in a rational assessment of costs and benefits, it would still seem that public policy initiatives by unions to impose greater penal-ties on labor law violators, or to expand the set of prohibited activities, are destined to have at best modest effects. Unions need to keep ahead of employers by continually developing new organizing initiatives and techniques that will catch antiunion management off guard. In the past unions were able to rely on relatively few tried-and-true organiz-ing techniques. Given determined management opposition, any method, no matter how successful in the short run, is apt to be effectively neutralized by countervailing employer strategies once management understands what is happening.

If unions are to take the initiative in organizing new units, as well as in precluding deunionization in established units, it is imperative that effective strategy formulation processes be put in place. Structures and procedures must be introduced that promote the rapid and unbiased assimilation of information and the realistic appraisal of options. But we know that these changes, often readily effected within business organizations, are difficult at best to carry out in unions. The political realities within unions often create nearly insurmountable barriers to change. Although Heckscher (1988, 234–237) goes so far as to suggest that only new unions not encumbered by these pressures have sufficient leeway to be truly creative and responsive, it is not clear that such organizations are likely to arise in large numbers. Thus, unions that have been successful in experimenting with innovative strategic decision-making systems ought to become models for other unions. The AFL-CIO should also expand efforts to improve the quality of union strategic decision making, though this could well be received as another threat to national union autonomy.

STRATEGIES AND OUTCOMES

The manner in which employers and unions implement strategies in various phases of the U/DU process has been considered in some detail (chapters 6–8). The intention has been to identify the more significant substrategies and tactics utilized on each side, positioning these within the overall conceptual framework. Of course, not all of the many activities unions and employers engage in could be examined. Yet the treatment is sufficient to provide the reader with a broad overview of the most relevant issues. In addition, research concerning the impact of these activities has been reviewed and evaluated (chapter 9).

THE NONUNION PHASE

Union success or failure in organizing new units seems to depend increasingly on events that transpire long before a formal campaign is ever initiated. Employers are now quite sensitive to the effects of personnel management systems in nonunion settings on the likelihood of employees developing an interest in bargaining. The design and implementation of preemptive strategies is a major focus of employer union-avoidance activity, the hope being that an organizing campaign will never occur. Unions are also increasingly sensitive to the significance of events that occur during this stage.

Employers

Although much is known regarding the manner in which em-ployer preemptive strategies are implemented, more research is needed on the impact of preemptive measures on outcomes. The research to date, however, indicates that "positive" labor relations programs substantially reduce the potential for unionization within a bargaining unit.

Preemptive strategies raise significant public policy concerns, even though they tend not to involve clearly illegal conduct. That preemptive strategies emphasize influence efforts and that these aspects seem most effective would suggest that such programs often work primarily by means of manipulation. Shifts in the employment-at-will doctrine in state courts provide one means of promoting the good faith of management implementing these programs. However, law firms representing employers may develop personnel manuals that are designed to limit the employer's liability while appearing to grant employees considerable rights. It may be that statutes are needed, perhaps at the federal level, regulating the content of formal employment policies in nonunion settings and ensuring that stated rights are also substantive rights—what amounts to a "truth in employment" act. Although nonunion employers would not in any way be obligated to implement any of the regulated personnel prac-tices, those that do would be required to state clearly the terms and conditions of employment, the rights of the employee, and the condi-tions under which the employer could alter the terms of employment. Of particular significance should be the regulation of participative management systems and grievance systems, as these most closely parallel the services provided to workers by unions. The NLRB and the courts have generally held that such activities do not violate the NLRA. Although it does not seem desirable, nor feasible, that such programs should be disallowed in nonunion settings, one approach might be to amend the NLRA to permit employees to bring unfair labor practice charges against employers who fail to follow through on commitments or who use these programs in an abusive or manip-ulative manner. More generally, implicit contracts could be made enforceable in federal courts under the same provisions of Title III of the NLRA that apply to negotiated contracts, thus establishing na-tional standards.

Certain aspects of preemptive strategies do involve efforts to thwart the provisions of the NLRA. For example, employee selection policies that discriminate against likely union supporters are not uncommon. Although a potential violation of section 8(a)(3) of the

NLRA, these policies rarely affect unions directly, since they frequently are put in place long before a union is present. That these policies will ever be detected, much less remedied, by the NLRB, is questionable. The solution to this problem is unclear, though greater attention to employer policies by unions engaged in target cultivation strategies may help. To date, there have only been a handful of preemployment discrimination cases brought before the NLRB. This is but one form of discrimination that may follow from abusive screening practices and is thus linked to other issues, such as genetic screening and the administration of polygraph tests. As suggested by a congressional investigation, this problem may be best addressed by legislation dealing with all aspects of preemployment screening and data collection (U.S. Congress 1981, 1–22).

Unions

Some labor organizations are now quite concerned with strengthening target selection strategies and developing long-term target cultivation strategies. The extent of these changes is not known, and studies dealing with the receptivity of international union organizing staff and local union leaders to new programs, especially those related to target cultivation strategies, are needed. In addition, there are really no data so far that could be used to assess the impact of these new approaches, which provides another useful avenue for research.

The concept of associate membership is perhaps the most controversial of all of the innovative organizing techniques promoted in recent years. Should associate membership programs become widespread, this might well raise interesting questions regarding the fundamental nature of union representation. Since associate memberships may include some assistance by union staff in handling work-related problems, associate members may come to expect more of these services in return for their dues, leading to pressures for a relaxation in the practice of exclusive representation (though appropriate changes would presumably have to be incorporated into the NLRA). The partial or complete abandonment of exclusive representation may, in fact, be precisely what is needed to salvage a faltering American labor movement. Union representation as an all-or-nothing proposition made sense at a time when unions had widespread appeal and gained recognition in a high proportion of cases. But unions now win less than 50 percent of all certification elections, and the number of elections held has dropped dramatically in recent years. If the law allowed for alternative, nonexclusive forms of recognition, then unions could provide some degree of representation for the significant proportion of unorganized American workers who favor unionization. Nonexclusive representation has been practiced in nonunion settings in many public sector jurisdictions for some time, so we have a model upon which to build a private sector approach.[1] We might expect to see practices emerge that are akin to public sector meet-and-confer procedures, and unions may provide assistance to associate members in company grievance procedures and wrongful discharge cases. This approach is not without its drawbacks. Contracts are likely to be nonexistent or extremely weak, and it would encourage the nemesis of "dual unionism." Yet nonexclusive representation, seemingly a step backward, could provide a viable remedy for eroding union strength. Heckscher (1988, 179–185) extends this line of reasoning considerably, proposing what he terms "associational unionism," which he sees as the logical extension of new practices such as associate membership.

THE CAMPAIGN PHASE

Research and analysis is most extensive on employer and union activities during representation election campaigns, though much more work has been published concerning employer conduct.

Employers

Several distinct employer campaign strategies are identified in the empirical analysis reported in chapter 7. In general, strategies that involve "reconciliation" objectives are much more common than suppression strategies. The analysis reported in chapter 9 suggests, however, that, at least when evaluated at the bargaining unit level, suppression strategies are much more effective in reducing the likelihood of union victory than are more benign strategies emphasizing influence or monitoring tactics. Conversely, and despite the claims of union-avoidance consultants and specialists, employers are probably not getting much of a payoff from captive audience speeches and flashy media presentations. Heavy investment in supervisor training and monitoring efforts would not seem to be cost efficient either. That related techniques seem to work quite effectively in preemptive strategies is probably the consequence of the much longer time horizon over which such programs are conducted.

These findings would support calls for stricter enforcement of NLRA provisions that already prohibit most of the activities research studies have repeatedly shown to be related to declines in union success in certification campaigns; in addition, stricter penalties, such as those proposed in the Labor Law Reform Act of the 1970s, would also seem warranted. But as was argued above, such measures may have only minimal effects. The actions of employers, especially the most aggressively antiunion, may be driven by ideology and emotion rather than rational reflection. Moreover, much of the research that has looked at the impact of campaign activities on election outcomes is narrowly focused and fails to control for endogenicity problems. Thus, the observed effects may be somewhat spurious. Some evidence also supports the existence of a backfire effect, which suggests that the relationship between employer campaign activity and election outcomes may be complex and dependent on the presence of various facilitating conditions. Under some circumstances overly aggressive employer opposition may actually mobilize employee support for unionization. Although this hypothesis requires additional analysis before it can be confirmed, it also suggests that stricter enforcement of National Labor Relations Act provisions and the imposition of substantial penalties for misconduct may not have the effect of increasing union organizing success.

Unions

Research suggests that the degree of effort organizers invest in election campaigns is strongly related to the likelihood of union victory. Unlike the work that has been done on employer campaign strategy, however, little research deals with the effects of union strategies and tactics on success in organizing campaigns, although it does seem that the personal characteristics of organizers affect campaign outcomes. Thus, there is considerable need for research on this topic.

An important development of the union side has been the use of innovative organizing techniques, particularly corporate campaigns and programs of interunion cooperation. Yet these techniques appear to be used relatively infrequently. Both approaches generate certain political problems within and between unions. Moreover, anecdotal evidence indicates that these techniques are not always effective. Thus, research studies, perhaps involving intensive case studies of particular programs, would be quite useful here.

Assertions that innovative campaign techniques will enhance union organizing effectiveness constitute at best informed speculation on the part of union officials. The labor movement is clearly searching for a formula that will work, and approaches such as the corporate campaign are highly experimental. This is not to denigrate these undertakings, as organizations confronting turbulent and uncertain environments must often implement programs based on incomplete information. The danger for the labor movement lies primarily in the conventional decision-making processes of unions outlined in chapter 3. If there is a tendency toward rationalization and rigidity, then new programs that ought to be treated as experiments may continue despite failure, particularly if championed by those who are politically influential.

Although corporate campaigns may prove to be quite effective in organizing drives, it is not clear that fundamental public policy objectives are always well served through the use of this method. Neutrality agreements obtained by coercive means may eliminate egregious employer misconduct. Yet employee free choice would also seem to be hampered by a complete absence of employer involvement in the campaign. Employer statements, though self-serving, may balance equally self-serving union propaganda. There are unquestionably circumstances in which union campaign promises will be totally unreasonable, or the union may be corrupt. Under these conditions employer campaigns can play a valuable role in bringing needed information to employees. An even more serious threat to free choice is created when corporate campaigns are used to secure recognition without an election, as employees are then also denied the opportunity to express their opinion through a secret ballot. Granted, employers cannot recognize a union without some demonstration of majority status. But if there is coercion, peer pressure, or misrepresentation during the card-signing drive, then employees are denied the opportunity to reconsider their support for bargaining. These same objections would not be so strong when employers voluntarily enter into neutrality agreements or extend recognition. Employers are only likely to do so if convinced that union support is so substantial that opposition would be futile.[2]

THE REPRESENTATION PHASE

Employers now actively pursue strategies designed to destabilize and remove incumbent unions with greater vigor than at any time subsequent to enactment of the National Labor Relations Act. A number of techniques are apparently common, though the true extent of employer deunionization efforts is unknown. Unfortunately, we have scant evidence of the impact of most of these techniques, and research is clearly needed. The impact of union responses to deunionization efforts is also not well researched, though some of the more commonly used methods (e.g., internal organizing, in-plant strategies, corporate campaigns) are fairly well identified.

AN EDITORIAL

Students of the American industrial relations system live in interesting, though turbulent, times. Only a few years ago some within the field were predicting, at least in private, that the labor movement would collapse by the end of the century. But union membership has stabilized and appears to be once again increasing (though only slightly). More significant, union leaders are beginning to respond in creative ways to the threat posed by the aggressive antiunionism of contemporary management. Thus, I am not sure if this book chronicles events in the final days of the labor movement (at least as we have known it over the past half-century) or provides a study of the reawakening of a vital social force in American life.

The question of why management is now so aggressively antiunion remains unanswered, though many suggest it is rooted in shifting values and ideologies. I think those of us who teach in the industrial relations and business fields must take care to reflect on the values that our academic programs bolster. In particular, much of what is taught as human resource management advances an almost arrogant view of management as omnipotent in controlling the destinies of organizations. Although seeming to promote participation and mutuality, the human resource management model often implicitly builds a case for managerial unilateralism and denies the legitimacy of unions. In recent years we have seen increased sensitivity in business schools to questions of ethics, largely as a consequence of scandals in the finance industry. Perhaps the time has come to reflect also on the ethical implications of what is taught in this field.

There likewise is need to be concerned about some of the methods unions are using in trying to turn things around. That a technique works in enhancing the ability of unions to organize or to thwart deunionization efforts does not mean that it is desirable from either an ethical or a public policy perspective. As noted above, corporate campaigns raise some troubling questions about worker free choice. Depending upon how they are conducted, corporate campaigns may largely remove employees from direct involvement in the organizing process. Unlike such self-help activities as organizing strikes or within-plant strategies, they are prone to be less exercises in industrial democracy than expressions of the institutional power some unions may possess. And some corporate campaigns have been almost extortion-like in character. Unions are also relying heavily on influence techniques, which may manipulate and coopt. Efforts that stress image management and largely utilize the techniques of Madison Avenue, though potentially quite effective, may serve to rob the labor movement of substance. The substitution of union paternalism for corporate paternalism in no way serves the interests of workers, who ought to define the organizations that represent them.

Cluster Analysis of Employer Campaign Tactics

The AFL-CIO field report data base contains complete information on campaign tactics, themes, and consultant or attorney involvement for 177 elections (out of about 200 in the total sample). Dummy variables code each of the tactics listed in table 7.2 and each of the major campaign themes (bargaining impact, antiunion, and promanagement) in table 7.3, as well as the involvement of attorneys and consultants as campaign advisers. Hierarchical cluster analysis was used to identify homogeneous activity groupings that define empirically derived strategic categories. Although the clustering variables are all qualitative in character, the Euclidean distance measure is appropriate as a measure of similarity between objects (elections) and was used here for purposes of clustering (Romesburg 1984).[1]

Cluster analysis is a heuristic technique, and determining the proper number of clusters within a given set of data is essentially a matter of judgment. The number of clusters should be sufficiently small so that meaningful categories emerge, though not so few in number as to lack internal homogeneity. Initially, all cases form separate clusters; as clustering proceeds, cases are gathered together until a single cluster results, with the distances increasing between the clusters formed at each iteration. One way of establishing meaningful clusters is to stop clustering when the distances between joined groups becomes relatively large. Diagram A-1 depicts the intercluster distances for the last sixty clusters formed. One criterion used to stop clustering is an abrupt increase in the distance between merged clusters (indicative of increasing heterogeneity within clusters). For the elections in this sample the Euclidean distance increases gradually from sixty down to about fifteen clusters, at which point a small plateau is followed by substantially increasing distances after the cases have been merged into ten clusters. Thus, a reasonable stopping point would seem to be ten clusters. In addition, the clustering tree diagram (not reproduced) indicated that cluster formation down to ten clusters involved building several common clusters. These com-

Diagram A-1. Cluster analysis of employer activities.

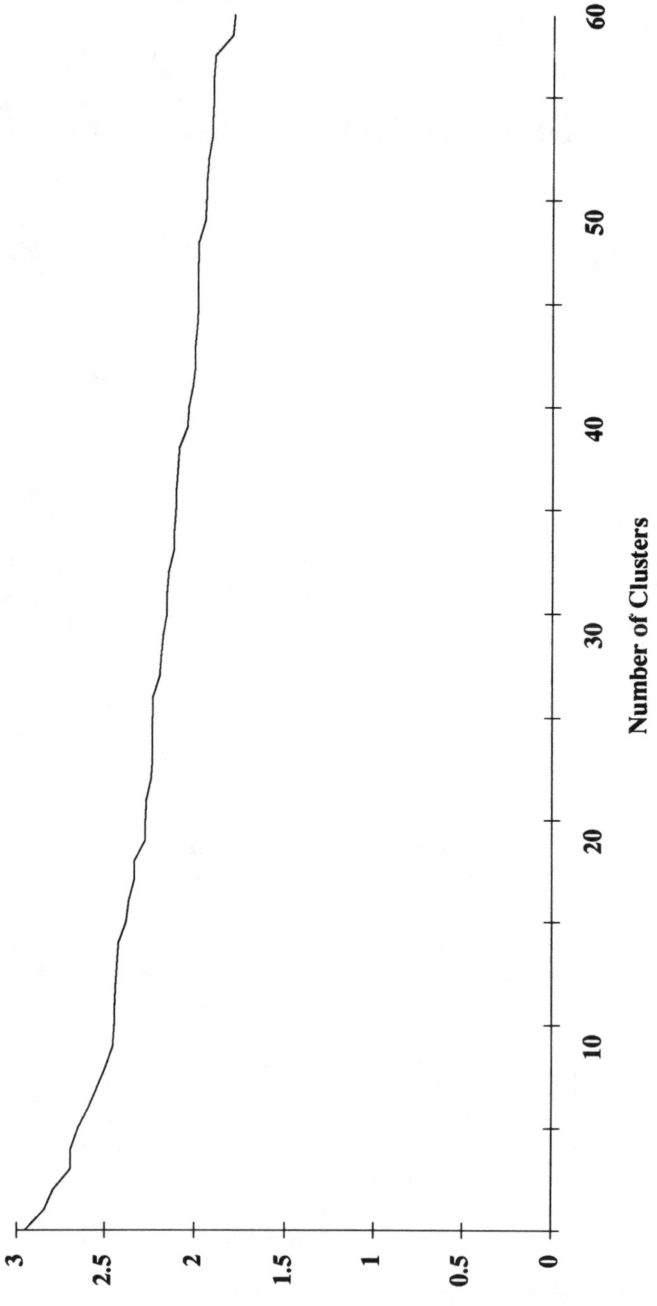

mon clusters were eliminated with fewer than ten clusters, leaving one large cluster and several very small clusters, which also suggests ten clusters to be most meaningful conceptually.

The ten clusters formed using this technique can be divided into three major clusters (containing seventy-eight, thirty-nine, and thirty-nine cases, respectively) and seven minor clusters (three to six cases each). The major clusters define *core strategies*, and the smaller clusters represent *outlier strategies*. Having identified activity clusters, the next step is to characterize these in terms of dominant campaign activities. This is accomplished using discriminant analysis, since multiple attributes can be collapsed into far fewer dimensions that differentiate among the clusters.[2] These dimensions (discriminant functions) are derived in a manner similar to factor analysis. The discriminant functions are linear combinations of the attributes used in the cluster analysis; the discriminating method forms these functions to optimally differentiate among the clusters. The value for a particular function for a given case may be expressed as

$$(A - 1) \quad F_{hj} = \Sigma_i f_{ih} X_{ij}$$

where F_{hj} = discriminant function h for case j; X_{ij} = value of attribute i for case j $(i = 1, 2, 3, \ldots N)$; f_{ih} = discriminant function coefficient for function h and attribute i.

Given the small number of cases in the outlier clusters, discriminant analysis could not be used to differentiate among all ten clusters. Moreover, the outliers, in general, tended to be closer to one another than to the core clusters. Thus, four groups were used in the discriminant analysis: the three core clusters and a residual cluster of the outliers $(N = 21)$. This approach allows us to characterize the differences among the core strategies, as well as differences between the core strategies and outlier strategies. The discriminant functions measure the extent to which an employer utilizes certain combinations of campaign activities that define substrategies (see chapter 2).

The Impact of Unionization/ Deunionization Strategies and Tactics:
Results of Selected Studies

Individual Level Studies

Dickens (1983)	Phase:[1] Campaign Dependent variable: Voting behavior in representation elections Sample: Reanalysis of Getman, Goldberg, and Herman data Principal Findings: *Negative impact on prounion vote exerted by both legal and illegal employer influence tactics
Evansohn (1989)	Phase: Nonunion Dependent variable: Employee desire for unionization Sample: 600+ nonunion employees, Quality of Employment Survey (1977) Principal Findings: *Innovative and rationalized personnel practices reduce probability of nonunion employee supporting unionization

Getman, Goldberg, and Herman (1976)	Phase: Champaign
	Dependent Variable: Voting behavior in representation elections
	Sample: Approximately 1000 employees in 33 NLRB certification elections (1972–1973)
	Principal Findings:
	  *No impact by legal or illegal employer influence tactics (meetings, letters, speeches, threats, etc.)
	  *Weak impact by legal union influence tactics (meetings, letters, speeches, etc.)
	  *Little change in employee voting intentions over course of campaign

Walker and
Lawler (1986)

Phase: Campaign
Dependent Variable: Voting behavior in representation elections
Sample: 285 faculty, California State University system (1981)
Principal Findings:
*No impact by influence tactics of competing unions (meetings, letters, speeches, personal contact)
*Little change in faculty voting intentions over a five-year period between first and second wave interviews

Bargaining Unit Studies

Anderson, Busman,
and O'Reilly (1982)

Phase: Representation
Dependant Variable: Union win/loss
Sample: 114 NLRB decertification elections, California (1978–1979)
Principal Findings:
*Employer influence tactics do not decrease probability of union victory (may have opposite effect)
*Presence of management consultant in election unrelated to probability of union victory
*Union influence tactics increase probability of union victory

Becker and
Miller (1981)

Phase: Campaign
Dependent Variable: Union win/loss
Sample: 1000+ NLRB certification elections, hospitals (1974–1978)
Principal Findings:
*Interunion competition slightly (though insignificantly) increases probability of union victory

Cooke (1983)

Phase: Campaign
Dependent Variable: Union win/loss and proportion of prounion vote
Sample: 3000+ NLRB certification elections, blue-collar workers (1979)
Principal Findings:
*Election delays reduce probability of union victory and prounion vote
*Consent elections (versus directed and stipulated) increase probability of union victory and prounion vote

Cooke (1985a)

Phase: Representation
Dependent Variable: Union attainment of initial contract after certification

Sample: 118 bargaining units, Indiana (1979–1980)
Principal Findings:
    *Postelection procedural delays reduce probability of contract attainment
    *Postelection unfair labor practices by employers (both 8(a)(3) and 8(a)(5)) reduce probability of contract attainment

Cooke (1985b)   Phase: Campaign
Dependent variable: Union win/loss
Sample: 225 NLRB certification elections, Indiana (1979–1980)
Principal Findings:
    *Discriminatory discharges in violation of Section 8(a)(3) of NLRA reduce probability of union victory
    *Election delays not significantly related to election outcome
    *Successful employer challenges to unit composition proposed by union increase probability of union victory

Cooper (1984)   Phase: Campaign
Dependent Variable: Union win/loss
Sample: 791 NLRB certification elections, upper Midwest (1978–1980)
Principal Findings:
    *Election delays slightly decrease probability of union victory
    *Employer unfair labor practices unrelated to probability of union victory
    *Proportion of employees signing authorization cards only weakly associated with election outcome
    *Presence of management consultant or attorney in election reduces probability of union victory; union consultants tend to increase probability of union victory

Delaney (1981)   Phase: Campaign
Dependent Variable: Union win/loss and proportion of prounion vote
Sample: 835 NLRB certification elections, hospitals (1974–1978)
Principal Findings:
    *Interunion competition slightly (though insignificantly) increases probability of union victory; strongly increases prounion vote

Dickens, Wholey, and Robinson (1987)	Phase: Campaign and representation Dependent Variable: Proportion of prounion vote Sample: 11,000+ NLRB certification elections and 1200+ NLRB decertification elections (1977-1979) Principal Findings: *Election delays reduce prounion vote in both certification and decertification elections *Consent elections (versus directed and stipulated) increase prounion vote (but only significantly for certification elections) *Mixed effects found for union organizing effort in certification elections (number of elections union participates in decreases prounion vote, but number of workers in organizing drives increases prounion vote); effects insignificant in decertification elections *Size of national union (as indicator of resources) unrelated to prounion vote
Florkowski and Shuster (1987)	Phase: Campaign Dependent variable: Union win/loss and proportion of prounion vote Sample: 15,000+ certification elections (1974-1979) Principal Findings: *Election delays reduce probability of union victory and prounion vote, but effect tapers off rapidly the longer the delay *Consent elections (versus directed and stipulated) increase probability of union victory and prounion vote
Hurd and McElwain (1988)	Phase: Campaign Dependent Variable: Proportion prounion vote Sample: 622 NLRB certification elections, clerical workers (1979) Principal Findings: *Consent elections (versus directed and stipulated) increase prounion vote *Election delays not significantly related to prounion vote *Interunion competition increases prounion vote
Lawler (1984)	Phase: Campaign Dependent Variable: Union win/loss Sample: 130 NLRB certification elections, midwestern retail grocery outlets (1972-1979)

Principal Findings:
*Presence of consultant in election decreases proba-
bility of union victory
*Generalized employer opposition to bargaining
positively related to probability of union victory

Lawler and
Walker (1984a)

Phase: Campaign
Dependent Variable: Union win/loss
Sample: 138 NLRB and state certification elections,
university and college faculty members (1970-1978)
Principal Findings:
*Interunion competition positively but insignifi-
cantly related to probability of union victory

Lawler and
West (1985)

Phase: Campaign
Dependent variable: Proportion of prounion vote
Sample: 175 NLRB certification elections, AFL-CIO
field reports (1975-1982)
Principal Findings:
*Several employer tactics studied, which generally
had negative impact on prounion vote
*Strongest negative effects exerted by small group
meetings, *Excelsior*-list violations, attitude surveys
*Effects of election delays, directed elections, threats
and promises generally weak
*Consultant effect observed, but complex[2]

Maranto and
Fiorito (1987)

Phase: Campaign
Dependent Variable: Proportion of prounion vote
Sample: NLRB elections, 22,000+ blue-collar and
2,400+ white-collar units (1972-1980)
Principal Findings:
*Generalized employer opposition to bargaining de-
creases prounion vote
*Interunion competition decreases prounion vote in
blue-collar units but increases it in white-collar
units
*Size of national union (as indicator of resources)
increases prounion vote

Mortimer,
Johnson,
and Weiss
(1975)

Phase: Campaign
Dependent Variable: Union election defeats
Sample: Case studies of 28 certification elections in
colleges and universities in which faculty unions
were defeated (1970-1975)
Principal Findings:
*Most union defeats associated with some degree of
strong public opposition to the union by administrators

Porter and Murrmann (1983)	Phase: Campaign
	Dependent variable: Union win/loss
	Sample: 52 NLRB certification elections (no other details provided)
	Principal Findings:
	  *Only simple correlations reported for several employer campaign and preventive labor relations tactics
	  *Most influence tactics reduced probability of union victory
	  *Contextual control tactics designed to create barriers to organizing had mixed effect on probability of union victory
	  *Consultant decreased probability of union victory

Reed (1989a)	Phase: Campaign
	Dependent Variable: Union win/loss and prounion vote
	Sample: 300+ certification elections (1982–1986)
	Principal Findings:
	  *Several personality characteristics of organizers significantly related to prounion vote and probability of union victory (e.g., self-esteem [+], desire for control [+], "Machiavellianism" [−])
	  *Social and demographic characteristics of organizers strongly related to prounion vote but not probability of union victory

Reed (1989b)	Phase: Representation
	Dependent Variable: Union attainment of initial contract after certification
	Sample: 107 bargaining units
	Principal Findings:
	  *Union organizers with personality profiles associated with manipulativeness, social conformity, and rigidity reduce probability of contract attainment
	  *Organizer experience unrelated to probability of contract attainment
	  *Management consultant involvement in election unrelated to probability of contract attainment
	  *Election delays and consent election unrelated to probability of contract attainment
	  *Employer unfair labor practices during campaign and postelection refusal to bargain reduce probability of contract attainment
	  *Some union campaign tactics increase probability of contract attainment

Sandver (1982)	Phase: Campaign

	Dependent Variable: Union win/loss and proportion of prounion vote

Dependent Variable: Union win/loss and proportion of prounion vote
Sample: 42,000+ NLRB certification elections, north versus south (1973-1978)
Principal Findings:
 *Consent elections increase probability of union victory and prounion vote

Seeber (1983)
Phase: Campaign
Dependent Variable: Proportion of prounion vote
Sample: 6800+ certification elections, manufacturing (1973-1979)
Principal Findings:
 *Interunion competition increases prounion vote

Stephan and
Kaufman (1987)
Phase: Campaign
Dependent Variable: union win/loss
Sample: 12,000+ NLRB certification elections (1973 and 1981)
Principal Findings:
 *Consent elections increase probability of union victory
 *Election delays decrease probability of union victory
 *Interunion competition increases probability of union victory
 *Statewide employer unfair labor practice rate unrelated to probability of union victory

Organizational Level Studies[3]

Fiorito, Lowman,
and Nelson (1987)
Phase: Nonunion
Dependent Variable: New plants opened ultimately organized and union win rate in elections in company
Sample: Panel study, 270+ companies (Conference Board survey)
Principal Findings:
 *"Union substitution" personnel practices generally reduce union organizing success
 *Some techniques increase organizing success (e.g., work sharing)
 *Influence tactics (participation, communications) most effective in reducing organizing effectiveness

Jenkins and
Perrow (1977)
Phase: Campaign
Dependent Variable: Outcome of farm worker organizing drives
Sample: Case analyses of the National Farm Labor Union and the United Farm Workers

Principal Findings:
*Resources available to support union organizing drive most important in determining success of the effort

Kochan, McKersie, and Chalykoff (1986)

Phase: Nonunion
Dependent Variable: New plants opened ultimately organized and number of workers organized
Sample: Panel study, 200+ companies (Conference Board survey)
Principal Findings:
*Number of innovative personnel policies decreases organizing success
*Commitment to union-avoidance strategy by management decreases organizing success

Reed (1989d)

Phase: Campaign and representation
Dependent Variable: Union organizing effectiveness and union attainment of initial contract after certification
Sample: Survey of sixty-four organizers in eight unions
Principal Findings:
*"Progressive" unions more successful than "traditional" unions in attaining initial contracts[4]
*Yield on organizing effort (effective number of employees organized per day of campaigning) slightly higher (but not significantly) in progressive unions

Voos (1983)

Phase: Campaign
Dependent Variable: Proportion of nonunion workers organized within national union's traditional jurisdiction
Sample: Time-series/cross-sectional data for a sample of national unions (1964–1977)
Principal Findings:
*Union expenditures per organizable worker increase the proportion organized
*Election delays unrelated to organizing outcomes

Aggregate Level Studies

Dworkin and Fain (1989)

Phase: Campaign
Dependent Variable: Annual national average union victory rate and proportion of prounion vote
Sample: All NLRB elections (1977–1985)
Principal Findings:
*Interunion competition associated with higher probability of union victory and greater prounion vote

Elliott and Hawkins (1982)	Phase: Representation Dependent Variable: Aggregate annual decertification elections lost per million union members Sample: Aggregate NLRB decertification election data (1948–1979) Principal Findings: *Investment of union resources in organizing of new units increases likelihood of decertification in established units
Freeman (1986)	Phase: Campaign Dependent Variable: Proportion of workers organized in certification elections within industries Sample: Pooled time-series/cross-sectional data for NLRB certification elections (1950–1980) Principal Findings: *Employer discrimination (8(a)(3) cases per election) reduces proportion organized
Hunt and White (1985)	Phase: Campaign Dependent Variable: Union victory rate and proportion of prounion vote Sample: NLRB certification election data, 96 Standard Metropolitan Statistical Areas (SMSAs) (1972–1976) Principal Findings: *Consent elections increase union victory rate and prounion vote *Election delays decrease union victory rate and prounion vote *Employer unfair labor practices slightly increase prounion vote, but unrelated to victory rate *Use of postelection procedures by management decreases prounion vote, but unrelated to victory rate
Moore and Newman (1988)	Phase: Campaign Dependent Variable: Statewide union density Sample: Pooled cross-sectional/time-series (every ten years, 1950–1980) Principal Findings: *Employer unfair labor practices unrelated to union membership
Prosten (1979)	Phase: Campaign Dependent Variable: Union victory rate and proportion of workers organized in representation elections Sample: Aggregate NLRB certification election data (1962–1977)

	Principal Findings:
	*Stipulated (versus consent) elections reduce the probability of union victory
	*Election delays reduce the probability of union victory
Roomkin and Block (1981)	Phase: Campaign
	Dependent Variable: Union victory rate
	Sample: Aggregate NLRB certification election data (1971–1977)
	Principal Findings:
	*Election delays reduce union victory rate
Roomkin and Juris (1979)	Phase: Campaign
	Dependent Variable: Union victory rate
	Sample: Aggregate NLRB certificaton election data (1956–1976)
	Principal Findings:
	*Election delays reduce union victory rate
Seeber and Cooke (1983)	Phase: Campaign
	Dependent Variable: Proportion of prounion vote within states
	Sample: Pooled time-series/cross-sectional data for NLRB certification elections (1970–1978)
	Principal Findings:
	*Consent elections increase probability of union victory
Stepina and Fiorito (1986)	Phase: Campaign
	Dependent Variable: Relative change in total union membership
	Sample: Time-series data (1947-1982)
	Principal Findings:
	*Consent elections unrelated to changes in union membership
	*Employer unfair labor practices unrelated to changes in union membership

Notes

CHAPTER 1. INTRODUCTION

1. Of course, not all structural changes are unintentional or passive. For example, employers may open plants in areas with low rates of unionization or selectively hire employees with demographic characteristics associated with low union proneness. Purposeful efforts to shift or transform the environment within which unions, employers, and workers interact so as to affect U/DU outcomes are treated here as strategic moves and will be discussed extensively in later chapters.

2. Not all U/DU strategies involve efforts to undercut or defeat an opponent. For example, either out of principle or as a matter of expedience, an employer may choose not to oppose an organizing effort, either by entering into a "neutrality" agreement or by directly recognizing a union without demanding a representation election.

CHAPTER 2. UNIONIZATION, DEUNIONIZATION, AND STRATEGIC ACTION: A THEORETICAL FRAMEWORK

1. The model proposed here builds on the author's earlier work in this area (Lawler and West 1985; Lawler 1986).

2. In both instances, of course, the employer is required, in principle, to have some good faith basis for its action (i.e., a belief that the union in question does [or does not] represent the majority of bargaining unit employees).

3. A "bargaining unit" does not technically exist until a union is recognized or certified for a particular group of employees. During an organizing campaign, such a group is most appropriately termed an *election unit*. Prior to unionization and in the absence of any overt union activity, there really is no applicable term. To simplify matters, the terms *bargaining unit* and *unit* are used here to signify both potential and established bargaining units (including settings in which no union is currently active).

4. An employer might undertake to replace a militant incumbent union with a friendlier outside union, perhaps even going so far as to establish a "company union." Alternatively, an outside union might use the turmoil of a deunionization campaign to supplant an incumbent union.

5. For example, Ashenfelter and Pencavel (1969) rely extensively on Dunlop's article, despite its institutionalist perspective. More recently, Fiorito and Greer (1982) use Dunlop as a basis for structuring their extensive review of the union growth literature.

6. Examples of macro-level studies of this type include those by Ashenfelter and Pencavel (1969), Bain and Elsheikh (1976), Mancke (1971), Pencavel (1971), and Neumann and Rissman (1984). Micro-level studies include papers by Lee (1978), Farber and Saks (1980), Farber (1983), and Leigh (1985).

7. Examples include Stepina and Fiorito (1986) and Lawler and Hundley (1983).

8. See Brett and Hammer (1982) for a review of several studies of this type done in the 1970s. More recent behavioral research includes work by Zalesny (1985) and Youngblood et al. (1984).

9. Younger workers may see themselves as having greater job mobility than more senior workers; they may also think union seniority systems put them at a disadvantage. Older workers may not expect sufficient returns from unionization over their remaining work years to justify organization.

10. Some studies have included more precise measures of structure or technology or both in analyses of union victory chances in representation elections (e.g., Becker and Miller 1981; Lawler and Walker 1984a). Such variables have been found to affect outcomes significantly, even after controlling for unit size.

11. For a discussion of these factors and the results of various studies, see reviews by Block and Premack (1983), Fiorito and Greer (1982), and Heneman and Sandver (1983).

12. "Lorenzo Blasts Unions for Eastern's Problems, Says Labor Costs Must Be Lowered to Compete," *Daily Labor Report*, 20 April 1988, A13–A14.

13. "Eastern Charges Unions with 'Smear Campaign' in $1.5 Billion Suit under Racketeering Law," *Daily Labor Report*, 9 May 1988, A12.

14. Contextual control and conversion or intimidation tactics may complement one another. That contextual conditions are changed does not guarantee that strategic targets will immediately recognize these changes. Persuasive and coercive statements may be used to make new conditions salient.

15. The union and employer might negotiate certain contractual provisions that have implications for the long-term viability of union representation (e.g., union security clauses, changes in bargaining structure, superseniority for union stewards and officers, a neutrality agreement).

16. For example, the Lou Harris organization has conducted polls for the AFL-CIO of worker attitudes regarding unions.

17. Not all U/DU tactics involve activities directed at achieving the organization's preferred outcome. Some tactics entail attempts to cut potential losses, as in the case of a union withdrawing from a bargaining unit. Similarly, employers may grant recognition to a union without an election being held.

CHAPTER 3. RIGIDITY AND RENEWAL: STRATEGIC CHOICE PROCESSES IN UNIONS

1. For example, the creation of multiunion organizing committees or restrictions on the involvement of management consultants in representation elections are examples of changes in decision-making structures that might have profound effects on subsequent strategic choices.

2. *Risk* is generally taken to mean conditions in which the relationships among the elements of a decision model are only known with certain probabilities. In contrast, *uncertainty* involves conditions in which probabilities are either unknown or highly unreliable. As an example of risk, a union may be able to use past experience to predict its likelihood of victory as its investment in the organizing effort varies. Yet if the union were to become involved in an industry with little prior organizing activity (e.g., high--

technology manufacturing), there would likely be little reliable information upon which to estimate success probabilities, which would constitute pure uncertainty. More generally, risk and uncertainty can be viewed as measures of a decision maker's lack of information.

3. Minimax, maximin, and related approches are useful when a decision maker is able to identify outcome possibilities but not the probabilities of those outcomes obtaining. A minimax approach involves selecting a course of action that minimizes the maximum loss that might occur, and a maximin approach maximizes the minimum gain. The choice of techniques depends, in part, on the risk-taking propensities of the decision makers.

4. Although perhaps not as likely in the period studied by Block, some unions avoid the election approach to certification, preferring to push for direct recognition. Block's measure would thus substantially underestimate organizing expenditures for any union acting in this fashion. In addition, there may well be an inverse relationship between average unit size and elections per one thousand members. If a union allocates a fixed proportion of its annual budget to organizing and, as seems reasonable, the cost of organizing campaigns is proportional to unit size, then the larger the average unit size, the fewer elections a union will be able to afford. Hence, Block's measure is apt to underestimate organizing expenditures for unions that are involved in jurisdictions characterized by particularly large election units.

5. The rate of employment change in the union's primary jurisdiction and the proportion of a union's contracts with union security clauses are also included in the analysis as control variables.

6. Given the theoretical curvilinear relationship between organizing activity and both union density and membership concentration, it would have seemed appropriate for Block to have included squared terms for both of those variables. This was not done on the tenuous assumption that since most unions studied had relatively high unionization rates the sample would tend to be situated in the negative region of the function.

7. There is some controversy over the appropriate deflator to use in adjusting nominal expenditures for inflation. Voos used the consumer price index, though Freeman and Medoff (1984, 229) argue that a wage deflator ought to be used to control for the labor intensity of organizing activity. Voos (1984) questions their approach but also reports figures computed using the wage deflator. That approach suggests a substantial *decline* in expenditures per organizable worker over the period.

8. This is not to suggest that employees do not affect organizational goals through political action. However, profitability and related financial considerations are likely to be dominant.

9. Pfeffer and Salancik build on the earlier work of Yuchtman and Seashore (1967), who proposed a framework for assessing organizational effectiveness in terms of an organization's ability to secure a continual flow of critical resources from its environment.

10. The concept of dependence and social power is rather more complex than this, and the reader is referred to chapter 3 of Pfeffer and Salancik for a thorough treatment of these issues.

11. This is reminiscent of the *dual loyalty* problem frequently discussed in the industrial relations literature.

12. For an overview of general themes in the behavioral decision literature, see Ungson, Braunstein, and Hall (1981).

13. Walton and McKersie (1965) discuss at some length the difference between the "behavioral" and "substantive" expectations of constituents during negotiations. Negotiators, seeking both a politically acceptable and workable settlement, may pacify

constituents by conforming to their behavioral expectations (e.g., issuing strike threats and acting aggressively in public) while making concessions on substantive matters. Thus, if properly accomplished, intraorganizational bargaining can generate perceptions of achievement where true achievement may be lacking.

14. For a thorough treatment of "sense making" and related cognitive processes in organizational settings, see Sims, Gioia, and Associates (1986).

15. See pages 15–31 of the report. The approaches unions have taken in implementing these suggestions, as well as their possible effects, are considered in later chapters.

16. "Convention Report Spells Out Organizing, Bargaining Goals," *AFL-CIO News*, 26 October 1985, 21.

17. See, for example, Harry Bernstein, "AFL-CIO Seeks Greater Role with Affiliates," *Los Angeles Times*, 5 March 1986, sec. 4, 1.

18. As quoted in Bernstein, "AFL-CIO Seeks Greater Role with Affiliates."

19. As quoted by Peter Perl, "Labor Leaders Adopt Blueprint for Change," *Washington Post*, 22 February 1985, sec. A, 4.

20. "Trades Cool to Plan Offering New Benefits," *Engineering News-Record*, 21 November 1985, 49.

21. Leonard Apcar, "AFL-CIO's Novel Program to Expand Union Membership Meets Resistance," *Wall Street Journal*, 30 October 1985, 7.

22. See chapters 6–8 for more detailed discussion of these experiments.

23. The latter issue is taken up in chapter 7.

24. "Steelworkers Plan for Survival," *Union Labor Report*, 11 August 1988, 8.

CHAPTER 4. SEIZING THE INITIATIVE: EMPLOYER STRATEGY FORMULATION

1. This theme has been developed by many authors. For a recent treatment see Piore and Sabel (1984).

2. See comments by Seymour M. Lipset in Burton (1988).

3. See comments by George Strauss in Burton (1988).

4. Recall that, in chapter 3, similar false attributions and distortions were argued to promote rigidity on the union side.

5. A *nonrational* decision is one that is suboptimal but still potentially beneficial to the decision maker. *Irrational* decisions are choices that are so ill-considered as to generate deleterious consequences as a matter of course.

6. The concept of a backfire effect is discussed in greater detail in later chapters. See also Lawler (1984).

7. For a review of this literature see Pfeffer (1982, 221–224).

8. The UPC is affiliated with the American Federation of Teachers (AFT), and the CFA was formed out of a coalition of the American Association of University Professors, the National Education Association, and the California State Employees' Association. The CFA ultimately won recognition in a closely contested election held in 1981. Prior to the election the CFA, which had established an institutional identity of its own, changed its name from the Congress of Faculty Associations.

9. See Walker and Lawler (1979) for a discussion of the ideological differences between the UPC and the CFA.

10. The latter variable has some obvious limitations, since firms may be unionized or not unionized for many reasons apart from an employer's attitudes toward collective bargaining. Unionization was included as a proxy for union sentiments given the strong correlation between these variables in both the 1977 and 1983 Conference Board surveys.

CHAPTER 5. LABOR RELATIONS CONSULTANTS

1. The increasing role of consultants began to be highlighted by the press in the late 1970s and early 1980s. For example, see "A New Breed of Antiunion 'Experts,' " *U.S. News and World Report* (30 January 1978): 82; "Labor Fights Back against Union Busters," *U.S. News and World Report* (10 December 1979): 96; "When the Boss Calls in This Expert, the Union May Be in Real Trouble," *Wall Street Journal* (19 November 1979): 1; and "The Union Busters," *Newsweek* (29 January 1980): 67. Not unexpectedly, the labor press voiced early concern with the expanding presence of what labor leaders disparagingly termed "union busters" (Payne 1977; McDonald and Wilson 1979). In addition, congressional hearings on employer antiunion activity (U.S. Congress 1981) pointed to the growth of consultant involvement in the labor relations area.

2. Rogers, the architect of the J. P. Stevens campaign in the late 1970s, has designed and managed a number of subsequent corporate campaigns. Not all of these have been so successful, and he has come under fire in recent years from some within the labor movement. Most controversial was the campaign directed against Hormel as part of a contract dispute at its Austin, Minnesota, plant.

3. See Michael Verespej, "The New Battleground," *Industry Week* (6 April 1987): 40–41.

4. See "Unions Test Marketing Waters," *Advertising Age*, 27 February 1984, 1ff., and "$13 Million Advertising Campaign Will Be Largest in AFL-CIO History," *Daily Labor Report*, 30 December 1987, A2–A3.

5. The McClellan Committee focused in particular on the activities of Chicago-based Labor Relations Associates, which had several hundred clients and earned some $2.5 million dollars in fees and retainers over the period 1950–1956 (Payne 1977). The company made extensive use of behavioral management techniques and related methods to help clients avoid unionization. For example, attitudinal surveys were used to identify union sympathizers, and committees of employees were established to work against organization.

6. See also "From Brass Knuckles to Briefcases: The Changing Art of Union-Busting in America," a pamphlet prepared in 1979 by the Center to Protect Workers' Rights.

7. Although there have long been law firms specializing in union-avoidance activity, many of the country's leading management labor law firms developed reputations in the postwar period of being "tough but fair." That is, although acting as spirited advocates for their clients, they did not challenge a union's fundamental legitimacy. In recent years, however, it would appear that a significant proportion of even these elite firms have moved into the union-avoidance area to at least some extent. One example of this transformation would seem to be the case of Chicago-based Seyfarth, Shaw, Fairweather and Geraldson, probably the country's largest labor law firm, whose activities have often been highlighted in AFL-CIO literature (e.g., McDonald and Wilson 1979; AFL-CIO *RUB Sheet* (Report on Union Busters), no. 2 (March 1979); AFL-CIO *RUB Sheet*, no. 29 (October 1981).

8. In the Wagner Act era (1935–1947) the NLRB had initially held that almost any employer action to influence the outcome of a campaign involved illegal interference with employee free choice. The Supreme Court later held (*NLRB* v. *Virginia Electric and Power*, 314 U.S. 469 [1941]) that an absolute prohibition against all statements could not be imposed by the NLRB. Though standards were relaxed in this area after *Virginia Electric*, section 8(c) provided even greater freedom for employers by holding that no statement made by an employer with regard to collective bargaining could be construed as unfair labor practice *unless* they contained threats of promises of benefit.

In implementing Taft-Hartley, the NLRB established certain standards of conduct that applied to election campaigns and that were intended to preserve "laboratory conditions" (*General Shoe Corporation*, 77 NLRB 124 [1948]). In particular, the NLRB held that conduct that did not constitute an unfair labor practice could still be the basis for nullifying the results of an election should that conduct interfere substantially with the outcome of the election. For a further discussion of the development of the NLRB campaign standards, see Taylor and Whitney (1987, 283–324).

9. 27 LRRM 2012 (1950).

10. For a discussion of evolving NLRB policy, see Schlossberg and Scott (1983, 166–173). Card-based bargaining orders may, of course, be issued as remedies in certain unfair labor practice cases under the *Gissel* doctrine (71 LRRM 2481 [1969]).

11. AFL-CIO *RUB Sheet*, no. 8 (September 1979).

12. Consultants and employers are obliged under the Landrum-Griffin Act (Labor Management Reporting and Disclosure Act, 1959) to file annual statements with the Labor Department when a consultant is hired to engage in certain activities related to the exercise of employee rights under the NLRA. Reportable activities may be perfectly legal, although failure to file the necessary reports is a violation of the law. Very few firms actually do file, however, and Labor Department enforcement is lax. Reporting and other issues related to the regulation of consultant activity are discussed later in this chapter.

13. Modern Management Methods was not, of course, connected to 3M Corporation.

14. AFL-CIO *RUB Sheet*, no. 16 (May 1980).

15. AFL-CIO *RUB Sheet*, no. 15 (April 1980).

16. Even though union sources of information on consultants are problematic, the BNA report (1985a) also noted that unions are the only organizations regularly monitoring and collecting information on consultants. National directories of consultants do list labor relations and human resource consultants, but these are self reports that do not clearly identify the range of activities of the firms.

17. One of the functions of the AFL-CIO *RUB Sheet* is to provide just this sort of intelligence to field organizers.

18. The author was told of one situation, by a management representative involved, in which the consultant avoided even visiting the employer's facilities. All communications from the consultant were sent in plain envelopes to a post office box maintained by the employer under a fictitious name.

19. "NLRB Finds No Atmosphere of Fear Existed from Posting of Management Consultant Memo," *Daily Labor Report*, 13 June 1986, A1–A2.

20. Sally Obringer, "Decertification in Mass Transit" (tutorial paper, University of Illinois, Institute of Labor and Industrial Relations, May 1985.) This paper is on file at the institute's library.

21. The states studied included Minnesota, North Dakota, South Dakota, Wisconsin, Iowa, Michigan, and Indiana.

22. "Unions and Management Representatives Disagree on Extent of Consultants' Influence," *Daily Labor Report*, 19 April 1988, C1–C3.

23. See *Daily Labor Report*, "Unions and Management Representative Disagree."

24. See *Daily Labor Report*, "Unions and Management Representative Disagree."

25. These analyses were based on a subsample of the cases, since client industry and union were not always reported.

26. The study covered a period prior to the formation of United Food and Commercial Workers (UFCW), which involved a merger of the Retail Clerks and Meatcutters.

27. It was not possible to determine whether attorneys or management consultants were used in some of the field reports in the sample; such cases were deleted from the analysis.

28. See *Daily Labor Report*, "Unions and Management Representative Disagree."

29. "Captive audience" speeches are so termed because management is in a position to require employees to attend such meetings during work hours. Unions, on the other hand, are not guaranteed this type of access to bargaining unit employees. Captive audience presentations are subject to certain restrictions under NLRB election procedures (e.g., a captive audience speech may not be given within the twenty-four hours preceding an election).

30. Cases falling into the second, third, and fourth categories in table 5.5 were scored as having a campaign adviser involved.

31. For more on factors linked to employer use of consultants, see chapter 4.

32. The backfire effect is discussed in more detail in chapter 9.

33. For various perspectives on enforcement under the Reagan administration, see "Union Organizers Tell of Frustrations in Getting Labor Consultant Reporting," *Daily Labor Report*, 8 February 1984, A8–A9; "Report Charges Labor Department Has Abandoned Labor Consultant Reporting Rules under LMRDA," *Daily Labor Report*, 7 February 1984, A5–A6; "Labor Department Official Defends Policies on Enforcing Landrum-Griffin Consultant Rules," *Daily Labor Report*, 9 February 1984, A13–A24; and "NLRB Chairman Dotson Challenges Assertion That Labor Department Was Lax on Consultants," *Daily Labor Report*, 10 February 1984, A8–A9.

34. See "Court Orders Stricter Enforcement of LMRDA Reporting Requirements," *Daily Labor Report*, 8 February 1988, A8–A9.

35. "Unions, Employers, Are Monitoring Closely Case on Employer Consulting Activity," *Daily Labor Report*, 6 January 1989, CC1–CC3.

CHAPTER 6. IMPLEMENTING UNIONIZATION/DEUNIONIZATION STRATEGIES IN NONUNION SETTINGS

1. Such meaning construction and enactment processes are similar to those processes discussed in chapter 3 in relation to union decision making and strategic rigidity.

2. Unfortunately, the Porter and Murrmann sample was relatively small (fifty-two companies) and geographically concentrated, so it is not clear how reliable or generalizable their results are.

3. Discrimination with respect to union proneness, like other forms of discrimination, may occur even though upper management has not established such a policy. Supervisors and personnel officers may act on their own, though the failure of executives to prohibit such practices may be taken by lower-level managers as signaling approval. Over time, discriminatory criteria may become institutionalized even without upper management's knowledge or approval.

4. For a discussion of some of the legal issues relating to independent contractor status and the duty to recognize a union, see Gale (1981, 96–146) and Jansonius (1985).

5. About 33 percent of the firms in the Porter and Murrmann (1983) study trained supervisors in the detection of possible organizing efforts.

6. See, for example, Alfred Vadnais, "The Fifteen Early Warning Signs of Union Organizing Activity," *Personnel Administrator* (April 1986): 14ff.

7. Arbitration is usually restricted to discharge cases.

8. About half of the firms in the Porter and Murrmann (1983) study reviewed employee complaints with the intention of discovering possible organizing activity. Only about 12 percent similarly reviewed personnel records, looking for signs of employee discontent such as increased absenteeism and turnover.

9. See, for example, Favius O'Brien and Donald Drost, "Nonunion Grievance Procedures: Not Just an Antiunion Strategy," *Personnel* (September–October 1984): 61–69.

10. An attorney with a leading management-labor law firm explained to the author that most of his company's work in the positive labor relations side involves designing handbooks that promise a great deal but legally bind the employer to little or nothing.

11. Some examples, which are documents prepared by the Food and Beverage Trades Department of the AFL-CIO, include "Basic Organizing Research for Private Companies" and "Lodging Industry Research Manual."

12. Robert Whiting, "Lessons for the AFL-CIO's Houston Organizing Project," *Personnel Administrator* (January 1984): 83ff.

13. Diversification is also a consequence of increased union mergers in recent years (see Warren Brown, "Like Corporations, Unions Merge and Diversify for Survival," *Washington Post*, 9 April 1980, 2).

14. "Steelworkers Report Focuses on Organizing," *Daily Labor Report*, 26 September 1984, A10.

15. See BNA (1985b, 113–118) and "Unions Test Marketing Waters," *Advertising Age*, 27 February 1984, 1ff. Advertising campaigns are also used, for a somewhat different purpose, during corporate campaigns (see discussion of corporate campaigns in chapters 7 and 8) and election campaigns.

16. See "$13 Million Advertising Campaign Will Be Largest in AFL-CIO History," *Daily Labor Report*, 30 December 1987, A2–A3.

17. See "AFL-CIO Releases Poll Showing Rise in Public Approval Rating of Unions," *Daily Labor Report*, 24 August 1988, A4–A5.

18. See James Warren, "Portrayals of Labor Don't Do the Job," *Chicago Tribune*, 1 March 1989, sec. 2, 1ff.

19. See, for example, Jonathan Tasini, "Big Labor Tries the Soft Sell," *Business Week* (13 October 1986): 126, and Carey W. English, "Now It's Unions Offering Fringe Benefits to Workers," *U.S. News and World Report* (11 November 1985): 86.

20. See "Effectiveness of New Union Strategies Urged by AFL-CIO Still Open Question," *Daily Labor Report*, 1 June 1987, C1–C3.

21. See "Teachers Union Reports Initial Success under AFL-CIO's Program for Associate Membership," *Daily Labor Report*, 30 March 1988, A1–A2.

CHAPTER 7. ELECTION CAMPAIGN STRATEGIES

1. Exceptions involve voluntary recognition by the employer and NLRB-ordered recognition, which can occur even without an election as a remedy for certain employer unfair labor practices. Since employers may legitimately refuse a demand for recognition in virtually all circumstances (see discussion in chapter 5) and NLRB-ordered recognition is a rarity, elections are generally mandatory.

2. Union victory rates in these elections remained unchanged, at about 48 percent.

3. Alex Kotlowitz, "Labor's Turn?" *Wall Street Journal*, 28 August 1987, 1ff.

4. "Changing Economy May Improve Climate for Union Organizing, Attorney Warns," *Daily Labor Report,* 14 November 1986, A7–A9.

5. Employer campaign strategies typically involve extensive legal maneuvering, both before and after elections, which is the responsibility of management attorneys. Management must clearly coordinate a wide range of intraunit activities with legal initiatives, however, so these two aspects of campaign strategy are linked. Moreover, management must generally make the final decision on how hard and when to push on the legal front.

6. Theodore Sares, "Precinct Techniques in NLRB Elections," *Personnel Administrator* (June 1983): 11ff.

7. Of course, the NLRA requires only a 30 percent showing of interest to petition for an election. Most organizers would view petitioning for an election, especially these days, without at least 50 percent support as courting disaster.

8. Under the *Livingston Shirt* rule (33 LRRM 1156 [1953]), employers may use captive audience speeches and deny equal access to unions if they do not also enforce broad "no-solicitation" rules that disallow the union other means of communication with bargaining unit members in the workplace (Williams 1985, 269–288). In addition, the *Peerless Plywood* rule (33 LRRM 1151 [1953]) bars both employer and union captive audience speeches for a full twenty-four hours prior to an election ("twenty-four-hour rule").

9. Drotning's reliance on election interference charges as a data source is questionable, since the decision to bring such charges is itself a strategic decision. Obviously, very few union objections will be raised in elections in which the union won, and objections may be exaggerated in elections that unions have lost.

10. See, for example, "Delta Catfish Workers Vote for Union at Mississipppi Plant," *Daily Labor Report,* 15 October 1986, A9–A10.

11. These categories are similar to those suggested by Fulmer (1982, 65–73), who listed four major employer campaign themes: (a) generalized antiunion messages, (b) antiunion messages related to the union or unions involved in the specific campaign, (c) procompany messages, and (d) low-key messages encouraging employees to oppose bargaining as a matter of personal choice. Fulmer suggests, impressionistically, that categories b and c are most common, also noting that these themes may also be associated with specific issues (e.g., compensation, worker control, etc.).

12. Of course, not all directed elections are the consequence of employer actions. There may be circumstances in which a union would prefer the directed election route, which is especially likely when two or more unions are in competition. In general, however, the union-avoidance literature recommends that employers use NLRB procedures in the manner described above. This provides both the opportunity to delay the election and the resolution of the case (a clear advantage to the employer should the union win the election) and gives the employer more opportunities to challenge the union both before and after the election. In contrast, experienced organizers generally recommend that the union seek an election at the earliest possible date and avoid the complications of NLRB procedures.

13. For a description of NLRB procedures in certification and decertification elections, see Lawler (1990).

14. There are some obvious exceptions to this rule. For example, an incumbent union that faces a challenge for recognition by an outside union or as the result of a decertification petition would probably find a delaying effort to its advantage.

15. Simple consent election cases are resolved by regional directors, generally within a matter of days after the election. In stipulated consent cases appeals may be taken to the NLRB. Although stipulated cases may not result in preelection delays as lengthy as in direct election cases, considerable opportunity exists for postelection delays and also for the nullification of election results should the union win.

16. The AFL-CIO reports did not contain information on the use of rules to contain organizing activity, though Porter and Murrmann (1983) report frequencies for some restrictive practices. For example, only 20 percent of the firms imposed limitations on workplace organizing by employees.

17. Supervisors, especially those drawn from the ranks of bargaining unit employees, may empathize with the problems of their subordinates and view middle and upper management as a common enemy. In addition, supervisors may anticipate that negotiated improvements in compensation and working conditions for bargaining unit employees will be extended to management (though they may also fear an erosion in their authority under bargaining). Indeed, prounion activity by supervisors during campaigns is so sufficiently common an issue as to be the basis for several important NLRB cases (Williams 1985, 242–246).

18. Of course, these actions often involve particularly subjective interpretations by the respondents of employer actions and the motives behind them.

19. Roughly 90 percent of the discrimination cases involved allegations of discharge for union activism.

20. For more on union use of neutrality agreements, see the discussion of corporate campaigns below.

21. Another objective of monitoring tactics may be to identify union supporters for retaliatory measures, an important reason for NLRB restrictions on interrogation and surveillance.

22. Individual and group meetings, categorized above as influence tactics, may also have surveillance objectives.

23. As with many campaign practices, the NLRB position on the legality of different monitoring tactics has shifted over time, generally in the direction of being more permissive. Of course, all of the monitoring techniques mentioned above may, under the right circumstances, constitute both election interference and unfair labor practices (8(a)(1), since they create an atmosphere of restraint or coercion) (Williams 1985, 191–226).

24. Of course, attorneys and consultants are not hypothesized to be directly related to U/DU outcomes in the model proposed in chapter 2. Yet the decision to retain an attorney or consultant to act as a campaign adviser is a strategic decision, and activity clusters used to define strategic types should include consultant or attorney activity. Moreover, the inclusion of indicators of attorney or consultant involvement can serve as proxies for unmeasured tactics and campaign themes. In addition, a consultant or an attorney may affect the manner in which tactics are implemented and campaign themes expressed.

25. Recall in chapter 2 that a *substrategy* is defined as an identifiable complex of elementary tactics, though not fully self-contained and limited in scope.

26. The "X" in each cluster in diagram 7.3 marks the group centroid (average value on each dimension). The lines from the centroid to the axes indicate the coordinates of the centroid.

27. For a general discussion of corporate campaign techniques from a labor perspective, see "Developing New Tactics: Winning with Coordinated Corporate Campaigns," a pamphlet published in 1985 by the Industrial Union Department of the AFL-CIO. For other perspectives on corporate campaigns, see Marks (1985), Mishel (1985), and Michael Verespej, "The New Battleground," *Industry Week*, 6 April 1987, 40–41.

28. See, for example, "Paperworkers Launch Boycott of Bank as Part of Campaign against International Paper Co.," *Daily Labor Report*, 6 June 1988, A12–A13.

29. One such method of inserting a labor issue into the agenda of a shareholders' meeting is through public interest proxy resolutions, though this avenue has not often been used by unions (Thompson 1988). Recent changes in SEC rules make such shareholder resolutions more difficult to initiate; thus, they will probably be even less common in the future.

30. See, for example, "Pension Fund Clout Used to Form Union," *Pensions and Investment Age* (26 May 1986): 3ff.

31. A recent example of an apparently effective, though protracted, boycott was the one conducted against Adolph Coors by the AFL-CIO (see "Organizing Campaigns at Coors Brewery Begin, Renew in Wake of AFL-CIO Agreement," *Daily Labor Report*, 1 September 1987, A6–A7).

32. See "Union Organizing Conference Urged to Adopt 'Corporate Strategy,' " *Daily Labor Report*, 10 April 1981, A1–A4. One example of the use of potentially embarrassing information in a corporate campaign involves a union that allegedly threatened to disclose preferential interest rates a bank had granted to a hotel the union was endeavoring to organize unless the bank pressured the hotel to recognize the union (Gilberg and Abrams 1987).

33. This approach is hardly new, though perhaps not recently used. John L. Lewis, for example, promoted the idea of prohibiting federal contracts to labor law violators.

34. The Industrial Union Department issued a pamphlet in 1985 entitled "Developing New Tactics: Winning with Coordinated Corporate Campaigns" to be used as a planning guide for unions in structuring corporate campaigns. Other examples include documents prepared by the Food and Beverage Trades Department of the AFL-CIO, (e.g., "Basic Organizing Research for Private Companies" and "Lodging Industry Research Manual") that detail methods for acquiring financial and other data to be used in campaigns.

35. See "Union Organizing Conference."

36. "Steelworkers Report Focuses on Organizing," *Daily Labor Report*, 26 September 1984, A10.

37. See "AFL-CIO Soon to Open New Office to Develop Organizing Strategies," *Daily Labor Report*, 3 April 1986, A1–A3.

38. See "Labor's New Arsenal," *Newsweek* (23 May 1988): 48.

39. See Gagala (1985) and Jeremy Main, "The Labor Rebel Leading the Hormel Strike," *Fortune* (9 June 1986): 105ff.

40. See Janet Novack, "Publish and Be Damned," *Forbes* (13 July 1987): 380ff.

41. From a report entitled "National Campaign to Counter Union Corporate Strategy and Intimidation Tactics," presented at the 1 December 1987 meeting of the ABC's board of directors.

42. See "Organizing Campaigns at Coors."

43. "How OSHA Helped Organize the Meatpackers," *Business Week* (29 August 1988): 82ff.

44. See "It's Union vs. Union in the Scramble for Members," *Business Week* (3 September 1984): 27, and "Improved Climate for Airline Organizing Prompts Fierce Competition among Unions," *Daily Labor Report*, 23 February 1981, A8–A11.

45. See "Strong Support for Merger Found in Small Unions," *AFL-CIO News*, 4 January 1986, 5.

46. See "Cement Workers' Merger into IBB Coming Unglued; New Independent Union Winning Disaffiliation Votes," *Daily Labor Report*, 21 May 1987, A5–A7.

47. See "Court Fight over Union Merger Jeopardizes Major Organizing Drive," *Daily Labor Report*, 13 February 1989, A1–A2.

48. See "AFL-CIO Orders Health Care Union to Withdraw from Election in Ohio," *Daily Labor Report*, 26 August 1985, A5–A6, and "Sanctions Imposed by Kirkland against Hospital Workers," *Daily Labor Report*, 18 September 1985, A2.

49. See "AFSCME Asks AFL-CIO for $700,000 Penalty against Union Election Rival," *Daily Labor Report*, 25 February 1986, A6–A7.

50. See "AFL-CIO Bars National Hospital Union from Participating in Blues Campaign," *Daily Labor Report*, 28 May 1986, A2.

51. See "Organizing Accord Plan Adopted," *AFL-CIO News*, 22 February 1986, 1.

52. The union must either be able to demonstrate that it undertook organizing within the unit significantly before the other union or unions involved in the case or, should this condition not be met, that it has a much greater chance of winning than the other union or unions.

53. "Teamsters Are Awarded Organizing Rights among Adolph Coors Company Employees," *Daily Labor Report*, 31 March 1988, A9–A10.

54. See "Fraser Makes Initial Arbitration Award under AFL-CIO Mediation-Arbitration Plan," *Daily Labor Report*, 5 June 1986, A3–A4.

55. See "AFL-CIO Officials Predict Long Life for Organizing Project in Houston," *Daily Labor Report*, 10 May 1982, A9–A10.

56. See "Joan Walsh, 'Down in the Valley: Hi-Tech Unions,' " *In These Times*, 30 October–5 November 1985, 7, and "High Tech Lures Union Organizers," *Business Week* (11 April 1983): 101–102.

57. See "Unions Launch Campaign to Organize IBM; Task Likened to Putting 'Man on the Moon,' " *Daily Labor Report*, 22 January 1987, A1–A3. The Communications Workers (CWA) is the lead American union in this effort.

58. See Perry (1987) and "Unions Targeting Beverly Enterprises Say Election Win Rate is 71 Percent," *Daily Labor Report*, 15 March 1985, A6–A7.

59. See BNA (1985b, 96–97) and "Stepped-Up Organizing Produces Gains," *AFL-CIO News*, 14 November 1981, 5.

60. See "AFL-CIO Organizing Project in Atlanta Yielded Meager Gains in 1982 Voting," *Daily Labor Report*, 10 February 1983, A7–A9.

61. See "Unions Still Dividing Territory for Blues Organizing Campaign," *Daily Labor Report*, 7 February 1986, A2–A3.

62. See "AFL-CIO's IUD Points to Success of Southern Organizing Drives," *Daily Labor Report*, 11 November 1988, A4.

CHAPTER 8. DEUNIONIZATION STRATEGIES AND UNION COUNTERMEASURES

1. In any event, the employer would still be obligated to negotiate over the effects of the relocation.

2. *Textile Workers Union* v. *Darlington Manufacturing*, 380 U.S. 263 (1965).

3. Plant relocations accompanied by offers to relocate affected employees are exempt from the WARN notification requirements.

4. See "Acting Labor Solicitor Defends DOL Rule on Content of Notices Provided under WARN," *Daily Labor Report*, 3 February 1989, A12–A14.

5. See, for example, "Transportation: Union Busters Exploit Chapter 11," *The Machinist* (October 1983): 8.

6. See *Border Steel Rolling Mills*, 204 NLRB 814 (1973). For a discussion of the relevant case law, see Bernstein and Cooper (1985) and Miscimarra (1983, 186–189).

7. See, for example, "The Name Game," *Solidarity* (16–31 January 1983): 11–14.

8. The employer may also incur significant costs if permanent replacements are hired during a strike precipitated by employer violations of 8(a)(5). As unfair labor practice strikers, union workers would be entitled to reinstatement and back pay.

9. See table 12 in the *Annual Report of the National Labor Relations Board* (various issues, 1978–1986).

10. See "CWA Official Points to Renewed Organizing Efforts," *Daily Labor Report*, 5 August 1987, A5–A6.

11. "Eastern Charges Unions with 'Smear Campaign' in $1.5 Billion Suit under Racketeering Law," *Daily Labor Report*, 9 May 1988, A12.

12. See "Labor's New Arsenal," *Newsweek* (23 May 1988): 48.

CHAPTER 9. STRATEGIC CHOICES AND UNIONIZATION/DEUNIONIZATION OUTCOMES

1. This study and the Conference Board surveys are explained in greater detail in chapter 4.

2. The "backfire" effect is discussed more extensively later in this chapter.

3. For a review of earlier studies see Brett and Hammer (1982).

4. Workers vary in how job satisfaction facets are most salient in generating support for bargaining. For example, Kochan (1979) finds that blue-collar workers are more likely to support unionization as a result of dissatisfaction with wages and other extrinsic rewards. Conversely, white-collar workers, particularly professional ones, are more responsive to intrinsic sources of dissatisfaction, especially lack of autonomy and influence.

5. *Hollywood Ceramics Co.*, 51 LRRM 1600 (1962).

6. This model is developed more extensively in Brett and Hammer (1982).

7. The California State University election is discussed in greater detail in chapter 4.

8. The author is indebted to suggestions made by Mal Walker, with whom he collaborated in the original study in which these data were collected.

9. Unless otherwise noted, the manner in which the variables in this analysis were constructed is covered in greater detail in Walker and Lawler (1986).

10. The explained variance for each equation is as follows:

$$CB_{81} : R^2 = .66$$
$$UPC_{81} : R^2 = .49$$
$$CFA_{81} : R^2 = .22$$

11. Several variables were included in each category (see Walker and Lawler 1986); these control variables are treated as a group here to simplify presentation of the results.

12. Three different measures of influence tactics were used for each union (degree of personal contact with bargaining unit members, extent of written communications, and frequency of meetings and social gatherings). Each measure was included as a separate variable, and none was statistically significant in any of the equations. They are treated as a single category for each union to simplify presentation of the results.

13. Getman, Goldberg, and Herman (1976) examine the effects of some unfair labor practices that fall into these categories (e.g., discriminatory discharge, interrogation) that are found to be unrelated to voting behavior. However, only selected and clearly illegal contextual control tactics are analyzed.

14. Results of some additional studies not included in Appendix B, most of which report only simple correlations, are summarized in Freeman and Medoff (1984, 234–235).

15. Reed (1989a) also controls for union and employer campaign tactics in his analysis. Unfortunately, parameter estimates for those variables were not reported in the prepublication version of the paper made available to the author.

16. For a discussion of the impact of stress on performance, see McGrath (1975).

17. The Lawler and West study included several measures of employer tactics, with the overall equation being statistically significant. Because of multicollinearity problems, the authors focused their attention largely on the signs and magnitudes of the individual coefficients, rather than on the significance levels.

18. The logit function used to estimate the parameters in table 6.8 is specified as

$$\ln(\% \text{YES}/\% \text{NO}) = a0 + a_1 X_1 + \ldots + a_m X_m + u$$

where: $\% \text{YES}$ = percent yes votes in election;
$\% \text{NO}$ = percent no votes in election;
X_1 = independent variables; a_1 = parameters;
u = error term.

The probability of employees voting in favor of bargaining is a nonlinear transformation of this function:

Let $Z = \% \text{YES}/\% \text{NO}$, then
$$\% \text{YES} = \exp(Z)/(1 + \exp(Z))$$

where: exp( ) represents exponentiation.

It can be readily shown that the first derivative of the probability function with respect to a given independent variable is:

$$d\% \text{YES}/dX_1 = (\% \text{YES})(\% \text{NO})(a_1).$$

19. Because of the nonlinear nature of the probability function, it is necessary to simulate outcomes in the following manner. First, the logarithm of the log-odds ratio for each case is computed for each assumed level of the suppression index. The vote is then computed through the logit transformation, and the simulated election outcome is determined. These numbers are then averaged over the entire sample.

CHAPTER 10. STRATEGY, TACTICS, AND OUTCOMES: AN ASSESSMENT

1. Nonexclusive representation as practiced in the private sector in Europe is not likely to be an especially useful model for the United States, given the differences in ideology and political power that exist between the American and European labor movements.

2. Even this may not always be true, particularly in firms with established bargaining relationships that wish to maintain the good will of the union at the bargaining table.

APPENDIX A. CLUSTER ANALYSIS OF EMPLOYER CAMPAIGN TACTICS

1. For purposes of cluster analysis objects are compared according to some index of similarity (or dissimilarity). The Euclidean distance between any two objects is a standard dissimilarity index; that is, the smaller the Euclidean distance, the greater the

similarity between any two objects. The familiar formula for computing the hypotenuse of a right triangle (which is the Euclidean distance between any two points in a two-dimensional space) generalizes to any n-dimensional space. Given n election attributes (tactics, themes, attorney or consultant activity), the Euclidean distance between elections j and k can be calculated as

$$D_{jk} = \sqrt{[\Sigma_i(X_{ij} - X_{ik})^2]}$$

where D_{jk} = Euclidean distance between objects j and k and $X_{i\cdot}$ = value of ith attribute ($i = 1, 2, \ldots, n$).

This measure is then used to cluster cases; cases are added to groups in an iterative fashion, with the least dissimilar objects joined on any given iteration.

2. The attributes in this study are all dichotomous variables. Although discriminant analysis is based on the assumption that attributes are continuous and normally distributed, the technique is generally considered sufficiently robust to allow use of ordinal variables.

APPENDIX B. THE IMPACT OF UNIONIZATION/DEUNIONIZATION STRATEGIES AND TACTICS: RESULTS OF SELECTED STUDIES

1. See chapter 2 for definitions of three U/DU phases (nonunion, campaign, and representation) used to classify studies here.

2. See chapter 5 for discussion.

3. These examine strategies or tactics on an employerwide or unionwide basis (rather than on a bargaining unit basis).

4. See text for a discussion of distinction between "progressive" and "traditional" unions.

Bibliography

AFL-CIO. 1983. *The future of work.* Washington, D.C.: AFL-CIO.

AFL-CIO. 1985. *The changing situation of workers and their unions.* Washington, D.C.: AFL-CIO.

AFL-CIO. 1989. *AFL-CIO organizing survey: 1986-1987 NLRB elections.* Washington, D.C.: AFL-CIO.

Abraham, Katherine G. Forthcoming. The role of flexible staffing arrangements in short-term workforce adjustment strategies. In *Employment, unemployment, and hours of work,* ed. Robert A. Hart. London: George Allen and Unwin.

Adams, A., and J. Krislov. 1974. New union organizing: A test of the Ashenfelter-Pencavel model of trade union growth. *Quarterly Journal of Economics* 88: 304-311.

Anderson, John C., Gloria Busman, and Charles A. O'Reilly, III. 1982. The decertification process: Evidence from California. *Industrial Relations* 21: 178-195.

Anderson, John C., Charles A. O'Reilly, III, and Gloria Busman. 1980. Union decertification in the U.S.: 1974-1977. *Industrial Relations* 19: 100-107.

Ashenfelter, Orley, and John Pencavel. 1969. American trade union growth: 1900-1960. *Quarterly Journal of Economics* 83: 434-448.

Atherton, W. 1973. *Theory of union bargaining goals.* Princeton, N.J.: Princeton University Press.

BNA. 1985a. *Labor relations consultants: Issues, trends, and controversies.* Washington, D.C.: Bureau of National Affairs.

BNA. 1985b. *Unions today: New tactics to tackle tough times.* Washington, D.C.: Bureau of National Affairs.

Bain, George Sayers, and Farouk Elsheikh. 1976. *Union growth and the business cycle: An econometric analysis.* Oxford: Blackwell.

Balanoff, Tom. 1985. The Cement Workers' experience. *Labor Research Review,* no. 7: 5-33.

Balanoff, Tom. 1987. In-plant strategies—continued. In *Union power in the future—A union activist's agenda,* ed. Ken Gagala, 163-168. Ithaca, N.Y.: Cornell University, Labor Studies Program.

Barbash, Jack. 1967. *American unions: Structure, government, and politics.* Madison: University of Wisconsin.

Barbash, Jack. 1984. *The elements of industrial relations.* Madison: University of Wisconsin Press.

263

Barczyk, Casimir. 1987. The effect of symbolic action on productivity and job satisfaction. Ph.D. diss., University of Illiniois, Urbana.

Beaird, J. Ralph. 1986. Employer and consultant reporting under the LMRDA. *Georgia Law Review* 20: 533–563.

Becker, Brian E., and Richard U. Miller. 1981. Patterns and determinants of union growth in the hospital industry. *Journal of Labor Research* 2: 309–328.

Bellinger, William K. 1989. A utility-production model of union behavior. *Journal of Labor Research* 10: 135–146.

Bensman, David. 1988. BAC's Comeback: The bricklayers' renewal program. *Labor Research Review*, no. 7: 59–69.

Berkowitz, Monroe. 1954. The economics of trade union organization and administration. *Industrial and Labor Relations Review* 7: 575–592.

Bernstein, Jules. 1980. Union busting: From benign neglect to malignant growth, *University of California (Davis) Law Review* 14: 3–77.

Bernstein, Jules. 1985. Management consultants: A labor perspective. *Trial* 21: 32–36.

Bernstein, Robert H., and Richard Cooper. 1985. Labor law consequences of the sale of a unionized business. *Labor Law Journal* 37 (June): 326–336.

Bethel, Terry A. 1984. Profiting from unfair labor practices: A proposal to regulate management representatives. *Northwestern University Law Review* 79: 506–565.

Block, Richard N. 1980. Union organizing and the allocation of union resources. *Industrial and Labor Relations Review* 34: 101–113.

Block, Richard N., and Steven L. Premack. 1983. The unionization process: A review of the literature. In *Advances in industrial and labor relations*, ed. David B. Lipsky and Joel M. Douglas, vol. 1, 31–70. Greenwich, Conn.: JAI Press.

Block, Richard N., and Myron Roomkin. 1982. A preliminary analysis of the participation rate and margin of victory in NLRB elections. In *Proceedings of the thirty-fourth annual meeting of the Industrial Relations Research Association*, ed. Barbara Dennis, 220–226. Madison: IRRA.

Block, Richard N., and Benjamin W. Wolkinson. 1986. Delay in the union election campaign revisited: A theoretical and empirical analysis. In *Advances in industrial and labor relations*, ed. David B. Lipsky and David Lewin, vol. 3, 43–81. Greenwich, Conn.: JAI Press.

Boden, Margaret. 1977. *Artificial intelligence and natural man.* New York: Basic Books.

Bok, Derek C., and John T. Dunlop. 1970. *Labor and the American community.* New York: Simon and Schuster.

Bower, Joseph L., and Yves Doz. 1979. Strategy formulation: A social and political process. In *Strategic management: A new view of business policy and planning*, ed. Dan E. Schendel and Charles W. Hofer, 152–166. Boston: Little, Brown and Company.

Brett, Jeanne, 1980. Behavioral research on union and union-management systems. In *Research in organizational behavior*, ed. Barry M. Staw and L. L. Cummings, 177–214. Greenwich, Conn.: JAI Press.

Brett, Jeanne, and Tove Hammer. 1982. Organizational behavior and industrial relations. In *Industrial relations research in the 1970s: Review and appraisal*, ed. Thomas A. Kochan, Daniel Mitchell, and Lee Dyer, 221–282. Madison: IRRA.

Brief, Arthur, and Dale Rude. 1981. Voting in union certification elections: A conceptual analysis. *Academy of Management Review* 6: 261–267.

Bulmer, Charles, and John L. Carmichael, Jr. 1980. Toil and trouble: Reform of the labor law. In *Employment and labor-relations policy*, ed. Charles Bulmer and John L. Carmichael, 143–150. Lexington, Mass.: Lexington Books.

Burton, John F. 1988. Review symposium: *The transformation of American industrial relations. Industrial and Labor Relations Review*, 41: 439-455.

Bush, Robert. 1986. Consultant reporting requirements under the labor-management reporting and disclosure act of 1959: How much is enough? *Labor Law Journal* 37 (March): 180-186.

Cappelli, Peter, and John Chalykoff. 1986. The effects of management industrial relations strategy: Results of a recent survey. In *Proceedings of the thirty-eighth annual meeting of the Industrial Relations Research Association*, ed. Barbara Dennis, 171-178. Madison, Wis.: IRRA.

Cappelli, Peter, and Robert McKersie. 1985. Labor and the crisis in collective bargaining. In *Challenges and choices facing American labor*, ed. Thomas A. Kochan, 227-245. Cambridge, Mass.: MIT Press.

Chafetz, I., and C. R. P. Fraser. 1979. Union decertification: An exploratory analysis. *Industrial Relations* 18: 59-69.

Chaffee, Ellen Earle. 1985. Three models of strategy. *Academy of Management Review* 10: 89-91.

Chaison, Gary. 1986. *When unions merge.* Lexington, Mass.: Lexington Books.

Chandler, Alfred D. 1962. *Strategy and structure.* New York: Anchor.

Child, John. 1972. Organizational structure, environment, and performance: The role of strategic choice. *Sociology* 6: 2-22.

Chilton, Kenneth W., and Ronald J. Penoyer. 1984. *Labor relations in transition: Bankruptcy law versus labor law.* St. Louis, Mo.: Center for the Study of American Business.

Cohen, Yinon, and Jeffrey Pfeffer. 1986. Organizational hiring standards. *Administrative Science Quarterly* 31: 5-24.

Cooke, William N. 1983. Determinants of the outcomes of union certification elections. *Industrial and Labor Relations Review* 36: 402-413.

Cooke, William N. 1985a. Failure to negotiate first contracts. *Industrial and Labor Relations Review* 38: 163-178.

Cooke, William N. 1985b. The rising toll of discrimination against union activists. *Industrial Relations* 24: 421-441.

Cooke, William N., and Frederick H. Gautschi, III. 1982. Political bias in NLRB unfair labor practice decisions. *Industrial and Labor Relations Review* 35: 539-549.

Cooper, Laura. 1984. Authorization cards and union representation election outcome: An empirical assessment of the assumption underlying the Supreme Court's "Gissel" decision. *Northwestern University Law Review* 79: 87-139.

Craft, James A., and Suhail Abboushi, 1983. The union image: Concept, programs, and analysis. *Journal of Labor Research* 4: 299-314.

Craft, James A., and Marian M. Extejt. 1983. New strategies in union organizing. *Journal of Labor Research* 4: 1-32.

Craver, Charles B. 1978. The application of the LMRDA "Labor consultant" reporting requirements to management attorneys: Benign neglect personified. *Northwestern University Law Review* 73: 605-640.

Curtin, William J. 1986. Airline labor relations under deregulation. In *Proceedings of the thirty-eighth annual meeting of the Industrial Relations Research Association*, ed. Barbara Dennis, 158-164. Madison: IRRA.

Cyert, Richard M., and James G. March. 1963. *A behaviorial theory of the firm.* Englewood Cliffs, N.J.: Prentice-Hall.

DeMaria, Alfred T. 1980. *How management wins union organizing campaigns.* New York: Executive Enterprises.

DeMaria, Alfred T. 1982. *The process of deunionization.* New York: Executive Enterprises.

Delaney, John T. 1981. Union success in hospitals representation elections. *Industrial Relations* 20: 149–161.

Devanna, Mary Anne, Charles J. Fombrun, and Noel M. Tichy. 1984. A framework for strategic human resource management. In *Strategic human resource management,* ed. Charles J. Fombrun, Noel M. Tichy, and Mary Anne DeVanna, 33–56. New York: John Wiley.

Dickens, William T. 1983. The effect of company campaigns on certification elections: Law and reality once again. *Industrial and Labor Relations Review* 36: 560–575.

Dickens, William T., and Jonathan S. Leonard. 1985. Accounting for the decline in union membership: 1950–1980. *Industrial and Labor Relations Review* 38: 323–334.

Dickens, William T., Douglas Wholey, and James Robinson. 1987. Correlates of union support in NLRB elections. *Industrial Relations* 26: 240–252.

Donovan, Ronald. 1983. Review of *Preventative labor relations* by John G. Kilgour. *Industrial and Labor Relations Review* 36: 676–677.

Dougherty, James L. 1974. *Union-free supervisor.* Houston: Gulf Publishing.

Dougherty, James L. 1980. *Union-free labor relations: A step-by-step guide for staying union-free.* Houston: Gulf Publishing.

Douglas, Sara. 1986. *Labor's new voice: Unions and the mass media.* Norwood, N.J.: Ablex Publishing.

Drotning, John E. 1965. The union representation election. *Monthly Labor Review* 88: 938–943.

Dunlop, John T. 1948. The development of labor organization: A theoretical framework. In *Insights into labor issues,* ed. Richard A. Lester and Joseph Shister, 163–193. New York: Macmillan.

Dunlop, John T. 1958. *Industrial relations systems.* New York: Holt, Rinehart, Winston.

Dunlop, John T. 1990. *The management of labor unions: Decision making with historical constraints.* Lexington, Mass.: Lexington Books.

Dutton, John M., and Richard Freedman. 1985. External environment and internal strategies: Calculating, experimenting and imitating. In *Advances in strategic management,* ed. Robert Lamb and Paul Shrivastava, 39–67. Geeenwich, Conn.: JAI Press.

Dworkin, James B., and Marian Extejt. 1980. Recent trends in union decertification/deauthorization elections. In *Proceedings of the thirty-second annual meeting of the Industrial Relations Research Association,* ed. Barbara Dennis, 226–234. Madison: IRRA.

Dworkin, James B., and James R. Fain. 1989. Success in multiple union elections: Exclusive jurisdiction vs. competition. *Journal of Labor Research* 10; 91–102.

Dyer, Lee. 1984. Studying human resource strategy: An approach and an agenda. *Industrial Relations* 23: 156–169.

Dyer, Lee, and Gerald Holder. 1987. *Toward a strategic perspective of human resource management.* Ithaca, N.Y.: Cornell University, Center for Advanced Human Resource Studies.

Eames, Patricia. 1976. An analysis of the union voting study from a trade unionist's point of view. *Stanford Law Review* 28: 1181–1193.

Edelstein, J. David, and Malcolm Warner. 1976. *Comparative union democracy.* New York: John Wiley.

Edwards, Richard. 1979. *Contested terrain: The transformation of the workplace in the twentieth century.* New York: Basic Books.

Elliott, R., and B. Hawkins. 1982. Do union organizing activities affect decertification? *Journal of Labor Research* 3: 153–161.

Evansohn, John. 1989. The effects of mechanisms of management control on unionization. *Industrial Relations* 28:91–103.

Farber, Henry. 1983. Worker preferences for union representation. In *Research in labor economics*, ed. Joseph D. Reid, Jr., supplement 2, 171–205. Greenwich, Conn.: JAI Press.

Farber, Henry. 1984. *The analysis of union behavior.* Working paper, no. 1502. Cambridge, Mass.: NBER.

Farber, Henry and Daniel Saks. 1980. Why workers want unions: The role of relative wages and job characteristics. *Journal of Political Economy* 88: 349–369.

Fiorito, Jack, and Charles Greer. 1982. Determinants of U.S. unionism: Past research and future needs. *Industrial Relations* 21: 1–32.

Fiorito, Jack, and Wallace Hendricks. 1987. The characteristics of national unions. In *Advances in industrial and labor relations*, ed. David B. Lipsky and David Lewin, vol. 4, 1–42. Greenwich, Conn.: JAI Press.

Fiorito, Jack, Christopher Lowman, and Forrest D. Nelson. 1987. The impact of human resource policies on union organizing. *Industrial Relations* 26: 113–127.

Fishbein, Martin, and Icek Ajzen. 1975. *Belief, attitude, intention, and behavior: An introduction to theory and research.* Reading, Mass.: Addison-Wesley.

Flanagan, Robert. 1976. The behavioral foundations of union election regulation. *Stanford Law Review* 28: 1195–1205.

Flanagan, Robert J. 1987. *Labor relations and the litigation explosion.* Washington, D.C.: Brookings Institution.

Florkowski, Gary, and Michael Shuster. 1987. Predicting the decisions to vote and support unions in certification elections: An integrated perspective. *Journal of Labor Research* 8: 191–208.

Fombrun, Charles. 1983. Strategic management: Integrating the human resource systems into strategic planning. In *Advances in strategic management*, ed. Robert Lamb, vol. 2, 191–210. Greenwich, Conn.: JAI Press.

Forbes, Frank S., and Ida M. Jones. 1986. A comparative, attitudinal, and analytical study of dismissal of at-will employees without cause. *Labor Law Journal* 37 (March): 157–168.

Foulkes, Fred. 1980. *Personnel policies of large nonunion companies.* Englewood Cliffs, N.J.: Prentice-Hall.

Fox, Jeremy, and Kent Murrmann. 1986. NLRA Section 7 protection in nonunion settings: Meyers Industries and after. *Labor Law Journal* 37 (January): 34–40.

Freedman, Audrey. 1978. *Managing labor relations.* Report no. 765. New York: Conference Board.

Freedman, Audrey. 1982. A fundamental change in wage bargaining. *Challenge* 25: 17–77.

Freedman, Audrey. 1985. *The new look in wage policy and employment relations.* Report no. 865. New York: Conference Board.

Freeman, R. Edward, and Peter Lorange. 1985. Theory building in strategic management. In *Advances in strategic management*, ed. Robert Lamb and Paul Shrivastava, 9–38. Greenwich, Conn.: JAI Press.

Freeman, Richard B. 1985. Why are unions faring poorly in NRLB representation elections? In *Challenges and choices facing American labor*, ed. Thomas A. Kochan, 45–64. Cambridge, Mass.: MIT Press.

Freeman, Richard B. 1986. The effect of the union wage differential on management opposition and union organizing success. *American Economic Review* 76: 92–96.

Freeman, Richard B., and James L. Medoff. 1979. New estimates of private sector unionism in the United States. *Industrial and Labor Relations Review* 32: 143–174.

Freeman, Richard B., and James L. Medoff. 1984. *What do unions do?* New York: Basic Books.

Friedman, Abraham. 1970. The American trade union leader: A collective portrait. In *Trade union government and collective bargaining,* ed. Joel Seidman, 207–240. New York: Praeger.

Fulmer, William E. 1978. When employees want to oust their union. *Harvard Business Review* 56: 163–170.

Fulmer, William E. 1981. Step by step through a union campaign. *Harvard Business Review* 35: 94–102.

Fulmer, William E. 1982. *Union organizing: Management and labor conflict.* New York: Praeger.

Fulmer, William E., and John J. Coleman. 1984. Do quality-of-work-life programs violate section 8(a)(2)? *Labor Law Journal* 35 (November): 675–685.

Gagala, Ken. 1983. *Union organizing and staying organized.* Reston, Va.: Reston Publishing.

Gagala, Ken. 1985. A Wobbly-bred campaign in Minnesota. *Labor Research Review,* no. 7: 81–90.

Gale, Edward R. 1981. Unionism, leasing, litigation, and regulation in the Chicago taxicab industry: An historical inquiry. AM thesis, University of Illinois, Institute of Labor and Industrial Relations.

Garbarino, Joseph W. 1986. Faculty collective bargaining: A status report. In *Unions in transition: Entering the second century,* ed Seymour M. Lipset, 265–286. San Francisco: Institute for Contemporary Studies.

Geissner, James. 1978. The management campaign: A case study. *Public Personnel Management* 7: 324–336.

Getman, Julius G., Stephen B. Goldberg, and Jeanne B. Herman. 1976. *Union representation elections: Law and reality.* New York: Russell Sage Foundation.

Gilberg, Kenneth, and Nancy Abrams. 1987. Union organizing: New tactics for new times. *Personnel Administrator* 32: 52–56.

Goldberg, Stephen B., Julius G. Getman, and Jeanne M. Brett. 1984. The relationship between free choice and labor board doctrine: Differing empirical approaches. *Northwestern University Law Review* 79: 721–735.

Gordon, Michael E., and Robert E. Burt. 1981. A history of industrial psychology's relationship with American unions: Lessons from the past and directions for the future. *International Review of Applied Psychology* 30: 137–156.

Gordon, Michael E., and Aaron J. Nurick. 1981. Psychological approaches to the study of unions and union-management relations. *Psychological Bulletin* 90: 293–306.

Gordon, Michael E., John W. Philpot, Robert E. Burt, Cynthia A. Thompson, and William E. Spiller. 1980. Commitment to the union: Development of a measure of and examination of its correlates. *Journal of Applied Psychology Monograph* 65: 479–499.

Grant, John H., and William R. King. 1979. Strategy formulation: Analytical and normative models. In *Strategic management: A new view of business policy and planning,* ed. Dan E. Schendel and Charles W. Hofer, 109–122. Boston: Little, Brown and Company.

Green, James, and Chris Tilly. 1987. Service unionism: Directions for organizing. *Labor Law Journal* 38 (August): 486–495.

Greer, Charles R., and Stanley A. Martin. 1978. Calculative strategy decisions during union organization campaigns. *Sloan Management Review* 19: 61–74.

Grenier, Guillermo J. 1988. Quality circles in a corporate antiunion strategy: A case study. *Labor Studies Journal* 13: 5-27.

Gross, James A. 1985. Conflicting statutory purposes: Another look at fifty years of NLRB law making. *Industrial and Labor Relations Review* 39: 7-18.

Harbrant, Robert. 1987. Comprehensive campaigns. In *Union power in the future—A union activist's agenda*, ed. Ken Gagala, 134-146. Ithaca, N.Y.: Cornell University, Labor Studies Program.

Harvard Law Review. 1984. The liability of labor relations consultants for advising unfair labor practices. *Harvard Law Review*. 97: 529-546.

Heckscher, Charles. 1988. *The new unionism: Employee involvement in the changing corporation.* New York: Basic Books.

Heider, Fritz. 1958. *The psychology of interpersonal relations.* New York: Wiley.

Heneman, H. G., and M. N. Sandver. 1983. Predicting the outcome of union certification elections: A review of the literature. *Industrial and Labor Relations Review* 36: 537-551.

Hill, Andrew D. 1987. *Wrongful discharge and the derogation of the at-will employment doctrine.* Philadelphia: Industrial Research Unit, Wharton School.

Hills, Stephen M. 1985. The attitudes of union and nonunion male workers toward union representation. *Industrial and Labor Relations Review* 38: 179-194.

Hirsch, Barry, and John Addison. 1986. *The economic analysis of unions: New approaches and evidence.* Boston: Allen and Unwin.

Hogarth, Robin. 1987. *Judgment and choice.* 2d ed. New York: John Wiley.

Hogler, Raymond. 1984. Employer involvement programs and *NLRB v. Scott and Fetzer Co.*: The developing interpretation of section 8(a)(2). *Labor Law Journal* 35 (January): 21-27.

Hrebiniak, Lawrence, and William Joyce. 1985. Organizational adaptation: Strategic choice and environmental determinism. *Administrative Science Quarterly* 30: 336-349.

Hughes, Charles. 1976. *Making unions unnecessary.* New York: Executive Enterprises Publications.

Hundley, Greg. 1988. Who joins unions in the public sector? The effects of individual characteristics and the law. *Journal of Labor Research* 9: 301-325.

Hunt, Janet C., and Rudolph A. White. 1985. The effects of management practices on union election returns. *Journal of Labor Research* 6: 389-403.

Hurd, Richard, and Jill K. Kriesky. 1986. "The rise and demise of PATCO" reconstructed. *Industrial and Labor Relations Review* 40: 115-121.

Hurd, Richard, and Adrienne McElwain. 1988. Organizing clerical workers: Determinants of success. *Industrial and Labor Relations Review* 41: 360-373.

Industrial Union Department. 1986. *The inside game: Winning with workplace strategies.* Washington, D.C.: AFL-CIO.

Ichniowski, Casey, and David Lewin. 1988. Characteristics of grievance procedures: Evidence from nonunion, union, and double-breasted businesses. In *Proceedings of the fortieth annual meeting of the Industrial Relations Research Association*, ed. Barbara Dennis, 415-424. Madison: IRRA.

Irving, John S., Jr. 1984. Plant relocations and transfers of work: The NLRB's "inherently destructive" approach. In *Plant closings: Public or private choices?*, ed. Richard B. McKenzie, 233-252. Rev. ed. Washington, D.C.: CATO Institute.

Jacoby, Sanford M., and Daniel J. B. Mitchell. 1982. Development of contractural features of the union-management relationship. *Labor Law Journal* 33 (August): 512-518.

Janis, Irving L., and Leon Mann. 1977. *Decision making: A psychological analysis of conflict, choice, and commitment.* New York: Free Press.

Jansonius, John V. 1985. Use and misuse of employee leasing. *Labor Law Journal* 35 (January): 35–41.

Jenkins, J. Craig, and Charles Perrow. 1977. Insurgency of the powerless: Farm worker movements (1946–1972). *American Sociological Review* 42: 249–268.

Juris, Hervey, and Myron Roomkin. 1980. *The shrinking perimeter.* Lexington, Mass.: Lexington Books.

Kahneman, Daniel, Paul Slovic, and Amos Tversky. 1982. *Judgment under uncertainty: Heuristics and biases.* Cambridge: Cambridge University Press.

Karsh, Bernard. 1982. *Diary of a strike.* 2d. ed. Urbana: University of Illinois Press.

Karsh, Bernard, Joel Seidman, and Daisy Lilienthal. 1953. The union organizer and his tactics: A case study. *American Journal of Sociology* 50: 113–122.

Kassalow, Everett. 1984. The future of American unionism: A comparative perspective. *Annals of the American Academy of Political and Social Science.* 473: 52–63.

Kellock, Susan. 1985. Time and timing in corporate campaigns: *IBEW 1446* v. *Southern Ohio Electric. Labor Research Review,* no. 7: 91–97.

Kilgore, Peter. 1984. No-solicitation/no-distribution rules: The word battle of "Time" versus "Hours" continues. *Labor Law Journal* 35 (November): 671–674.

Kilgour, John G. 1981. *Preventive labor relations.* New York: AMACOM.

Kilgour, John G. 1983. Union organizing activity among white-collar employees. *Personnel* 60: 18–27.

Kilgour, John G. 1987. Decertifying a union: A matter of choice. *Personnel Administrator* 32: 42–51.

Kistler, Alan. 1984. Union organizing: New challenges and prospects. *Annals of the American Academy of Political and Social Science* 473: 96–107.

Klein, Janice, and David Wanger. 1985. The legal setting for the emergence of the union-avoidance strategy. In *Challenges and choices facing American labor,* ed. Thomas A. Kochan, 75–88. Cambridge, Mass.: MIT Press.

Kleiner, Morris. 1984. Unionism and employer discrimination: Analysis of 8(a)(3) violations. *Industrial Relations* 23: 234–243.

Kochan, Thomas A. 1979. How American workers view labor unions. *Monthly Labor Review* 102: 23–31.

Kochan, Thomas A. 1980. *Collective bargaining and industrial relations.* Homewood, Ill.: Richard Irwin.

Kochan, Thomas A. 1985. *Challenges and choices facing American labor.* Cambridge, Mass.: MIT Press.

Kochan, Thomas A., and Harry C. Katz. 1988. *Collective bargaining and industrial relations.* 2d. ed. Homewood, Ill.: Irwin.

Kochan, Thomas A., Harry C. Katz, and Robert B. McKersie. 1986. *The transformation of American industrial relations.* New York: Basic Books.

Kochan, Thomas A., and Robert B. McKersie. 1983. SMR forum: Collective bargaining—Pressures for change. *Sloan Management Review* 24: 59–65.

Kochan, Thomas A., Robert B. McKersie, and Peter Cappelli. 1984. Strategic choice and industrial relations theory. *Industrial Relations* 23: 16–39.

Kochan, Thomas A., Robert B. McKersie, and John Chalykoff. 1986. The effects of corporate strategy and workplace innovations on union representation. *Industrial and Labor Relations Review* 39: 487–501.

Korn, Sarah. 1984. Property rights and job security: Workplace solicitation by non-employee union organizers. *Yale Law Journal* 94: 374–393.

Kravetz, Dennis. 1988. *The human resources revolution.* San Francisco: Jossey-Bass.

Lagerfeld, Steve. 1981. The pop psychologist as union buster. *American Federationist* 88: 6–12.

Latham, Joseph, Jr. 1980. Susceptibility to a successful union organizing campaign— The seven warning signals. *Employee Relations Law Journal* 6: 228–238.

Lawler, John J. 1980. Labor consultants in the upper Midwest: A profile. University of Minnesota, Industrial Relations Center, Minneapolis. Working paper.

Lawler, John J. 1982. Collective bargaining and market uncertainty. *Industrial Relations* 21: 33–52.

Lawler, John J. 1983. Trade union strategy in a time of adversity. In *Proceedings of the thirty-fifth annual meeting of the Industrial Relations Research Association*, ed. Barbara Dennis, 40–45. Madison: IRRA.

Lawler, John J. 1984. The influence of management consultants on the outcome of union certification elections. *Industrial and Labor Relations Review* 38: 38–51.

Lawler, John J. 1986. Union growth and decline: The impact of employer and union tactics. *Journal of Occupational Psychology* 59: 161–176.

Lawler, John J. 1990. Union organizing and representation. In *Employee and Labor Relations*, ed. John A. Fossum, in press. Washington, D.C.: Bureau of National Affairs.

Lawler, John J., and Gregory Hundley. 1983. Determinants of certification and decertification activity. *Industrial Relations* 22: 335–348.

Lawler, John J., and J. Malcolm Walker. 1984a. Representation elections in higher education: Occurrence and outcomes. *Journal of Labor Research* 5: 63–80.

Lawler, John J., and J. Malcolm Walker. 1984b. Union campaign effects in university faculty representation elections. In *Proceedings of the thirty-sixth annual meeting of the Industrial Relations Research Association*, ed. Barbara Dennis, 327–336. Madison: IRRA.

Lawler, John J., and Robin West. 1985. Impact of union-avoidance strategy in representation elections. *Industrial Relations* 24: 406–420.

Lawrence, Paul. 1985. The history of human resource management in American industry. In *Human resource management trends and challenges*, Walton and Paul Lawrence, 15–34. Boston: Harvard Business School Press.

Lawson, J. W. 1977. *How to meet the challenge of the union organizer.* Chicago: Dartnell.

Lee, Lung-Fei. 1978. Unionism and wage rates: A simultaneous equations model with qualitative and limited dependent variables. *International Economic Review* 19: 415–433.

Lehr, Richard I., and David J. Middlebrooks. 1987. *The new unionism: A blueprint for the future.* New York: Executive Enterprises.

Leigh, Duane E. 1985. The determinants of workers' union status: Evidence from the national longitudinal surveys. *Journal of Human Resources* 20: 555–566.

Lester, Richard. 1958. *As unions mature.* Princeton, N. J.: Princeton University Press.

Lewin, David. 1987. Industrial relations as a strategic variable. In *Human performance and the performance of the firm*, ed. Morris W. Kleiner, Richard N. Block, Myron Roomkin, and Sidney Salsburg, 1–42. Madison: IRRA.

Lewis, Robert. 1986. Union decertification: A new look at management's role. *Labor Law Journal* 37 (February): 115–122.

Lichtenstein, Nelson. 1982. Industrial democracy, contract unionism, and the National War Labor Board. *Labor Law Journal* 33 (August): 524–531.

Lindblom, C. E. 1959. The science of muddling through. *Public Administration Review* 19: 79–88.

Lipset, Seymour Martin, Martin Trow, and James Coleman. 1956. *Union democracy*. New York: Anchor-Doubleday.

Lynch, Lisa M., and Marcus H. Sandver. 1987. Determinants of the decertification process: Evidence from employer-initiated elections. *Journal of Labor Research* 8: 85–91.

Lynn, Monty L., and Jozell Brister. 1989. Trends in union organizing: Issues and tactics. *Industrial Relations* 28: 104–113.

MacMillan, Ian C. 1979. Commentary. In *Strategic management: A new view of business policy and planning*, ed. Dan E. Schendel and Charles W. Hofer, 166–172. Boston: Little, Brown and Company.

Mancke, Richard B. 1971. "American trade union growth, 1900–1960": A comment. *Quarterly Journal of Economics* 85: 187–193.

Maranto, Cheryl L., and Jack Fiorito. 1987. The effect of union characteristics on the outcome of NLRB certification elections. *Industrial and Labor Relations Review* 40: 225–240.

Marks, Nancy, 1985. The corporate strategy: A new course for labor? *Labor Center Review* 7: 32–35.

Mason, Richard O., and Ian I. Mitroff. 1983. A teleological power-oriented theory of strategy. In *Advances in strategic management*, ed. Robert Lamb, vol. 2, 31–41. Greenwich, Conn.: JAI Press.

Masters, Marick F., and John T. Delaney. 1982. The AFL-CIO's political record, 1974–1980. In *Proceedings of the thirty-fourth annual meeting of the Industrial Relations Research Association*, ed. Barbara Dennis, 351–359. Madison: IRRA.

Masters, Merick F., and John T. Delaney. 1985. The causes of union political involvement: A longitudinal analysis. *Journal of Labor Research* 6: 341–362.

McDonald, Charles. 1987. The AFL-CIO blueprint for the future—A progress report. In *Proceedings of the thirty-ninth annual meeting of the Industrial Relations Research Association*, ed. Barbara Dennis, 276–283. Madison: IRRA.

McDonald, Charles, and Dick Wilson. 1979. Peddling the "union free" guarantee. *American Federationist* 86: 12–19.

McGrath, Joseph. 1975. Stress and behavior in organizations. In *Handbook of industrial and organizational psychology*, ed. Marvin Dunnette, 1351–1396. Chicago: Rand-McNally.

Metzgar, Jack. 1985. "Running the plant backwards" in UAW Region Five. *Labor Research Review*, no. 7: 35–43.

Meyer, John W., and Brian Rowan, 1978. The structure of educational organizations. In *Environments and organizations*, ed. Marshall W. Meyer, 78–109. San Francisco: Jossey-Bass.

Miles, Raymond E. 1975. *Theories of management*. New York: McGraw-Hill.

Miles, Raymond E., and Charles C. Snow. 1978. *Organizational strategy, structure, and process*. New York: McGraw-Hill.

Mills, Daniel Quinn, and Mary Balbaky. 1985. Planning for morale and culture. In *Human resource management trends and challenges*, ed. Richard Walton and Paul Lawrence, 255–284. Boston: Harvard Business School Press.

Mintzberg, Henry. 1979. Organizational power and goals: A skeletal theory. In *Strategic management: A new view of business policy and planning*, ed. Dan E. Schendel and Charles W. Hofer, 64–80. Boston: Little, Brown and Company.

Mintzberg, Henry. 1989. *Mintzberg on management*. New York: Free Press.

Mintzberg, Henry, D. Raisinghani, and A. Theoret. 1976. The structure of "unstructured" decision processes. *Administrative Science Quarterly* 21: 246–275.

Miscimarra, Philip. 1983. *The NLRB and managerial discretion: Plant closings, relocations, subcontracting, and automation.* Philadelphia: Industrial Research Unit, Wharton school.

Mishel, Lawrence. 1985. Corporate campaigns: Strengths and limits of nonworkplace strategies. *Labor Research Review*, no. 7: 69–79.

Moore, William J., and Robert J. Newman. 1975. On the prospects of American trade union growth: A cross-sectional analysis. *Review of Economics and Statistics* 57: 435–445.

Moore, William J., and Robert J. Newman. 1988. A cross-section analysis of the postwar decline in American trade unionism. *Journal of Labor Research* 9: 139–148.

Mortimer, Kenneth P., Mark D. Johnson, and David A. Weiss. 1975. "No representative" victories in faculty collective bargaining elections. *Journal of College and University Personnel Association* 26 (January-February): 34–47.

Murray, Alan I., and Yonatan Reshef. 1988. American manufacturing unions' stasis: A paradigmatic perspective. *Academy of Management Review* 13: 615–626.

Myers, M. Scott. 1976. *Managing without unions.* Reading, Mass.: Addison-Wesley.

Neumann, George R., and Ellen R. Rissman. 1984. Where have all the union members gone? *Journal of Labor Economics* 2: 175–191.

Nye, David. 1988. *Alternative staffing strategies.* Washington, D.C.: Bureau of National Affairs.

O'Keefe, Edward P., and Seamus M. Touhey. 1984. Economically motivated relocations of work and the National Labor Relations Act: A three-step analysis. In *Plant closings: Public or private choices?* ed. Richard B. McKenzie, 253–308. Rev. ed. Washington, D.C.: CATO Institute.

Payne, Phillis. 1977. The consultants who coach the violators. *AFL-CIO American Federationist* 84: 22–30.

Pearce, Thomas, and Richard Peterson. 1987. Regionality in NLRB decertification cases. *Journal of Labor Research* 8: 253–270.

Pencavel, John H. 1971. The demand for union services: An exercise. *Industrial and Labor Relations Review* 24: 180–190.

Pennings, Johannes M. 1985. *Organizational strategy and change.* San Francisco: Jossey-Bass.

Perras, Richard A. 1984. Effective responses to union organizing attempts in the banking industry. *Labor Law Journal* 35 (February): 92–102.

Perry, Charles. 1987. *Union corporate campaigns.* Philadelphia: Industrial Research Unit, Wharton School.

Perry, Charles R., Andrew M. Kramer, and Thomas J. Schneider. 1982. *Operating during strikes.* Philadelphia: Industrial Research Union, Wharton School.

Pestillo, Peter J. 1979. Learning to live without the union. In *Proceedings of the thirty-first annual meeting of the Industrial Relations Research Association,* ed. Barbara Dennis, 233–239. Madison, IRRA.

Pfeffer, Jeffrey. 1981. *Power in organizations.* Marshfield, Mass.: Pitman.

Pfeffer, Jeffrey. 1982. *Organizations and organization theory.* Cambridge, Mass.: Ballinger.

Pfeffer, Jeffrey, and John J. Lawler. 1980. Effects of job alternatives, extrinsic rewards and behavioral commitment on attitude toward the organization: A field test of the insufficient justification paradigm. *Administrative Science Quarterly* 25: 38–56.

Pfeffer, Jeffrey, and Gerald R. Salancik. 1978. *The external control of organizations.* New York: Harper and Row.

Pierce, Jon L., John W. Newstrom, Randall D. Dunham, and Alison W. Barber. 1989. *Alternative Work Schedules.* Boston: Allyn and Bacon.

Piore, Michael, and Charles Sabel. 1984. *The second industrial divide*. New York: Basic Books.

Porter, Andrew A., and Kent F. Murrmann. 1983. A survey of employer union-avoidance practices. *Personnel Administrator* 12: 66–72.

Preston, Lee. 1980. The manufacturing environment in the 1980s. In *The shrinking perimeter*, ed. Hervey Juris and Myron Roomkin, 3–34. Lexington, Mass: Lexington Books.

Prosten, Richard. 1979. The longest season: Union organizing in the last decade, aka how come one team has to play with its shoelaces tied together? In *Proceedings of the thirty-first annual meeting of the Industrial Relations Research Association*, ed. Barbara Dennis, 240–249. Madison: IRRA.

Pulliam, Mark. 1985. The collision of labor and bankruptcy law: Bildisco and the legislative response. *Labor Law Journal* 36 (July): 390–401.

Quaglieri, Philip. 1988. The new people of power: The backgrounds and careers of top labor leaders. *Journal of Labor Research* 9: 207–221.

Raskin, A. H. 1979. Management comes out swinging. In *Proceedings of the thirty-first annual meeting of the Industrial Relations Research Association*, ed. Barbara Dennis 223–233. Madison: IRRA.

Raskin, A. H. 1986. Labor: A movement in search of a mission. In *Unions in transition: Entering the second century*, ed. Seymour M. Lipset, 3–38. San Francisco: Institute for Contemporary Studies.

Reed, Thomas F. 1989a. Do organizers matter?: Individual characteristics and representation election outcomes. *Industrial and Labor Relation Review*, 41: 103–119.

Reed, Thomas F. 1989b. Nice guys don't always finish last: The impact of the union organizer on the probability of securing a first contract. *Industrial Relations*, forthcoming.

Reed, Thomas F. 1989c. Profiles of union organizers from manufacturing and service unions. *Journal of Labor Research*, forthcoming.

Reed, Thomas F. 1989d. Union attainment of first contracts: Do service unions possess a competitive advantage? *Journal of Labor Research*, forthcoming.

Reed, Thomas F. 1989e. Union organizing department characteristics: Representation campaign tactics. Texas A & M University School of Business Administration. Working paper.

Rehmus, Charles. 1986. The future of industrial relations in the United States. *Labour and Society* 11: 149–158.

Romesburg, H. Charles. 1984. *Cluster analysis for researchers*. Belmont, Calif.: Wadsworth.

Roomkin, Myron, and Richard Block. 1981. Case processing time and the outcome of representative elections: Some empirical evidence. *University of Illinois Law Review* 1: 75–97.

Roomkin, Myron, and Hervey A. Juris. 1979. Unions in the traditional sectors: The midlife passage of the labor movement. In *Proceedings of the thirty-first annual meeting of the Industrial Relations Research Association*, ed. Barbara Dennis, 212–221. Madison: IRRA.

Salancik, Gerald. 1977. Commitment and the control of organizational behavior. In *New directions in organizational behavior*, ed. Barry M. Staw and Gerald Salancik, 1–55. Chicago: St. Clair Press.

Salancik, Gerald, and Jeffrey Pfeffer. 1978. A social information processing approach to job attitudes. *Administrative Science Quarterly* 23: 224–253.

Sandver, Marcus H. 1982. South-nonsouth differentials in National Labor Relations Board certification election outcomes. *Journal of Labor Research* 3: 13–30.

Saposs, David J. 1918. Colonial and federal beginnings. In *History of labour in the United States*, ed. John R. Commons, Vol. 1, 25–326. New York: Macmillan.

Sayles, Leonard, and George Strauss. 1967. *The local union.* Rev. ed. New York: Harcourt, Brace.

Schendel, Dan E., and Charles W. Hofer. 1979. *Strategic management: A new view of business policy and planning.* Boston: Little, Brown and Company.

Schlossberg, Stephen I., and Judith Scott. 1983. *Organizing and the law.* 3rd ed. Washington, D.C.: Bureau of National Affairs.

Schmidman, John, and Kimberlee Keller. 1984. Employee participation plans as section 8(a)(2) violations. *Labor Law Journal* 35 (December): 773–780.

Schwartz, Arthur R., and Michele M. Hoyman. 1984. The changing of the guard: The new American labor leader. *Annals of the American Academy of Political and Social Science* 473: 64–75.

Seeber, Ronald L. 1983. Union organizing in manufacturing: 1973–1976. In *Advances in industrial and labor relations*, ed. David B. Lipsky and Joel M. Douglas, vol. 1, 1–30. Greenwich, Conn.: JAI Press.

Seeber, Ronald L., and William N. Cooke. 1983. The decline in union success in NLRB representation elections. *Industrial Relations* 22: 34–44.

Shister, Joseph. 1953. The Logic of Union Growth. *Journal of Political Economy* 61: 413–433.

Shrivastava, Paul. 1983. Variations in strategic decision-making processes. In *Advances in strategic management*, ed. Robert Lamb, vol. 2, 177–189. Greenwich, Conn.: JAI Press.

Sims, Henry, Dennis A. Gioia, and Associates. 1986. *The thinking organization.* San Francisco: Jossey-Bass.

Snow, Charles, and Raymond Miles. 1983. The role of strategy in the development of a general theory of organizations. In *Advances in strategic management*, ed. Robert Lamb, vol. 2, 231–259 Greenwich, Conn.: JAI Press.

Spizzo, James A. 1988. Public-sector union elections: A management perspective. *Illinois Public Employee Relations Report* 5: 1–6.

Staw, Barry M. 1977. Motivation in organizations: Toward synthesis and reflection. In *New directions in organizational behavior*, ed. Barry M. Staw and Gerald Salancik, 55–96. Chicago: St. Clair Press.

Staw, Barry M. 1983. The self-perception of motivation. In *Psychological foundations of organizational behavior*, ed. Barry M. Staw, 140–151. 2d. ed. Dallas: Scott, Foresman.

Staw, Barry M., Nancy Bell, and J. A. Clausen. 1986. The dispositional approach to job attitudes: A lifetime longitudinal test. *Administrative Science Quarterly* 31: 56–77.

Staw, Barry M., and Jerry Ross. 1985. Stability in the midst of change: A dispositional approach to job satisfaction. *Journal of Applied Psychology* 70: 469–480.

Stephan, Paula, and Bruce Kaufman. 1987. Factors leading to a decline in union win rates: 1973–1981. In *Proceedings of the thirty-ninth annual meeting of the Industrial Relations Research Association*, ed. Barbara Dennis, 296–305. Madison: IRRA.

Stephens, David B., and Paul R. Timm. 1978. A comparison of campaign techniques in contested faculty elections: An analysis of the Florida experience. *Journal of Collective Negotiations in the Public Sector* 7: 167–177.

Stepina, Lee P., and Jack Fiorito. 1986. Toward a comprehensive theory of union growth and decline. *Industrial Relations* 25: 248–264.

Stinchcombe, Arthur. 1965. Social structure and organizations. In *Handbook of organizations*, ed. James G. March, 142–193. Chicago: Rand-McNally.

Stratton, Kay, and Robert B. Brown. 1988. Strategic planning in U.S. labor unions. Paper presented at the forty-first annual meeting of the Industrial Relations Research Association, New York City.

Strauss, George. 1953. Factors in the unionization of a utilities company: A case study. *Human Organization* 12: 17–25.

Strauss, George. 1977. Union government in the U.S.: Research past and future. *Industrial Relations* 16: 215–242.

Sullivan, Frederick. 1978. Limiting union organizing activity through supervisors. *Personnel* 55 (July–August): 55–65.

Susser, Peter A. 1988. Election year politics and the enactment of federal "plant closing" legislation. *Employee Relations Law Journal* 14: 349–358.

Taylor, Benjamin J., and Fred Whitney. 1987. *Labor relations law* (fifth edition). Englewood Cliffs, N.J.: Prentice-Hall.

Terry, Larry D. 1987. The conference as an administrative strategy for building organizational commitment: The CWA experience. *Labor Studies Journal* 12: 48–61.

Thieblot, Armand, and Thomas Haggard. 1984. Union violence: The record and the response by courts. Philadelphia: Industrial Research Unit, Wharton School.

Thompson, James D. 1967. *Organizations in action.* New York: McGraw-Hill.

Thompson, Judith Kenner. 1988. Union use of public interest proxy resolutions. *Labor Studies Journal* 13: 40–57.

Triandis, Harry. 1976. Values, attitudes, and interpersonal behavior. *Nebraska Symposium on Motivation.* Lincoln, Neb.: University of Nebraska Press.

Troy, Leo. 1986. The rise and fall of American trade unions: The labor movement from FDR to RR. In *Unions in transition: Entering the second century*, ed. Seymour M. Lipset, 75–109. San Francisco: Institute for Contemporary Studies.

Troy, Leo, and Neil Sheflin. 1985. *Union sourcebook.* West Orange, N.J.: Industrial Relations data and Information Services.

Tucker, Jerry. 1987. In-plant strategies. In *Union power in the future—A union activist's agenda*, ed. Ken Gagala, 147–162. Ithaca, N.Y.: Cornell University, Labor Studies Program.

U.S. Congress. 1981. *Pressures in today's workplace: Report of the subcommittee on labor-management relations of the committee on education and labor, House of Representatives.* Washington, D.C.: U.S. Government Printing Office.

Ungson, G. R., D. N. Braunstein, and P. D. Hall. 1981. Managerial information processing: A research review. *Administrative Science Quarterly* 26: 116–134.

Verma, Anil. 1985. Relative flow of capital to union and nonunion plants within a firm. *Industrial Relations* 24: 395–405.

Voos, Paula B. 1983. Union organizing: Costs and benefits. *Industrial and Labor Relations Review* 36: 576–591.

Voos, Paula B. 1984. Trends in union organizing expenditures, 1953–1977. *Industrial and Labor Relations Review* 38: 52–63.

Voos, Paula B. 1987. Union organizing expenditures: Determinants and their implications for union growth. *Journal of Labor Research* 8: 19–30.

Walker, J. Malcolm. 1981. Unions as organizations: A respectable neomarxist perspective. Paper presented at annual meeting, Western Academy of Management, Monterey, Calif.

Walker, J. Malcolm, and John J. Lawler. 1979. Dual unions and political processes in organizations. *Industrial Relations* 18: 32–43.

Walker, J. Malcolm, and John J. Lawler. 1982. University administrators and faculty bargaining. *Research in Higher Education* 16: 353–372.

Walker, J. Malcolm, and John J. Lawler. 1986. Union campaign activities and voter preferences. *Journal of Labor Research* 7: 19–40.

Walton, Richard. 1985. Toward a strategy of eliciting employee commitment based on policies of mutuality. In *Human resource management trends and challenges*, eds. Richard Walton and Paul Lawrence, 35–68. Boston: Harvard Business School Press.

Walton, Richard, and Paul Lawrence, eds. 1985. *Human resource management trends and challenges*. Boston: Harvard Business School Press.

Walton, Richard, and Robert McKersie. 1965. *A behavioral theory of labor negotiations*. New York: McGraw-Hill.

Waterman, Donald A. 1986. *A guide to expert systems*. Reading, Mass.: Addison-Wesley.

Weick, Karl. 1979. *The social psychology of organizing*. 2d. ed. Reading, Mass.: Addison-Wesley.

Weiler, Paul, 1983. Promises to keep: Securing workers' rights to self-organization under the NLRA. *Harvard Law Review* 96: 418–476.

Weiler, Paul. 1984. Striking a new balance: Freedom of contract and the prospects for union representation. *Harvard Law Review* 98: 351–419.

Wessels, Walter J. 1981. Economic effects of right-to-work laws. *Journal of Labor Research* 2: 55–76.

Wheeler, Hoyt N. 1985. *Industrial conflict: An integrative theory*. Columbia: University of South Carolina Press.

Wheeler, Hoyt N. 1986. Management from an institutional/biological perspective. Paper presented at the Berlin-Toronto Symposium on Comparative Management, Berlin.

Williams, Robert E. 1985. *NLRB regulation of election conduct*. Philadelphia: Industrial Research Unit, Wharton School.

Youngblood, Stuart A., Angelo S. DeNisi, Julie L. Molleston, and William H. Mobley. 1984. The impact of work environment, instrumentality beliefs, perceived labor union image, and subjective norms on union voting intentions. *Academy of Management Journal* 27: 576–590.

Yuchtman, E., and S. E. Seashore. 1967. A system resource approach to organizational effectiveness. *American Sociological Review* 32: 891–903.

Zalesny, Mary. 1985. Comparison of economic and noneconomic factors in predicting faculty vote preference in a union representation election. *Journal of Applied Psychology* 70: 243–256.

Name Index

278

Subject Index

282

JC

JOS I